80 Proposals to

STOP Wrongful Convictions

Before the End of This Decade

by Morrison Bonpasse

BonPasse Exoneration Services. (a Maine non-profit corporation)
P.O. Box 390
Newcastle, ME 04553 USA
001-207-586-6078
Morrison Bonpasse, Executive Director
morrison@bonpasseexonerationservices.com
www.bonpasseexonerationservices.com

80 Proposals to STOP Wrongful Convictions Before the End of This Decade

by Morrison Bonpasse

ISBN-10 0-9906526-2-9
ISBN-13 978-0-9906526-2-5

TABLE OF CONTENTS

Glossary

Exoneration: In general, an exoneration occurs when a person who has been convicted of a crime is officially cleared based on new evidence of innocence. More precisely: A person has been exonerated if he or she was convicted of a crime and later was either:

(1) declared to be factually innocent by a government official or agency with the authority to make that declaration; or

(2) relieved of all the consequences of the criminal conviction by a government official or body with the authority to take that action.

The official action may be:

(i) a complete pardon by a governor or other competent authority, whether or not the pardon is designated as based on innocence;

(ii) an acquittal of all charges factually related to the crime for which the person was originally convicted; or

(iii) a dismissal of all charges related to the crime for which the person was originally convicted, by a court or by a prosecutor with the authority to enter that dismissal.

The pardon, acquittal, or dismissal must have been the result, at least in part, of evidence of innocence that either

(i) was not presented at the trial at which the person was convicted; or

(ii) if the person pled guilty, was not known to the defendant, the defense attorney and the court at the time the plea was entered. The evidence of innocence need not be an explicit basis for the official action that exonerated the person.

[Source: the National Registry of Exonerations - https://www.law.umich.edu/special/exoneration/Pages/glossary.aspx]

Exoneree: A person who was convicted of a crime and later officially declared innocent of that crime, or relieved of all legal consequences of the conviction because evidence of innocence that was not presented at trial required reconsideration of the case. [Source: the National Registry of Exonerations https://www.law.umich.edu/special/exoneration/Pages/glossary.aspx]

Innocence: Status of being innocent in either or both of the meanings below of "innocent." [Source: the author of this book]

Innocent: (two meanings)

1. Virginal, pure, unknowing, not-involved. Synonyms here are the rhyming "actually innocent" and "factually innocent."
2. Not found guilty beyond a reasonable doubt in a court of law. Synonym here is "legally innocent." [Source: the author of this book]

Presumption Of Innocence: One of the most sacred principles in the American criminal justice system, holding that a defendant is innocent until proven guilty. In other words, the prosecution must prove, beyond a reasonable doubt, each essential element of the crime charged. [Source:http://www.nolo.com/dictionary/presumption-of-innocence-term.html]

Wrongful Conviction: A criminal conviction, whether by trial or by guilty plea, of a person for a crime s/he did not commit beyond a reasonable doubt. [Source: the author of this book]

Foreword

It could be said that this book began when my friend, Bill Bunting, called me in December, 2002, and asked me to read the book, *Human Sacrifice*, about the 1989 wrongful conviction of Dennis Dechaine for murder in Maine. Written by James Moore, a retired ATF (Alcohol Tobacco & Firearms) agent, the book described how the police and prosecutors came to believe that Dennis abducted and murdered 12-year old Sarah Cherry of Bowdoin, Maine. Then, Moore described how the police theories and the conviction were incorrect. Despite considerable evidence of another perpetrator, including DNA of an unknown male underneath Sarah's thumbnail, Dennis remains in prison. However, the struggle to free this innocent man continues.

Bill had called me because he knew I was trained as a lawyer at Boston University Law School and that my wife had been a judge in Massachusetts. However, although I passed the Mass. bar exam, I had not practiced law and was certainly not a criminal lawyer – in part because I feared the possibility of seeing an innocent client convicted. When my wife and I moved to Maine, she passed the required bar exam, and I declined to take it.

Reading *Human Sacrifice* and meeting the author led to thousands of hours of my volunteer work for Dennis, along with Bill Bunting and many other members of Dennis's support organization, Trial and Error. We created the website for Dennis, www.trialanderrordennis.org. After two full-time years, I was forced to resign from the organization because Dennis's lawyer, whom I had originally recruited, disagreed with my view that the struggle for Dennis's exoneration[1] was a political as well as legal campaign. Such campaigns should, in my view, seek support from all quarters, including the police, the public and the victim's family and friends, if discreetly and humanely possible. Dennis's lawyer felt that the struggle was between lawyers and that she would cease representing Dennis if I was not removed from the organization.

Shortly after my separation from Trial and Error, but not my continued private efforts directly with Dennis, I was contacted by David Wallace of Brunswick, Maine. He told me that his half-brother, Alfred Trenkler, had been wrongly convicted in Massachusetts Federal District Court in 1993. After some investigation, it was soon apparent that Alfred was completely innocent of the crimes which sent him to prison for life. We created the website, www.alfredtrenklerinnocent.org along with the support organization, the Alfred Trenkler Innocent Committee. I wrote the book, *Perfectly Innocent - The Wrongful Conviction of Alfred Trenkler*, and we contacted as many stakeholders as possible, including his jurors. However, presenting the truth has not yet been enough, just as it has not been enough, so far, for Dennis Dechaine after the publication of *Human Sacrifice.*

The New England Innocence Project accepted Alfred's case in 2010 and in 2011 Judge Nancy Gertner retired from the bench to become a professor at Harvard Law School. At the same time, she joined and led the effort to exonerate Alfred.

---

1. Exoneration is defined as the vacating of a wrongful conviction. For a complete definition see the Glossary.

In 2009, I became a licensed private investigator in Maine in the belief that such certification would assist my efforts on behalf of the wrongly convicted, including Dennis Dechaine and Alfred Trenkler.

In November 2009, Chad Evans read a front page *Boston Herald* article about Alfred Trenkler's case and of the then-existing plan by the Boston Police Dept. to re-investigate the case. Chad was an inmate in the New Hampshire State Prison, serving 43 years-to-life for the purported murder of 21-month old Kassidy Bortner. Kassidy was the daughter of Chad's live-in woman-friend, Amanda Bortner. Once again, a website, www.chadevanswronglyconvicted.org, was created and I wrote a book, *EYE CONTACT- The Mysterious Death of Kassidy Bortner and the Wrongful Convictions of Chad Evans and Amanda Bortner.* Amanda was wrongly convicted and sentenced to two years in prison for endangering Kassidy's life by not stopping Chad from abusing and murdering her. Chad had done neither.

I worked with Chad and a former Massachusetts attorney to prepare a habeas corpus petition for Chad to submit *pro se* to the New Hampshire Superior Court in early 2013. However, Chad felt uncomfortable in that *pro se* role and was advised by others that the draft habeas was too long and would not likely succeed, so we located an attorney to improve the habeas petition and then to file and argue it.

Early in 2010, the non-profit organization, BonPasse Exoneration Services, was established, with the hope of assisting more wrongly convicted inmates.

In April, 2013, I attended the annual Innocence Network Conference in Charlotte, North Carolina and presented my paper on the role of polygraphs in wrongful conviction exoneration cases. (It's discussed in the main text of this book.) That paper was previously presented to a Maine polygraph seminar sponsored by the American Polygraph Association.

In 2013, I collaborated with Jaykumar Menon of Montreal on his innovative efforts to expand the work of the Innocence Movement. He had been the key attorney in the David Wong exoneration case in New York.[2] The ideas that contributed to that effort led to the idea that much more is needed to be done in the U.S. to eradicate wrongful convictions and remedy those which had already occurred. The first collection of those ideas appeared in 2014 in my two companion utopian novels, *Jesus and Jesusa* and *2121.* Jesus and Jesusa were twins cloned from a relic of Jesus of Nazareth and who later became co-popes. In the first book, a man was wrongly convicted for an apparent assassination attempt on the co-popes. The novel *2121*, presented a man wrongly convicted of manslaughter who was finally exonerated in the year 2121. In that same year, his sister gave birth to the first human born on Mars. During the late 21st century in the book, *2121*, the U.S. had successfully reduced its wrongful conviction rate to less than .1 percent, which effort became the subject of this book.

On March 28, 2014 I wrote to several leaders of the Innocence Movement about achieving such a goal:

> I write to you as leaders of the Innocence Movement, with a recommendation that

2. "David Wong," National Registry of Exonerations, at http://www.law.umich.edu/special/exoneration/Pages/casedetail.aspx?caseid=3763

the Innocence Movement declare a two part national goal to nearly eliminate wrongful convictions within a reasonable time. First, we need a numerical standard for justice, which could be a .1% wrongful conviction rate, and second, we need a time frame, recommended at five years, to reflect the urgency of the need.

Last year, the movement was correctly proud of the record 87 exonerations recognized by the National Registry of Exonera-tions. Martin Yant wrote an article,[3] attached, on the Wrongful Convictions Blog about how exonerations were still difficult to achieve. I added the comment below:

Yes, exceedingly difficult. It's estimated that between 1-6% of inmates were wrongly convicted. Let's be conservative and use the 1% number, and apply that to an inmate population of 1.5 million. That works out to 15,000 INNOCENT people in prison. Given that number and normal turnover, it's likely that far more than 87 wrongly convicted people actually were SENT to prison last year, as compared to the 87 who were exonerated. Shouldn't there be some kind of a national goal to reduce the percentage of the wrongly convicted in prison to something like 1/10 of a percent?

---

3. Martin Yant, "Exonerations still exceedingly difficult to receive." On the "Wrongful Convictions Blog," February 7, 2014, at http://wrongfulconvictionsblog.org/2014/02/07/exonerations-still-exceedingly-difficult-to-achieve/

Doesn't that sound like a goal consistent with "beyond a reasonable doubt"? That means 1,500 inmates, and even that number should be intolerable and inexcusable. Now, if we had another goal to reduce the number of the wrongly convicted in prison from the estimated 15,000 to 1,500 in five years, that would mean exonerating 2,700 inmates a year (and not wrongly convicting anyone during that time).

Eighty-seven (87) may be the largest number so far, but it's no time for complacency. Martin is right. Exonerations are still much too hard to achieve.

To give more perspective on the 87 number, it was estimated by "the skeptical juror" in the attached 2010 article that there are 10,000 wrongful convictions every year in this country.[4] Most of them are below the radar because the sentences are short.

Given the incredible progress of the Innocence Movement since the Registry's date of 1989, or the founding of Centurion Ministries in 1983, is it now time to ask that there be a national campaign to reduce wrongful convictions? It's good that the Federal Government has established the National Commission on Forensic Science, and that Peter is on that Commission, but

---

4. "On the Rate of Wrongful Conviction," by the Skeptical Juror. August 25, 2010 at http://www.skepticaljuror.com/2010/08/on-rate-of-wrongful-conviction-chapter_25.html

forensic science is only one part of the wrongful conviction problem.

In 1962, President Kennedy set the goal for the United States to put a man on the moon by the end of the decade. At the time of the setting of that goal, only a maximum of seven years and three months in the future, the United States had launched only two people into orbit, beginning with John Glenn in January and Scott Carpenter in May, and neither flight lasted longer than five hours.

1. The Goal of .1%. Attorneys and judges have long been reluctant, to my knowledge, to attach a number to "beyond a reasonable doubt." This is unfortunate, because for many courts, that standard seems to have evolved into "probably." Attached is a 1992 Canadian Parliament report[5] on the problem of wrongful conviction which notes that "it has been claimed that in Great Britain, the wrongful conviction rate may be as high as .1%...." Also, the article notes that the U.S. percentage had, as of that early time in the Innocence Movement been estimated to be between .5% and 1%. Now, as we know from several U.S. studies, the percentage is more likely between 1% and 6%. For this memo, let's

---

5. "Wrongful Convictions in the Criminal Justice System," by Philip Rosen, Library of Parliament (Canada), Jan., 1992, at http://www.parl.gc.ca/Content/LOP/researchpublications/bp285-e.htm

use the range from the Innocence Project's[6] website: 2.3% to 5%.

There is a difference between a .1% wrongful conviction rate for all the criminal trials, and saying that .1% of all the convictions are wrongful; but let's assume they are the same here. Why can't we say that "beyond a reasonable doubt" = 99.9%? Despite the high publicity of losses of passenger planes, the safety rate for such travel is much higher than 99.9%. In 2009, the International Air Transport Assn. reported that there is one commercial plane accident every 1.4 million flights, which works out to 99.99992857%. For each person on these multi-passenger flights, the percentage is even higher. In any case, humans build these planes and humans fly these planes, just as humans designed the criminal justice system and humans run the system. Why can't we aim for a 99.9% accuracy rate for our criminal justice system?

2. The Goal of five years.

If the prison population is a conservative 1.5 million, that means that there are between 34,500 and 75,000 innocent people in prison [using the range of estimated percentage of wrongful

6. Where this book refers to the "Innocence Project" it is referring to the original Innocence Project founded by Barry Scheck and Peter Neufeld in 1992 and based in New York City within the auspices of the Cardozo School of Law. When other innocence projects in the Innocence Movement (www.innocencemovement.org) are cited, their full name and geographical responsibility will be identified.

convictions of 2.3% to 5%]. If you look at the total number of people under judicial or probation supervision for convictions, and they all suffer even if not in prison, the number is much larger.

Even if the current exoneration rate of 87 per year were multiplied by ten [deleted], we still would not be making a dent. President Kennedy didn't ask to send two more people into orbit per year in succeeding years. He urged a quantum leap, just as the Innocence Movement should do.

Using 50,000 as a round number, conservative average, it would take five years at 10,000 per year to bring that number down to the .1% number of 1,500. This work doesn't address what is needed to prevent any more than a few hundred new wrongful convictions a year. Ten thousand exonerations year sounds like a very large number, compared to 87, but the 365 days in a year sounds like a very large number to all those inmates, as you know more than most people.

Thus, I write to you to ask that you collectively, somehow, announce to the world, somehow, the two goals, .1% and five years, and ask the govern-ments of the United States to do their part to achieve those goals. It will take an effort like the Man-to-the-Moon, but the country can do it. Incidentally, in dollar terms, the Kennedy goal cost the country approximately $159 billion in 2012 dollars. At $30,000 per year, which is

> only one aspect of the total cost of the incarceration of the wrongly convicted, it costs $1.5 billion annually to support our wrongly convicted inmates, using the 50,000 estimate. It would take more than that to imple-ment the necessary changes to the criminal justice system, but likely not costing $159 billion.

The response to that email led to the writing of this book.

Selected Chronology of Wrongful Convictions and Innocence Movement

1819	Exoneration of the Boorn brothers in Vt., before their hanging for the murder of Russell Colvin, who returned alive.
1887	Hanging of William Jackson Marion in Nebraska for the murder of John Cameron.
1891	John Cameron reappeared in Nebr., alive.
1932	*Convicting the Innocent*, by Edwin Borchard
1952	*Court of Last Resort*, by Erle Stanley Gardner
1963	*The Vindicators*, by Eugene B. Block
1964	*The Innocents*, by Edward D. Radin
1970	Inmate population in U.S. prisons: 200,000 Estimated wrongly convicted @2%: 4,000
1989	First DNA Exoneration: Gary Dotson (Ill.)
1990	Inmate population in U.S. prisons: 770,000 Estimated wrongly convicted @2%: 15,400
1992	Founding of the Innocence Project
2005	Establishment of Innocence Network, originally with 21 founding member projects.
2010	Inmate population in US prisons: 1.6 million Estimated wrongly convicted @2%: 32,000
2014	December 31. Exonerees since 1989 in National Registry of Exonerations: 1,520.

Introduction

The United States has a large wrongful conviction problem, and it's a travesty. Putting it that way has the sound of telling a friend that s/he has a drinking problem, or a drug problem or an obesity problem, and then offering to help that friend overcome the problem. It's not an easy discussion to start or complete, but that's the purpose of this book.

The forensic DNA revolution, which produced its first wrongful conviction exoneration in 1989, has led to some changes in the U.S. criminal justice system but not nearly enough. During that milestone year, 200 years after the Bastille Day dawn of the French Revolution, the exoneration of Gary Dotson in Illinois led the first 25-year wave of exonerations in the United States. Both events were milestones in the march for human liberty. Previously, a criminal exoneration had been an occasional droplet into an otherwise tranquil sea of confidence in the U.S. justice system. That drop has turned into a stream, and this book seeks to turn it into a torrent.

Americans are fond of saying that our criminal justice system is the best in the world.[1] Fortunately, in this data-driven internet world the question of the quality of justice has been surveyed in the annual Rule of Law report of the World Justice Project. The eighth of the nine "factors" of justice which were surveyed is criminal justice and that factor uses seven sub-factors:

1. See, for example, the statement on the website of Congressman Tim Cole of Oklahoma: "The United States has perhaps the world's best criminal justice system with multiple safeguards in place to prevent innocent people from being unjustly convicted." at https://cole.house.gov/punishment-does-not-fit-crime.

8.1 Criminal investigation system is effective
8.2 Criminal adjudication system is timely and effective
8.3 Correctional system is effective in reducing criminal behavior
8.4 Criminal justice system is impartial
8.5 Criminal justice system is free of corruption
8.6 Criminal justice system is free of improper government influence
8.7 Due process of law and rights of the accused

In the 2014 survey, the U.S. ranked 22nd out of the 99 countries surveyed.[2]

The DNA revolution has revealed to everyone that a larger than widely known percentage of all criminal convictions in the U.S. have been wrongful, and that is another indication that the claims of "best criminal justice system" are misplaced.

In the history of criminal justice systems, the people wrongly convicted over the centuries always knew what had happened to them, but few others knew or cared. More recently, their lawyers probably knew, but they were usually able to rationalize the wrongful convictions of their clients, perhaps by saying that their own assessments might have been wrong. Another possibility was that lawyers rationalized that such injustice was unavoidable collateral damage in an otherwise excellent system. A related phenomenon is that defense lawyers tend to distance themselves from their innocent clients in order to protect themselves from the emotional burden of a wrongful conviction.

2. "Rule of Law Index – 2014," World Justice Project, at http://worldjusticeproject.org/sites/default/files/files/wjp_rule_of_law_index_2014_report.pdf

Despite such books as Edwin Borchard's 1932 classic, *Convicting the Innocent - Sixty-five Actual Errors of Criminal Justice,*[3] wrongful convictions were thought in the early 20th century to be improbable or extremely rare.

In 1963, Eugene Block published *The Vindicators,*[4] which, if written today, might have been named *The Exonerators*, to align with the current word usage. In that book, Block summarized the stories of many instances of injustice and injustice avoided, including 12 exonerations from wrongful convictions. One of the 12 was the wrongful conviction of James Montgomery, a successful Black factory worker in Illinois who lived in one home and had tenants in another.

Montgomery was convicted in 1923 of raping a 62-year old mentally unstable white woman who later died in a mental hospital. Through the extensive pro bono efforts of Luis Kutner, later a professor at Yale Law School and known as the creator of the "living will," Montgomery was finally released from prison 26 years later in 1949.

The *Chicago Sun-Times* editorialized about the case on August 16, 1949:

> "The case is so shocking, indeed that it should make Illinois citizens sick at heart. Assuming the facts are as Judge Igoe found them to be, James Montgomery was the victim of ghastly injustice. What can Illinois do about it? One obvious duty is to compensate Montgomery for the 25 years of useful life which the state took away from him. Beyond this looms the more important

3. Yale University Press, 1932.
4. Doubleday, 1963.

> question of how Illinois can attain a system of criminal law administration in which such cases won't happen. The fact that there has been one such case brings the question: How many other James Montgomery's are there in our prisons? How many other men are being victimized because their constitutional rights to a fair trial were flagrantly violated?"[5]

The newspaper asked the right questions, but the answers have proved elusive to this day.

Despite the horrific miscarriages of justice which Eugene Block described and which surely indicated that there were hundreds, if not thousands still to be reported, the author was optimistic about future avoidance of wrongful convictions. He wrote that wrongful conviction could occur to anyone,

> ...but that it is far less likely than ever before because of the many safeguards – scientific, legal, and moral – that have been set up in recent years to prevent such miscarriages of justice. A strong public conscience supports such advances.
>
> As has been stated before, probably the most significant progress has been made in the attitude and philosophy of law enforcement officers themselves, who have come to realize, more and more, that truth and justice are their main objectives, whether their work results in conviction or in vindication.[6]

5. Ibid. page 167. Bills were introduced in the Illinois Legislature and the Illinois Court of Claims approved the $150,000 claim for Montgomery, but he never received any compensation for his lost 25 years. He died in 1962.
6. Ibid. Page 237.

Such confidence was bolstered by others, including a member of the Pennsylvania Board of Pardons who stated publicly upon the exoneration of George Wentzel in 1951 that of the 15,000 cases he had reviewed since taking office, this was the first in which he was absolutely positive that the petitioning prisoner was entirely innocent.[7] A one-in-15,000 chance works out to .006 percent, but inmates who request pardons are discouraged from claiming innocence because contrition and remorse were the required emotions.

A year after Eugene Block's book, Edward Radin published *The Innocents,* which he began with a discussion of "The Myth," that "innocent people are not convicted for crimes they have not committed."[8] Radin went on to recount stories of much injustice in America, including 84 exonerations, or their equivalents, of the wrongly convicted. He wrote that for every "case that captures public attention there are literally hundreds of others that receive little, if any, press attention."[9]

In addition to the books by Borchard, Block, and Radin, there were a few others prior to 1989 that presented the truth to readers about wrongful convictions. The four Appendices of this book are lists of books relating to wrongful convictions before and after 1989.

Appendix A is a list of general books, with some articles about wrongful conviction, organized by

7. Ibid.
8. *The Innocents*, by Edward D. Radin, 1964. William Morrow and Co. Page 7. The phrasing of this myth is astonishingly similar to "Myth #2" of the eight myths presented 57 years later by Jim and Nancy Petro in their 2011 book, *False Justice: Eight Myths that Convict the Innocent*: "Our system almost never convicts an innocent person."
9. Ibid. Page 8.

date. Appendix B has a list of books about specific cases of exoneration organized by state and date. Appendix C has a list of books in support of claims of innocence by those convicted of crimes, also organized by state and date. Appendix D provides a short list of novels where wrongful conviction is an issue.

Because the exoneration of Gary Dotson occurred in 1989, that year has been informally designated by many as the pivotal year in the struggles for the wrongly convicted. For example, the National Registry of Exonerations[10] begins with exonerations achieved during that year.

Except for the occasional alive appearance of a person thought to have been murdered, or money thought to have been stolen, the DNA-based exonerations provided for the first time a level of certainty that was previously missing from claims of wrongful conviction.

By December 31, 2014, twenty-five years after Gary Dotson was exonerated by the vacating of his rape conviction, the count of exonerations in the National Registry of Exonerations had risen to 1,520, including 67 in 1989[11]. The second largest count, so far, is 91 from calendar 2013, but it's already been exceeded by the 2014 count of 98 as of December 31, 2014. Considering that six of the 2013 count of 91 were reported in 2014, the count for 2014 will likely approach 105 by the end of 2015.

The sad and intolerable truth is that even with the highly publicized exonerations of an ever-increasing number of people, but still fewer than

10. www.exonerationregistry.org.

11. The National Registry of Exonerations was launched two years earlier in May 2012 with a total of 891 exonerations since 1989. The December 31, 2014 count of 1,520 is used throughout this book.

100 per year, there are many more innocent people being convicted each year than are being exonerated. As will be seen in Chapter 1, that 100 is less than one percent of the people likely to suffer wrongful convictions every year. Thus, the vast majority (99+ percent) of wrongfully convicted people either serve their entire wrongful sentences or die in prison.

Those who emerge alive from jails and prisons must wear the permanent labels of "felon" affixed to their records, and most of those are never exonerated. One reason is that the scarce legal resources available for overturning wrongful convictions are devoted primarily to those who suffer the most, i.e. those who are in prison, and especially those who are on death rows.

This book presents a call-to-action to achieve two goals within five years:

1. **reduce wrongful convictions in the U.S. to .1 percent.**
2. **reduce the percentage of wrongly convicted inmates in prison to .1 percent, by liberating the thousands of wrongly convicted inmates.**

The last clause of title of this book, "before the end of this decade," comes from President John Kennedy's setting the goal for the United States to land a person on the Moon by the end of the 1960s. At the time of the creation of that Moon landing goal in a speech on September 12, 1962 at Rice University in Texas,[12] the end of the 60s decade was seven years and three months in the future. When Kennedy spoke, the United States had

12. See full speech at http://er.jsc.nasa.gov/seh/ricetalk.htm.

launched only two astronauts into orbit, beginning with John Glenn in January 1962, and Scott Carpenter in May, and neither flight lasted longer than five hours.

This book is being published in January 2015, which is only five years from the end of this decade of the 2010s, but the country now knows a lot more about the problems of wrongful convictions than the U.S. knew in 1962 about landing a person onto the Moon. Hopefully, this book will advance that knowledge.

There have been many calls to stop wrongful convictions, and quickly. On May 31, 2012, the New York State Bar Association and the Innocence Project, issued a joint press release, "Stop Wrongful Convictions, Now."[13]

For practical purposes, the book title's goal to "STOP" wrongful convictions is the same as "REDUCE TO .1%," which is one in one thousand.

The concept of STOPPING wrongful convictions isn't new to this book. The Jeffrey Deskovic Foundation for Justice,[14] once had a logo with a red STOP sign with the words "wrongful convictions" inside the sign and below "STOP."

John Grisham spoke at Wake Forest University in 2010 and the student newspaper headline credited his passion: "John Grisham: Stop Wrongful Convictions."[15]

However, STOPPING is an absolute and that's not as reasonable as the .1 percent proposed here.

13. http://www.innocenceproject.org/Content/Stop_Wrongful_Convictions_Now_Innocence_Project_and_New_York_State_Bar_Association_Call_to_Action.php

14. http://www.thejeffreydeskovicfoundationforjustice.org/

15. "John Grisham: StopWrongful Convictions," by Katie Phillips. Sept. 16, 2010, *Old Gold and Black*. At http://oldgoldandblack.com/?p=10212

A few words about words.

Among the most important words in this book is "innocent." The definition in the Glossary presents the definitions of the non-legal generic "innocent" and the legal sense of not guilty beyond a reasonable doubt.

In this book, "innocence" and "innocent" are used, or assumed to be used, in the legal sense. When it appears to be ambiguous, there may be an explanatory note accompanying such usage.

The difficulty with the words "innocent" or "innocence" in the context of criminal justice comes when a lay listener thinks that both meanings are intended, but in reality it is only the legal sense.

For example, consider the case of William Lee who was convicted in Michigan in 2007 of felonious assault and two counts of rape and sentenced to 15-30 years in prison. On appeal, a new trial was ordered because the state had mishandled exculpatory evidence by claiming that the rape kit was insufficient for DNA testing. Lee's counsel learned otherwise and obtained an order for DNA testing. Lee was re-tried and acquitted with a finding of not guilty beyond a reasonable doubt in 2010, but he remained in prison for three more years for an unrelated conviction for robbery.[16]

William Lee is listed as an exoneree in the National Registry of Exonerations and he is legally innocent. However, during the 2006 incident for which he was wrongly convicted, he was with the victim and another person and was fighting with that other person. Also, he was a robber. Some people would be reluctant to call William Lee "innocent" in the generic, virginal sense. However,

16. "William Lee," National Registry of Exonerations, at http://www.law.umich.edu/special/exoneration/Pages/casedetail.aspx?caseid=3377

in the legal sense he was innocent of the assault and rape as he was found not guilty beyond a reasonable doubt.

Marvin Mitchell was convicted in 1990 in Massachusetts for raping an 11-year old girl despite his dramatically different appearance from her initial description of her assailant. At his trial, the lab technician incorrectly summarized the statistical probability that Mitchell was the assailant. Mitchell served seven years in prison before a new attorney secured DNA testing which showed that Mitchell was not the rapist. A new trial was ordered, but the prosecutor declined to prosecute further.[17] Thus, Mitchell was returned to his pre-trial status of presumed legal innocence.

In 2005, the City of Boston finally agreed to settle Mitchell's lawsuit for $450,000. Such a settlement could be said to have explicitly established that Mitchell was factually, as well as legally, innocent.

Themes of this book.

The book provides 80 practical proposals for national reform of the criminal justice system in order to reduce the frequency of wrongful conviction to .1 percent or less. That's one in one thousand or 1 in 1,000. It's approximately the chance that a coin can be flipped 10 times and come up on the same side every time. There are several themes which permeate the book.

1. <u>Make Truth and Justice the highest priority goals of the Criminal Justice System and for its</u>

17. "Marvin Mitchell," National Registry of Exonerations, at http://www.law.umich.edu/special/exoneration/Pages/casedetail.aspx?caseid=3478

participants. While it is often said that truth is the objective of trials,[18] it sometimes happens that the application of legal rules reduces the windows to truth. For example, the interest in reducing the government's cost of justice has led to laws and rules which restrict the ability of inmates to petition the courts for further relief. Some laws and rules restrict the time periods within which petitions for new trials can be filed on the basis of new evidence. These laws are often fiscally misplaced because the costs of keeping innocent inmates in prison often outweigh the costs of re-investigations and re-trials.

Canon 7 of the American Bar Association Model Code of Professional Responsibility for attorneys states that a lawyer's obligations are to the lawyer's client and to the legal system, but it doesn't mention truth or justice. The word "truth" as applied to lawyers[19] appears only twice in the Code, not counting the extensive footnotes, and those instances are in the sections which govern attorney advertising, as in "truthfully" (EC 210) and publicity ("truthfulness,")DR 2-101(C).

A classic illustration of the lower priority for truth and justice when weighed against professional norms is the case where a lawyer will keep secret information shared with him/her by a client even when the disclosure of that information would prevent an injustice. For examples, see Chapter 13.

18. "Court proceedings are held for the solemn purpose of endeavoring to ascertain the truth which is the *sine qua non* of a fair trial." Estes v. State of Texas, 381 U.S. 532, 540 (1965), rehearing denied, 382 U.S. 875, 15 (1965).
19. For witnesses, Ethical Canon 7-28 provides that "Witnesses should always testify truthfully...."

2. Ameliorate the Adversary Process. Many of the causes of wrongful conviction arise from the adversarial structure of the Anglo-American criminal justice system, where one side wins and the other loses. In such a system, the constant temptation is to take actions, or not take action, in order to win the contest, regardless of the implications for obtaining truth and justice.

There is a twisted saying from the movie, "The Thin Blue Line," but which could have come from anywhere, and which no longer is said publicly by prosecutors, that "any prosecutor can convict a guilty man. It takes a great prosecutor to convict an innocent man."[20] Such sick humor illustrates the problem.

The goal of many of the proposals in this book is to assist the search for truth and justice as a first priority, rather than enabling one side to increase the probability of winning.

3. Take a systematic "organizational" look at the criminal justice process. While many of the proposals in this book relate to specific aspects of the criminal justice process, such as witness identification, others look at the entire system.

Since 1989 when the DNA-induced reality of wrongful conviction shook the criminal justice system, some have called for systemic review of errors, just as does the National Traffic Safety Board of all airplane accidents.

Most recently, the National Institute of Justice issued a report, *Mending Justice: Sentinel Event Reviews*, which presents several essays about fixing the criminal justice system, often from the

20. Said by the Attorney Melvyn Carson Bruder, playing himself in "The Thin Blue Line," at http://www.imdb.com/title/tt0096257/quotes

perspective of "sentinel events."[21] A "sentinel event" is a "bad outcome that no one wants repeated and that signals the existence of underlying weaknesses in the system." This terminology borrows from the worlds of medicine and transportation where a sentinel event might be an unexpected death after minor surgery or a plane crash.

Sentinel reviews treat errors of a system as "organizational errors," and not merely errors of one person. For example, a decision by a judge that a DNA statute does not authorize a new trial can be seen not just as an error by the judge or the arguments of the prosecution or the defense, but also as an error by the drafters of the DNA legislation and those who amended the language as it worked its way through to enactment.

Each of the proposals presented in this book could warrant a book by itself, or at least a scholarly article. The ideas are collected here in one volume to provide the public with a view of what **can** be done, and **should** be done, to stop wrongful convictions. Many of the proposals, such as legalizing recreational drugs, are supported by others for reasons entirely separate from the expected effect on the wrongful conviction rate.

There are two aspects of the U.S. society which are basic causes of injustice and wrongful convictions, but are far less amenable to short proposals. They are racism and income/wealth inequality. It is well-known that the burden of

21. *Mending Justice: Sentinel Event Reviews*, National Institute of Justice, 2014, at http://www.nij.gov/topics/justice-system/pages/mending-justice.aspx. This report is about systematically addressing all types of "organizational" or "sentinel" errors in the criminal justice system, including wrongful convictions.

wrongful convictions falls most heavily on non-whites and on the poor.[22] Some of the proposals here ameliorate the effects of racism and inequality, but the solutions of those problems go far beyond criminal justice.

These 80 proposals by no means include the complete set of possibilities, of which there are hundreds. Daniel Medwed has presented many proposed "reforms" and those of others in his excellent book, *Prosecution Complex.* Those reforms are aimed at the problem of wrongful conviction from the perspective of prosecutors. He listed four themes for his reforms, all of which are consistent with the proposals in this book:

1. that there should be greater transparency in most discretionary decisions made by prosecutors,
2. that courts and legislatures should raise the legal bar for prosecutors in justifying those discretionary choices,
3. that ethical rules should be more concrete and disciplinary agencies more inclined to penalize prosecutors for violating them, and
4. that prosecutors should construct internal review committees to evaluate major decisions to neutralize the grave effects of cognitive bias.[23]

22. See "Dealing with the Racial Nature of Wrongful Conviction," by David Love. *Huffington Post*, December 23, 2014, at http://www.huffingtonpost.com/david-a-love/dealing-with-the-racial-nature-of-wrongful-convictions_b_6337850.html. He wrote, "The vast majority of the wrongfully convicted who are exonerated through DNA evidence are people of color. The numbers don't lie."
23. *Prosecution Complex – America's Race to Convict and Its impact on the Innocent*, by Daniel S. Medwed. New York University Press. 2012. Page 4.

If only a few of the reforms in Medwed's book and a few of the proposals contained in this book are adopted, in whole or in part, and if only a few wrongful convictions are avoided or corrected, its writing will have been worth the effort.

Chapter 1: The Wrongful Size of the United States Wrongful Conviction Problem.

Statistics can be numbing, but they must be used in this book. Wrongful convictions are simply too large a problem to tell the story by anecdote or individual cases. This chapter presents the important categories which are quantified, and the ranges of estimates for each and the estimate to be used in this book.

The Categories

A. Annual convictions for felonies

In 2006, there were 1,132,290 convictions for felonies in state courts and 72,983 in Federal courts for a total of 1,205,273.[1] Included as felonies were: murder, rape, sexual assault, robbery, aggravated assault, burglary, larceny, fraud, forgery, drug possession, drug trafficking, weapons offenses and a category of "other" offenses. These are the crimes for which people are sent to prisons and jails.

For perspective, but beyond the scope of this book, in 2006, there were 11.5 million reported crimes within roughly the non-drug-related crimes specified above.[2] As convictions for these crimes constituted 47 percent of all felony convictions, it

1. U.S. Census Bureau, *Statistical Abstract of the United States*, 2011 – Table 346. See also the report of approximately 1 million felony convictions per year in Peter Yost's, "Criminal Exonerations: 2,000 Convicted Then Exonerated Over Last 25 Years, Says Study." Associated Press, 21 May 2012, at http://www.huffingtonpost.com/2012/05/21/criminal-exoneration-convicted-released-23-years-study_n_1531908.html.
2. U.S. Census Bureau, *Statistical Abstract of the United States, 2012* – Table 306. Data for the year 2006 was the most recent available.

can be estimated that the total number of felonies committed in 2006 was approximately 24 million. That would mean a conviction rate per reported crime of approximately 5 percent (1.2 million/24 million).

ESTIMATE: For this book, the annual felony conviction count for this decade, in the absence of adoption of the proposals here, is estimated to be 1 million.

B. Annual wrongful convictions.

In *The Innocents*, Edward Radin recounted a conversation with a "highly respected judge" who said to Radin, "Let us suppose for the sake of argument that justice does falter in five percent of the cases tried. In this imperfect world you certainly must admit that any system that renders justice ninety-five percent of the time is doing very well."[3]

Radin then extrapolated that in the 1960s there were approximately 280,000 convictions annually, and five percent of that number was an "astonishing" 14,000. Radin wrote, "It may be comforting to the judge to think in terms of ninety-five percent, but there is scant comfort in thinking of even 1,000 innocent persons being imprisoned"[4] every year.

In 1996, three authors, (C. Ronald Huff, Arye Rattner and Edward Sagarin), estimated that there were approximately 10,000 wrongful convictions per year.[5]

More recently, there have been several studies.

In 2007, Michael Risinger compared exonerations, as were known at the time, and convictions

3. *The Innocents* by Edward D. Radin, William Morrow & Co. 1964, page 8.
4. ibid, page 9.
5. The book was *Convicted But Innocent: Wrongful Conviction and Public Policy*, Sage Publications.

for capital rape and murder for the years 1982-1989. He calculated a wrongful conviction rate of 3.3 to 5.0 percent.[6]

In 2012, using an exhaustive review of previous studies and data, Marvin Zallman estimated that the wrongful conviction rate was between .5 percent and 1.0 percent.[7]

In 2013 Professor Samuel Gross, of the University of Michigan Law School and one of the founders of the National Registry of Exonerations, and author of several articles and compilations about wrongful conviction, estimated that the wrongful conviction rate for serious violent offenses was between 1-5 percent.[8]

In April 2014, a *Scientific American* article reported a National Academy of Sciences study which estimated a wrongful conviction rate of 4.1 percent for people sentenced to death since 1973.[9]

In June of 2014, the National Institute of Justice released a 2012 study conducted by the

6. "Innocents Convicted: An Empirically Justified Wrongful Conviction Rate," by D. Michael Risinger. *Journal of Criminal Law and Criminology*, Vol. 97, No. 3, 2007.
7. "Qualitatively Estimating the Incidence of Wrongful Convictions," by Marvin Zalman. *Criminal Law Bulletin*, Volume 48, No. 2, pp. 221-279. (2012). At http://globalwrong.files.wordpress.com/2012/04/qual-estimate-zal-clb-2012.pdf
8. "How Many False Convictions Are There? How Many Exonerations Are There?" by Samuel Gross, in *Wrongful Convictions and Miscarriages of Justice: Causes and Remedies in North American and European Criminal Justice Systems*, C.R. Huff & M. Killias, Editors. Routledge, 2013.
9. "Many Prisoners on Death Row are Wrongfully Convicted," by Dina Fine Maron, *Scientific American*, April 28, 2014. The cited article was "Rate of False Conviction of Criminal Defendants who are Sentenced to Death," by Samuel Gross, Barbara O'Brien, Chen Hu and Edward H. Kennedy, in the *Proceedings of the National Academy of Sciences*, April 28, 2014, at http://www.pnas.org/content/111/20/7230.full

Urban Institute of convictions for sexual assault in Virginia from 1973 through 1987. The study found wrongful convictions within the astonishing range of 8-15 percent.[10]

In November 2014, New York Federal District Court Judge Jed Rakoff wrote of his understanding that the wrongful conviction rate was between two and eight percent.[11]

In December 2014, exoneree and advocate Jeff Deskovic summarized the current conventional wisdom that the percentage of wrongful conviction is between 2-5 percent, but he added that on the basis of his own experience in prison, the number is closer to 15-20 percent. In a *Huffington Post* article, he listed 13 exonerees that he personally knew when he was in prison.[12]

At the other end of the spectrum are a few deniers of the problem, including Supreme Court Justice Antonin Scalia. In the 2006 case of Kansas v. Marsh, Justice Scalia wrote in his concurring opinion of "the .027% error rate for American verdicts...."[13] For that number he cited a widely discredited calculation by Oregon District Attorney,

10. "Post-Conviction DNA Testing and Wrongful Conviction," Urban Institute Justice Policy Center, by J. Roman and K. Walsh, as released by the National Inst of Justice, June 2014, at https://www.ncjrs.gov/pdffiles1/nij/grants/238816.pdf
11. "Why Innocent People Plead Guilty," by Jed S. Rakoff. November 20, 2014, *New York Review of Books*, at http://www.nybooks.com/articles/archives/2014/nov/20/why-innocent-people-plead-guilty/
12. "Recent Rash of Exonerations Only the Surface: Many More Remain Wrongfully Imprisoned," by Jeffrey Deskovic. *Huffington Post*, December 9, 2014. At http://www.huffingtonpost.com/jeffrey-deskovic/recent-rash-of-exoneratio_b_6296898.html
13. Kansas v. Marsh, 548 U.S. 163 (2006), at http://www.law.cornell.edu/supct/html/04-1170.ZS.html. Michael Lee Marsh II was not executed and remains in prison.

Joshua Marquis.[14] Twenty seven thousandths of a percent can be stated as one in 3,703.

Another person who downplays the seriousness of the problem is Scott Burns, former executive director of the National District Attorneys Association. He said in 2012 that prosecutors in the US had prosecuted about 400 million non-traffic-related cases during the same period studied by the National Registry of Exonerations, i.e. 1989-2012, or 23 years.[15] That's an average of 17.4 million per year. He said that the statistics from the Registry "give the gross perception that there is a serious problem with wrongful convictions in this country, and it is just not the case," Burns said.

There are about 30,000 prosecutors in the country in more than 2,000 offices of district attorneys, attorneys general and county attorneys.[16]

If the wrongful conviction rate was only one percent during that period, that would have meant 4 million wrongful convictions, during the period from 1989 through 2012. Four million.

ESTIMATE: This book will use the estimate of a wrongful conviction rate of two percent for all crimes. Applying the 2 percent estimate to the estimated number of 1 million felony convictions annually brings the estimate of 20,000 annual wrongful felony convictions.

14. "The Innocent and the Shammed," Op-Ed by Joshua Marquis. January 26, 2006, *New York Times*, at http://www.nytimes.com/2006/01/26/opinion/26marquis.html
15. "Wrongful convictions shine spotlight on judicial system," by Kevin Johnson. *USA Today*, May 20, 2012.
16. *Prosecution Complex – America's Race to Convict and Its Impact on the Innocent*, by Daniel Medwed. New York University Press, 2012. Introduction, page 5.

Paraphrasing what the authors of the Urban Institute study wrote about their 8-15 percent estimate, "whether the true rate of potential wrongful conviction is [2 percent]... is not as important as the finding that these results require a strong and coordinated response."[17] This book urges a "strong and coordinated response."

C. Inmates in prisons and jails.

The number of inmates in prison is a key number because it's the most extreme form of punishment in the United States, except for execution in 32 states and by the Federal Government.

In 2012, there were 1,571,013 inmates in Federal and state prisons.[18] The often reported number of two million people-plus in U.S. prisons includes those in local jails and juvenile facilities. Those additional inmates are not included here as many of them are pre-trial detainees.

The Economist has estimated that there were 721,000 inmates in U.S. jails as of June, 2012. Of those, 60 percent had been convicted of crimes, which results in a count of 432,600 convicted people in jails.[19] The others were awaiting trial.

These numbers far exceed those for all other countries in the world. With five percent of the world's population, the U.S. holds 25 percent of the

17. "Post-Conviction DNA Testing and Wrongful Conviction," op cit., Fn#10, at page 58.
18. "Prison Populations Down for Third Straight Year," by Ted Guest, 25 July, 2013, at http://www.thecrimereport.org/news/inside-criminal-justice/2013-07-prison-populations-down-for-third-straight-year
19. "America's prison population – Who, what, where and why," by J.F. in *the Economist.* March 13, 2014 at http://www.economist.com/blogs/democracyinamerica/2014/03/americas-prison-population

world's inmates.[20] In four U.S. states, more is spent on prisons than on education.[21]

ESTIMATE: For the purposes of future projections, this book uses the estimate of 1.5 million inmates in U.S. state (1.3 million) and Federal prisons (.2 million) and .5 million in jails.

D. Number of wrongly convicted inmates in prisons and jails.

Using the estimate of 2 percent for the rate of wrongful convictions, as derived above, the estimates used in this book are 30,000 wrongly convicted people in U.S. prisons and 10,000 in jails.

E. Number of people under criminal justice supervision, i.e. parole, probation or supervised release.

In addition to the numbers of the incarcerated, there were approximately 4.7 million adults on parole (.85 million), probation or supervised release (3.91 million) in 2013.[22] Although large, those numbers represented a fifth year of steady decline.

The turnover is also large, with approximately two million going onto correctional supervision and two million coming off every year, with the latter number slightly larger than the former.

20. "Changing the Priorities of a 'Prison-Happy Country,'" by Walter Holton, Jr. at *The Crime Report*, at http://www.thecrimereport.org/viewpoints/2014-11-changing-the-priorities-of-a-prison-happy-country
21. ibid. The states are California, Michigan, Oregon and Pennsylvania, but the state and local splits for funding education make a difference in the calculations.
22. "Probation and Parole in the United States, 2013," by Erinn Herberman and Thomas Bonczar, Bureau of Justice Statistics, U.S. Dept. of Justice at http://www.thecrimereport.org/news/articles/2014-10-new-report-probation-numbers-drop-parole-increases

ESTIMATES: As the number is declining, the estimates used in this book are four million people under correctional supervision and two million coming on and off each year.

Applying the two percent wrongful conviction rate to those numbers obtains a total of 80,000 wrongly convicted people under supervision, with 40,000 being added and subtracted every year.

It's estimated very roughly that there are 15 million Americans, mostly men, who have been either incarcerated otherwise subjected to correctional supervision. That's about two percent of the total U.S. population.

F. Annual exonerations of the wrongly convicted.

In 2013, there were 91 exonerations, according to the National Registry of Exonerations. Of those, 72 were released from prison, 12 were relieved of their parole or probation status and 7 were already free, but had their records expunged.

ESTIMATES: As the number of exonerations has been gradually increasing, it can be estimated that those numbers will continue to increase gradually, in the absence of implementing the proposals in this book, to the levels of 80, 20 and 10.

The percentages of their respective categories are:

80 from prisons (1.5 million) = .05 percent (or five out of every 10,000)
20 from parole/probation (4 million) = .00005 percent (or five out of every 1 million)
10 from a status of post-correctional supervision freedom. (no estimate of percentage made here.)

G. Annual reduction in count of annual wrongful convictions from 2 percent (20,000) to reach level of .1 percent (1,000) by the end of 2019.

There would have to be an annual reduction of 4,750 wrongful convictions annually to reach the annual rate of 1,000 at the end of 2019.

H. Annual exonerations of inmates required to reduce the number of wrongly convicted in our prisons from the current estimate of 30,000 to 1,500.

Even without an annual inflow of wrongly convicted people to prison, there would have to be an annual reduction of the wrongly convicted population in prisons by 7,125 annually to reach the population of 1,500 by the end of 2019. That is, there would have to be 7,125 exonerations per year of prison inmates.

However, if the projected annual inflow of estimate "G," above, is utilized, the annual exoneration rate would have to be the total of 4,750 plus 7,125, or 11,875. This is 118.75 times (11,875 percent) the current exoneration rate of approximately 100 per year.

I. Annual exonerations of people under correctional supervision required to reduce the count to .1%.

Very few (7 of 91 or 7.6%) of the annual exonerations involve non-supervised citizens, or free citizens. One reason for that is that there is less need, as compared to the powerful drive to remove the wrongly convicted from death row and from our prisons. That need is far more important than the desire of a person to clear his/her record of a criminal conviction – although that goal means a lot to millions of Americans.

The other reason for the low percentage of exoneration of people with criminal records is that their cases are usually very old and the evidence is often unavailable.

To move the number from 80,000 (2 percent of four million) to 4,000 (.1 percent) would require a vast undertaking.

Given the other priorities and the short five year project plan, this goal must have a lower national priority, except for those individuals who come forward with facts and arguments that make exoneration relatively easier.

J. Distribution of Wrongful Convictions among the States.

In short, some states have more wrongful convictions and exonerations than others. Also, it takes longer in some states to exonerate the wrongly convicted. In early 2014, the author generated a ranking of the U.S. states according to the frequency of exonerations and the lengths of wrongful imprisonment.[23] The six states with the most wrongful conviction activity were District of Columbia, Louisiana, Massachusetts, Mississippi, Nebraska and Illinois. At the other end of the chart are Delaware, Maine, New Hampshire, North Dakota, and South Dakota. However, the low ranking of these states is due in some part to their refusal to acknowledge and correct the wrongful convictions which have occurred there. Thus, the rankings are not necessarily those of better justice.

K. Costs of Wrongful Convictions in the U.S.

23. "Ranking of States by Frequency of Wrongful Conviction Exonerations and Lengths of Time Before Exoneration," by Morrison Bonpasse, January, 2014, at http://www.bonpasseexonerationservices.com/documents/140120ArticleonrankingofStatesforWCswsprdshts.pdf

Borrowing from the study of economics, a key concept for understanding the costs of wrongful convictions is whether costs are "internalized" or "externalized." When they are internalized, they are incorporated into the understanding of the true cost of an activity. For example, the requirement to obtain liability insurance for drivers of automobiles is a way of internalizing the potential costs of harm which an automobile might cause to others. Instead of externalizing the cost of such harm by relying upon the injured party to pay for his or her costs, the liability insurance provides a means of assessing those costs to the owner of the automobile, as spread out over all the owners of automobiles which are covered by the insurance policies of a particular insurance company.

In Illinois, which has suffered more than its share of wrongful convictions, the Better Government Association (BGA) released in 2011 a study of the costs of wrongful convictions. Using the records of 85 exonerations in Illinois since 1989, the BGA study, authored by John Conroy and Rob Warden, found that those 85 cases cost the taxpayers of Illinois $214 million. Included was the obvious cost of 926 years in prison which cost taxpayers $18 million at the estimated rate of approximately $20,000 per year per inmate. Other costs included the compensation paid to exonerees, and the costs of litigation. If the total costs of 16 lawsuits pending at the time of the study, and expected to be assessed soon, were included, the total bill was expected to be $300 million.[24]

24. "The High Costs of Wrongful Convictions," by John Conroy and Rob Warden. The Better Government Association, June 2011, at http://www.bettergov.org/investigations/wrongful_convictions_1.aspx.

Not included in the total costs were the externalized costs of the subsequent crimes committed by the real perpetrators of the crimes for which the 85 exonerees were wrongly convicted. The study identified 14 murders, 11 sexual assaults, 10 kidnappings and more than 62 other felonies committed by those real perpetrators. As the real perpetrators in 48 of the 85 cases were never identified, the number of subsequent crimes committed by all the real perpetrators should be roughly doubled.

This study did not include the internalized and externalized costs of the hundreds of claimants of wrongful convictions who will never be exonerated and will either die in prison or be released on schedule. Since the release of the June 2011 study, more than 100 additional Illinois citizens have been exonerated.[25]

Extrapolating from the ratio of 85 exonerees costing $300 million (or $3.5 million each), the estimated total cost to the United States of the 1,520 exonerations in the National Registry of Exonerations since 1989 as of December 31, 2014, @$3.5 million, is $5.4 billion.

This is a lot of money. As this estimate arises from Illinois, the saying misattributed to the late U.S. Senator Everett Dirksen from Illinois can be recalled, "You take a billion here. You take a billion there, and pretty soon, you're talking about real money."[26]

25. Nat'l Registry Exonerations at www.exonerationsregistry.org.
26. Wikiquote. Everett Dirksen, at http://en.wikiquote.org/wiki/Everett_Dirksen

Chapter 2: 80 Proposals for STOPPING Wrongful Convictions

Below are 80 proposals which have the common goal of stopping wrongful conviction in the U.S. In practical terms, this means bringing the frequency down to .1 percent or less, and bringing the percentage of wrongly convicted people in prison down to that same level.

Each proposal is presented once in a single chapter, but some proposals may be applicable to several stages in the criminal justice process. For example, Proposal 49, regarding the disappearance or destruction of evidence, is presented in Chapter 8, the trial chapter, but it is also applicable in the post-trial chapters as well.

The methods of implementing these proposals varies widely, from Constitutional Amendment (changing standard of guilt, Proposal 55) to judge's courtroom practices (colloquoy with prosecutors, Proposal 28) to changed police practices (interviews, Proposal 27).

Chapter 3. National Goal and National Registry

Proposal 1: That the United States establish a national goal of reducing wrongful convictions to .1 percent or fewer of all criminal convictions.

Proposal 2: That the President appoint a National Commission to recommend the changes necessary to prevent, and correct previous, wrongful convictions before the end of this decade with its report to be due in early 2016.

Proposal 3: That a national registry of claims of innocence be established.

Proposal 4: That the national DNA database, CODIS, be expanded to include all citizens and residents of the U.S.

Proposal 5: That the national fingerprint database, IAFIS, and its successor, the NGI, be expanded to include all citizens and residents of the U.S.

Proposal 6: That the country's citizens, corporations and governments utilize the decreasing cost of computer memory and processing to gather more data which can be used to deter and sanction crime.

Proposal 7: That every prosecutor's office have a "conviction integrity unit" to give that office a first review opportunity to detect or prevent wrongful convictions, and to review post-conviction claims of innocence.

Proposal 8: That every state, and the Federal Government, have within it at least one Innocence Project, or equivalent organization, which works on behalf of those claiming innocence.

Proposal 9: That every state have a statewide commission which reviews claims of wrongful conviction and makes recommendations to the judicial branch for exoneration based on innocence.

Proposal 10: That the subject of wrongful conviction be taught at every law school and police academy and that every continuing legal and professional education program for police, lawyers and judges provide further education about wrongful conviction.

Proposal 11: That forensic science standards utilized in all jurisdictions be consistent with those recommended by the National Commission on Forensic Science.

Proposal 12: That a National Forensic Science Agency be established within the Department of Justice.

Proposal 13: That spending for indigent defense be increased to a level whereby judges and juries cannot easily determine by the availability of expertise or the quality of the work performed and testimony given whether a defendant's case is privately or publicly funded.

Proposal 14: That all states abandon the practice of appointing private counsel for indigent defendants and move to the practice of universal state funding of public defender offices.

Proposal 15: That the Innocence Movement participate in the election and judicial nomination processes at every governmental level to promote the goals of preventing and correcting wrongful convictions.

Proposal 16: That biometric software be developed that will standardize and render more accurate eyewitness recollections, including generic photo arrays.

Proposal 17: That the goals be established that the annual level of crime be reduced to the levels of 1960 and/or the levels of crime for men be reduced to those of women and/or that the levels of crime be reduced to those of the United Kingdom.

Chapter 4. Reduce Crime and prison populations

Proposal 18: That all recreational drugs be legalized and regulated.

Proposal 19: That other victimless crimes, including prostitution and gambling, be legalized and regulated.

Proposal 20: That the length of prison sentences be adjusted to reasonable levels, approximating those in Europe.

Proposal 21: That mandatory prison sentencing, and mandatory minimums be eliminated.

Proposal 22: That the bail process be changed from a money-based system to a risk based system.

Proposal 23: That parole, and/or other processes of early release be established or re-established in those states which do not have them.

Proposal 24: That a claim of innocence during parole hearings not be an absolute bar to granting such parole.

Proposal 25: That the number and lethality of guns be reduced through taxation and regulation.

Proposal 26: That the death penalty be abolished.

Chapter 5. Investigation

Proposal 27: That all interviews and interrogations be recorded, preferably video recorded. Further, that no confession be admissible in court without a recording, preferably video, of the confession and the interview(s) preceding the confession.

Proposal 28: That in every criminal case there be full open file disclosure to the defense of everything in the files of the prosecution and police and their experts related to the case against the defendant, except information which may jeopardize the safety of one or more people.

Proposal 29: That the Office of the Coroner or Medical Examiner in each state be placed within that state's Health or Public Health Department.

Proposal 30: That DNA be collected at all crime scenes where the deposit of the perpetrator's DNA is probable.

Proposal 31: That for every investigation where there is an eyewitness identification, the witness's verbal description of all relevant aspects of the perpetrator be written and signed by the witness, and a drawing or other visual representation be created. And that these steps be taken before there is any lineup or other actual effort to have the eyewitness identify the perpetrator.

Proposal 32: That subsequent use of a physical lineup or photo-array process be conducted without any suggestion or hint regarding the possible perpetrator.

Proposal 33: That checklists be used by law enforcement, prosecutors, defense attorneys and others to ensure that best practices are followed.

Proposal 34: That polygraph examinations be made available to all defendants and witnesses on an ability-to-pay basis, with public funding paying the balance. And that if an exam result is not acceptable to the defendant, s/he may request a peer review of that exam, and/or another exam with a different examiner.

Proposal 35: That where internal and external experts are used by the police and prosecution to prove guilt, an amount of money equivalent to the costs of those experts should be made available to the defense for expert consulting and witnesses. And that if such funding is not made available, the evidence from the government's experts should not be allowed at trial.

Chapter 6. Grand Jury/Preliminary Hearing for Indictment

Proposal 36: That prospective defendants be invited to give testimony to grand juries or to prosecutors who are considering indictments.

Chapter 7. Pleas and Plea Bargaining

Proposal 37: That a prosecutor not proceed, nor continue, with a charge against a defendant unless s/he believes beyond a reasonable doubt that the defendant committed the crime, and that s/he believes that s/he could persuade a jury of the defendant's guilt beyond a reasonable doubt; and that the prosecutor sign a nationally standardized form affirming those beliefs.

Proposal 38: That a judge participate in the plea bargaining process and hear evidence, if necessary, to ensure fairness, and to protect where applicable a defendant's claim of innocence.

Proposal 39: That prosecutors meet with defendants, together with counsel for at least one hour in order that prosecutors understand that they will be prosecuting a human being with a life story. And that questions which prosecutors may ask would come from a national standardized list.

Proposal 40: That the Alford plea, which allows a defendant to plead guilty even while claiming innocence, be eliminated. Alternatively, no plea bargaining should be permitted for a defendant who claims innocence.

Chapter 8. Trial

Proposal 41: That jury training be at least one day in duration and include nationally produced videos, with emphasis on the meaning of "beyond a reasonable doubt" and the risks and causes of wrongful conviction.

Proposal 42: That no witness or victim be asked to identify the defendant at trial.

Proposal 43: That the testimony of defendants be encouraged, and that if a defendant is reluctant to testify the trial judge (in a jury trial, or other judge in a bench trial) intervene to negotiate the terms or boundaries of the defendant's testimony.

Proposal 44: That when a defendant testifies, the jury be instructed during the post-evidence charge to the jury that if it is leaning toward a guilty finding beyond a reasonable doubt, it must also find the defendant guilty of perjury and make specific findings that specific statements by the defendant were lies beyond a reasonable doubt.

Proposal 45: That when witnesses testified for an alibi defense, the jury be instructed during the post-evidence charge to the jury that if it is leaning toward a guilty finding beyond a reasonable doubt, it must also make specific findings that specific statements by the alibi witnesses were false beyond a reasonable doubt.

Proposal 46: That jurors be authorized by statute or court rule to ask questions during trials, but before deliberations.

Proposal 47: That jurors be authorized by statute or court rule to ask questions after deliberations have begun which may require the reopening of the evidentiary portion of the trial including the recalling of witnesses for providing additional testimony and/or the production of documents.

Proposal 48: That inmate informants not be utilized to present allegations at trial that during conversations in jail or prison a defendant admitted guilt or said anything else to the informant which was incriminating.

Proposal 49: That when potentially exculpatory evidence which was in the possession of the police or prosecution disappears or is destroyed, that evidence be construed to be favorable to the defendant.

Proposal 50: That where evidence of "consciousness of guilt" is allowed into a trial, the defendant be permitted to introduce evidence of "consciousness of innocence," or that in the alternative, the concept of "consciousness of guilt" be disallowed as evidence.

Proposal 51: That jury deliberations be structured by written guidelines from the court, with explicit provisions for voting procedures.

Proposal 52: That the number of jury votes on any indictment count be limited to three and if a vote leaves only one or two jurors in the minority, that s/he/they must be advised of the right to request the cessation of deliberations on the count at issue.

Proposal 53: That when a mistrial is declared due to the failure of a jury to agree on a defendant's guilt, and the jurors' positions are determined to be reasonable, that such mistrial be deemed to be a trial with a Not Guilty verdict and not subject to retrial.

Proposal 54: That jury deliberations be video recorded and be open to review by either party for up to one year. And that if any irregularities which may have influenced the verdict are identified, they should be brought to the attention of the trial judge to ensure that the jury verdict was fairly and legally reached.

Proposal 55: That the standard of "beyond a reasonable doubt" be restored to its proper meaning by defining it mathematically as 99.9 percent certain. OR, if that proves unfeasible, to change the standard of guilt to "beyond any doubt" or "no doubt."

Proposal 56: That juries be re-empaneled in the interest of justice when new evidence develops and that the available jurors be asked whether, for a Guilty verdict, the new evidence would have introduced sufficient reasonable doubt to prevent them from reaching a guilty verdict, or, for a Not Guilty verdict, whether the new evidence would have erased their previously expressed doubts.

Chapter 9. Post-Trial

Proposal 57: That judicial reviews of cases be permitted at any time, but at least every year, when claimants of innocence present new evidence or new interpretations of law, and that such reviews consider all the evidence in a case.

Proposal 58: That filing deadlines for motions for relief from wrongful convictions be waived in the interest of justice when the petitioner has presented a non-frivolous justification for the delay.

Proposal 59: That the standard for the post-trial vacating of a previous verdict be: whether the jury, or fact-finding judge, would have been likely to have had "reasonable doubt" or "any doubt" if all the evidence now available had been presented at trial.

Proposal 60: That in appeals from Guilty trial verdicts, every split decision at the appellate court level be interpreted as a reversal of the lower court's decision on the issues raised, or of the entire verdict.

Proposal 61: That when an appeals court or habeas court rules that a conviction must be reversed for reasons relating to the existence of reasonable doubt as to guilt, the case must be returned for the option of retrial without further appeal.

Proposal 62: That no evidence be discarded or destroyed or returned to owners until the death of a defendant or the end of his/her judicial penalty. But that in severe circumstances where storage is expensive and/or where property needs to be returned to owners, such disposition be with approval of the defendant and his/her counsel which approval shall not be unreasonably withheld.

Proposal 63: That post-trial recantations by witnesses be fairly evaluated for their truthfulness, and that subsequent charges of perjury be initiated only by judges in the interests of promoting truthfulness at all stages of the criminal justice system. And that polygraphs be utilized in that consideration.

Proposal 64: That post-trial reviews of cases utilize the maximum use of DNA testing and other up-to-date forensic knowledge where there was insufficient forensic expertise presented at trial.

Proposal 65: That jurors be encouraged to have a continuing interest in justice in a particular case, and that if they come to believe that the verdict for which they voted is unjust, they be encouraged to step forward individually or as a group with their views.

Proposal 66: That victims and their families be encouraged to continue to seek justice in their cases, which will sometimes involve claims of wrongful conviction.

Proposal 67: That defense attorneys, police, prosecutors and judges be encouraged to have a continuing interest in justice in a particular case, and that if they come to believe that the verdict in a case in which they participated is unjust, they be encouraged to proactively seek justice.

Chapter 10. Executive powers

Proposal 68: That Governors and the President administer their departments and bureaus of corrections and prisons in order to encourage that all claims of wrongful conviction by inmates, parolees and probationers be presented and fairly considered.

Proposal 69: That Governors and the President invite members of the Innocence Network or related organizations to establish offices within every prison system in the U.S. which can provide inmates with onsite confidential appointments to present and discuss their claims of innocence.

Proposal 70: That Governors and the President specifically proclaim to their corrections employees and to inmates, parolees and probationers that they will work proactively to ensure that there are no innocent people in their prisons by the end of the 2010s decade.

Proposal 71: That Governors and the President direct that the libraries of each of their prisons be connected electronically with the law library of a nearby law school and that inmates receive adequate training and assistance to maximize their utilization of the library's legal resources.

Proposal 72: That Governors and the President use their powers of Pardon and Clemency to release inmates or defendants whose claims of innocence have not received a fair decision before the judicial branch. And that the standard of pardon or clemency be the same as for the granting of a new trial, i.e. would it be likely that a contemporary jury, after hearing all the currently available evidence would find "reasonable doubt" or "any doubt" as to the culpability of the defendant.

Proposal 73: That when governors and the President and their delegates appoint judges and prosecutors, they should consider the proven record of sensitivity to the claims of innocence by defendants and those who have been wrongly convicted.

Chapter 11. Post Exoneration

Proposal 74: That fair compensation be paid to all defendants who suffered imprisonment and other deprivations due to wrongful convictions, and that such compensation begin, at some reasonable level, within 30 days after the inmate's release from prison or the vacating of the conviction.

Proposal 75: That all other vestiges of wrongful conviction be remedied for each exoneree, such as criminal records for the vacated wrongful conviction, immediately upon release from prison or the date of vacating of the conviction.

Proposal 76: That the 42 US Code 1983 statute be amended to change the absolute immunity from civil liability for prosecutors in their "advocative" functions to a qualified immunity, as already applies to their "non-advocative" functions.

Chapter 12. Substance and procedure in an Adversarial System.

Proposal 77: That wherever the adversarial system faces a choice between the system and its procedures, or truth and justice, that truth and justice prevail.
Proposal 78: That where the enforcement of a procedural rule is likely to deter the presentation of the truth and frustrate justice, a judge would be authorized to waive that enforcement.

Chapter 13. Conclusion

Proposal 79: That everyone involved in the criminal justice system accept a responsibility to ensure that truth and justice prevail.
Proposal 80: That enough of the previous 79 proposals be implemented to STOP and CORRECT wrongful convictions before the end of this decade.

Chapter 3: The National Problem of Wrongful Convictions Requires National Solutions

Although every wrongful conviction occurs at a local level, and there must be changes at every local level, the size of the wrongful conviction problem also requires national changes. This multi-level solution is similar to what was needed for success for the civil rights movement: national legislation and action and state and local legislation and action.

Proposal 1: That the United States establish a national goal of reducing wrongful convictions to .1 percent or fewer of all criminal convictions.

There are few "national goals" with which most citizens are familiar. Earlier in this book, the goal of putting men on the Moon before the end of the 1960s was noted.

In 1972, Congress passed the Clean Water Act with the national goal of "to restore and maintain the chemical, physical, and biological integrity of the Nation's waters."[1]

In 1988, Congress established "the national long-term goal" that "radon levels in buildings" be "as free of radon as the ambient air outside of buildings."[2]

In 2014 President Obama issued a memorandum "Establishing a National Goal and Developing Airport Specific Action Plans to

1. "The Clean Water Act," U.S. EPA, at http://water.epa.gov/action/cleanwater40/cwa101.cfm
2. 15 U.S.C. 2661 at http://codes.lp.findlaw.com/uscode/15/53/III/2661

Enhance the Entry Process for International Travelers to the United States."[3]

Given the low frequency and low visibility of current specific national goals, the time is right to establish the proposed goal of reducing wrongful convictions to .1 percent.

Proposal 2: That the President appoint a National Commission to research and recommend the changes necessary to prevent, and correct previous, wrongful convictions before the end of this decade with its report to be due in early 2016.

When the timing is right and the issue is ready for national change, the appointment of a national commission can be very helpful.

Among previous successful commissions was the "9/11 Commission." It was established in 2002 to recommend ways to avoid such "9/11" attacks in the future. It issued its final report in 2004, which led to several government reorganizations and changes in intelligence gathering.

The Warren Commission issued its final report on the assassination of President John Kennedy in September, 1964, less than a year after the assassination. While it didn't answer all public questions, it did reduce public uncertainty.

In February, 1968, the National Advisory Commission on Civil Disorders, known more familiarly as the Kerner Commission, issued its report on racial relations in the country, in light of

3. May 22, 2014. Presidential Press Release, at http://www.whitehouse.gov/the-press-office/2014/05/22/presidential-memorandum-establishing-national-goal-and-developing-airpor

the riots in cities in the 1960s. The report came only seven months after President Johnson created the Commission in July, 1967.

Thus, important commissions can work rapidly and they can influence the course of history.

In 2013, Attorney General Eric Holder announced the creation by the Departments of Justice and Commerce, through its National Institute of Standards and Technology, the National Commission on Forensic Science. The objectives of the Commission are to:

> provide recommendations and advice to the Department of Justice (DOJ) concerning national methods and strategies for: strengthening the validity and reliability of the forensic sciences (including medico-legal death investigation): enhancing quality assurance and quality control in forensic science laboratories and units: identifying and recommending scientific guidance and protocols for evidence seizure, testing, analysis, and reporting by forensic science laboratories and units; and identifying and assessing other needs of the forensic science communities to strengthen their disciplines and meet the increasing demands generated by the criminal and civil justice systems at all levels of government.

On the 33-member commission, only one person, Peter Neufeld of the Innocence Project, is clearly identified with the issue of wrongful convictions.

While improving forensic science is an important part of reducing wrongful convictions, the creation and operation of the Forensic Science

Commission will not be enough. The country needs, in addition, a National Commission on Wrongful Convictions (NCWC).

The NCWC should be commissioned to continue making recommendations until the achievements of the twin goals of reducing wrongful convictions to the effective stopping point of .1 percent and to reduce the percentage of wrongly convicted inmates in our prisons to .1 percent.

Proposal 3: That a national registry of claims of innocence be established.

Creating a national registry of claims of innocence (NRCI) would achieve several goals. First, it would help answer the question of how many inmates are actually innocent, by providing a base number of claimants. From that base, there could be further estimates of the numbers are actually innocent.

There will be some inmates who are actually innocent who don't bother to register or who are otherwise missed, but it's estimated that most of such claimants are actively claiming their innocence and will be in the Registry. Simultaneously, the Registry would track those who are exonerated. The next step will be to compare the counts of those exonerated to those who are claiming innocence, for the appropriate time periods. By so doing, we will come closer than any previous study to answering accurately the question, "How Many Wrongly Convicted People Are There?"

Such a registry now exists in testing form, at www.registryofclaimsofinnocence.org. There are fewer than one thousand names on the Registry for the U.S., as most of them have come from the internet. The names are listed by state and name, with a separate category for the Federal Government. Also listed with the names are the primary crime for which convicted and the year of conviction. Additional information for some of the claimants is available in linked documents.

Thousands of inmates claiming wrongful conviction have written for assistance to Innocence Projects and related members of the Innocence Network. A review by the author of data on the internet from nine such organizations showed that during the period 2008-2013, approximately 39,000 requests for assistance were received. Of those, the nine organizations achieved 89 exonerations, or .23 percent of the applications.

Surely, some of the 39,000 were duplicates and some were, on their face, unworthy of investigative resources. However, after a triage review, the vast majority of those 39,000 were set aside and effectively forgotten. It's not known how many inmates write to multiple organizations with the same plea, "Help me, I'm innocent." One such inmate was David McCallum, who was exonerated in October 2014 in New York City. Of his efforts a Center for Wrongful Convictions newsletter stated, "David McCallum never stopped fighting for his innocence, appealing his conviction with no luck in either the state or federal courts. He also wrote to innocence organizations around the country without success until one of his letters landed on the desk of the Canadian organization, Innocence International, and captured the attention of [Hurricane] Carter and [Ken] Klonsky."[4]

It could become a requirement that any applicant for assistance with the Innocence

4. Newsletter of the Center on Wrongful Convictions, October 15, 2014.

Network be first registered with the Registry of Claims of Innocence. Alternatively, every Innocence Network member could register the applications they receive for assistance with the Registry of Claims of Innocence. That would reduce the redundancy of applications for assistance from multiple sources.

Of the 91 exonerees recorded by the National Registry for Exonerations in 2013, 31 were due to the work of organizational members of the Innocence Network. If the .23 percent ratio calculated above for exonerations:applications were applied to these members, that would mean that the 31 exonerations arose from approximately 13,478 requests for assistance. What isn't known is how many of those inmates, or others under correctional supervision, applied to more than one member organization of the Innocence Network. Also, it isn't known for how long the .23 percent ratio has held. With average prison sentences in the U.S. of 63 months,[5] it seems reasonable to multiply the annual estimated number of requests for assistance by five years, for a total of 67,000. Beyond five years, on average, inmates leave their prisons.

Currently, those requests for assistance are viewed as confidential communications between potential legal clients and their potential attorneys, so very little is known about them, beyond the sheer numbers which are not systematically available. However, if future claimants to Innocence Network organizations were asked to consent, by the use of a form letter, to the release

5. "Finding Direction: Expanding Criminal Justice Options by Considering Policies of Other Nations," Justice Policy Institute. April, 2011, at http://www.justicepolicy.org/research/2322

of a bare minimum of information for the Registry of Claims of Innocence, that information could be transferred to the Registry, and the world would get a far better view of the size of the wrongful conviction problem.

Journalists, law schools, and even prosecutors need to know the size of the wrongful conviction problem in order to mobilize resources to solve it, i.e. reduce the frequency of wrongful conviction to .1 percent.

Proposal 4: That the national DNA database, CODIS, be expanded to include all citizens and residents of the U.S.

CODIS is the acronym for the national COmbined Dna Index System, which is maintained by the Federal Bureau of Investigation (FBI). The system includes the NDIS (National Dna Index System). CODIS was originally established as a database with coded information about 13 "markers" from DNA samples of convicted felons and unidentified DNA (called forensic profiles) from crime scenes throughout the country. CODIS now also contains information about the DNA of missing persons and arrestees (where authorized by individual states.)

As of August, 2014, the CODIS contained over 11 million offender profiles, close to 2 million arrestee profiles and close to .6 million forensic profiles. Combining the offender and arrestee files gives a total of 13 million, assuming that the FBI numbers have zero overlap. That 13 million is 6 percent of the U.S. adult population in 2013 of 214 million, and 4 percent of the entire population of 316 million.

The expansion of CODIS to include all Americans would constitute a major increase and would be controversial. Logistically, the easiest time for collection would be the sampling of DNA from all newborns in the U.S. For all others, border crossings would be a likely sampling point for visitors and immigrants.

The primary benefit to the country would be that nearly all crimes where DNA collected from a crime scene and ostensibly belonging to the offender would be solved. For example, it would mean that nearly all rapes where DNA was collected would be solved.

For the purposes of this book, it would mean that the rate of wrongful conviction would be substantially reduced. It would achieve that goal indirectly by identifying suspects whose DNA would currently be "unknown" because it belongs in the 94 percent of the adult population whose DNA is not in CODIS. That would lead more rapidly to solving the crime as compared to the current processes where other methods are used. Where suspects are located by those other methods, police often assume that the "unidentified" DNA is therefore meaningless, whereas it could be vitally important of the source were identified.

If the DNA of all Americans, including visitors and alien residents, were contained in the CODIS database, the chances of identifying perpetrators when DNA is collected would increase to nearly 100 percent. With such prospects for success, police would be encouraged to gather DNA at many more crime scenes, including those of minor misdemeanors.

In 2012, New York became the first state to require that DNA samples be taken from people convicted of all misdemeanors. Previously, the state's law extended to only 48 percent of the misdemeanors.[6] Twenty-plus other states have led the way with obtaining samples from felony arrestees. Maryland's practice of collecting DNA from felony arrestees was upheld in 2013 by the U.S. Supreme Court in the case, Maryland v. King.[7] For those arrestees from whom probable cause is not found, the DNA samples are destroyed.

In 2015, Wisconsin began collecting DNA from felony arrestees and from those convicted of misdemeanors. The state's additional DNA collection is expected to grow from 12,000 annually to 65,000.[8] It's expected that the other states will follow suit and continue to expand their DNA databases as the utility of that course continues to be demonstrated.

Some states will move faster than others. In December 2014, a three judge California appeals court ruled that the expansion of DNA collection to arrestees, as approved by voters in a 2004 referendum, violated the California state constitution. The court noted that 62 percent of people arrested for felonies in California were never convicted, and about 20 percent were not charged with crimes.[9] Unlike the Maryland statute which

6. "Governor Cuomo Signs Law to Expand New York's DNA Databank," Press release, Office of Governor Cuomo. March 19, 2012, at https://www.governor.ny.gov/press/03192012-Dna-Databank
7. 569 U.S. ____, 133 S.Ct. 1958 (2013) https://supreme.justia.com/cases/federal/us/569/12-207/
8. "Wisconsin preps for surge in DNA tests when crime law kicks in," by Todd Richmond, Associated Press in *Milwaukee Journal Sentinel*, at http://www.jsonline.com/news/crime/wisconsin-preps-for-surge-in-dna-tests-when-crime-law-kicks-in-b99396012z1-283632111.html
9. "Mandatory DNA collection during arrest is unconstitutional, court says," by Maura Dolan. *Los Angeles Times*, December 3, 2014, at

was upheld in King v. Maryland there is no provision for automatic withdrawal of a DNA sample if an arrestee is not convicted.

However, given the proposed goal of including everyone in the United States in a DNA database, whether a person is ultimately convicted or whether there is probable cause will make no difference. The court was incorrect in viewing the collection of the DNA as an invasion of privacy. It's not the collection but the possible improper use of such DNA that would be an invasion of privacy.

Collecting the DNA could be compared to the sound of a tree falling in the woods when no one is there to hear it. The sound of the falling would have no effect unless someone was there to hear it, just as the collection of DNA would have no effect upon a person, unless someone used it; and no ill effect unless someone used it improperly.

The collection of DNA is about our physical attributes, such as fingerprints rather than collecting the contents of our conversations or thoughts. The fears expressed by some critics of DNA expansion address not the collection but the possible use of such DNA, such as for studies or, worse, discriminatory treatment. The way to allay those concerns is not to reduce or limit collection, but to be very careful about how the DNA data is used and by whom.

Beyond the expansion of DNA databases for the purpose of crime solving, the more comprehensive justification for a universal DNA database comes from other sources, such as the need to identify unidentified bodies, or to help locate missing or amnesic people. The City of New York, for example has buried 1,200 unidentified bodies since 1990,

http://www.latimes.com/local/lanow/la-me-ln-dna-court-ruling-20141203-story.html

and is gathering their DNA for future matches when relatives and others come forward with samples to be matched.[10]

Another use will be to apprehend some proportion of the several million people who are currently fugitives from justice with their names on arrest warrants.[11]

At each such expansion, there will be concerns expressed about our rights to privacy.

Another issue about universal DNA collection and database maintenance is cost. At $30 per saliva sample, the one-time, but over time, collection of DNA from the 300+ million Americans not already in the CODIS database would cost approximately $9 billion. Thereafter, the annual cost would be for testing the approximately four million babies born in the U.S. and approximately one million legal immigrants, for $150 million.

Balanced against that cost would be the cost savings from reducing consecutive crimes by people. When arguing in 2012 for expansion of DNA testing in New York State to include testing for all people convicted of misdemeanors, Manhattan District Attorney, Cyrus Vance, Jr. cited the example of a man convicted in 2010 of assault and robbery. The man had been convicted in the early 2000s of several misdemeanors and would have been convicted of an assault and attempted rape in 2004 if his DNA had been in the CODIS database

10. "New York City Seeks to Put Names to Unidentified Bodies," by Corey Kilgannon. *New York Times*, November 9, 2014, at http://www.nytimes.com/2014/11/10/nyregion/new-york-city-seeks-to-put-names-to-unidentified-bodies.html
11. "For a million fugitives [from three states], freedom starts at county line," by Brad Heath. Aug. 6, 2014, *USA Today*, at http://www.usatoday.com/longform/news/nation/2014/08/06/fugitives-las-vegas-wont-pick-up/13607595/

at the time.[12] A conviction and incarceration in 2004 might have avoided the 2010 crimes.

It must be noted that DNA is not perfect, and that caution must still be exercised when DNA testing and results defy common sense. For example, while a person's DNA has been thought to be totally unique, it appears that there are limits to that rule. We don't yet fully understand the frequency and extent of chimeras, which are instances of people with at least two different DNA types.[13] This phenomenon can occur for twins who share blood during their fetal periods. Women who have had children can retain some DNA from those children. Bone marrow transplant recipients can retain the DNA of donors in some organs, but it's been determined that the hair of the recipient contains only the recipient's original DNA.

We are still early in the DNA and biometrics forensics revolutions. At some point the key 13 markers of our genetic code will become as available as our Social Security numbers are today – available, but reasonably secure. The DNA markers might be coded in such a way that our DNA-code might become the single national personal identifier of the future, displacing the pervasive Social Security number.

12. "Taking DNA From All Criminals Should Be Standard Procedure," by Cyrus R. Vance, Jr. *New York Times*, January 23, 2012. At http://www.nytimes.com/2012/01/24/opinion/collect-dna-samples-even-when-its-just-a-misdemeanor.html
13. "DNA Double Take," by Carl Zimmer. *New York Times*, September 16, 2013, at http://www.nytimes.com/2013/09/17/science/dna-double-take.html and "Chimera," Wikipedia, at http://en.wikipedia.org/wiki/Chimera_(genetics)

This proposal merits a large amount of further discussion and awaits several articles and books. The far-reaching proposal is not made lightly, but with the knowledge that wider DNA-testing will improve the quality of the criminal justice system, and will contribute thereby to the reduction of wrongful convictions.

Proposal 5: That the national fingerprint database, IAFIS, and its successor, the NGI, be expanded to include all citizens and residents of the U.S.

DNA has been called the "genetic fingerprint" of the human body. Thus, an expansion of the DNA database, CODIS, warrants a similar expansion of the fingerprint database, IAFIS (Integrated Automated Fingerprint Identification System).

Actually IAFIS is a misleading acronym, because the database has more than fingerprints. From the FBI comes this description:

> Not only fingerprints, but corresponding criminal histories; mug shots; scars and tattoo photos; physical characteristics like height, weight, and hair and eye color; and aliases. The system also includes civil fingerprints, mostly of individuals who have served or are serving in the U.S. military or have been or are employed by the federal government. The fingerprints and criminal history information are

submitted voluntarily by state, local, and federal law enforcement agencies.[14]

IAFIS has fingerprints for more than 75 million Americans, split almost evenly between criminal and civil collections. For some Americans, the idea of submitting to fingerprinting is an invasion of privacy and seems to brand the innocent as suspects, given the history of fingerprints as a forensic tool.

In June, 2001, a friend of the author resigned his school teacher position after 20 years of teaching, rather than submit to fingerprinting as required by a new state law which was designed to enable school system to perform criminal records checks to prevent the inappropriate hiring of criminals as teachers. This was before September 11, 2001 when the country showed an increased willingness to weigh personal and national security higher that previously held views of privacy and honor. The difference between the proposal here and the state law that offended my friend, and many other dedicated teachers, is that this proposal does not single out any particular person or group for fingerprinting. It is for everyone.

With minimal additional effort, such as at periodic automobile license or passport renewals, or voter registrations, fingerprints could be obtained.

The FBI is currently developing the Next Generation Information system, (NGI), which will include several other biometric identifiers, such as images of the irises of eyes and palm prints and facial biometrics. The cost effectiveness of capturing additional identifying information for an

14. "Integrated Automated Fingerprint Identification System," FBI, at http://www.fbi.gov/about-us/cjis/fingerprints_biometrics/iafis/iafis.

increasing sector of the population will have to be evaluated over time. Presently, it appears that the costs of gathering more information are still outweighed by the actual costs of unsolved crimes and wrongful convictions. Those latter costs do not include their incalculable emotional and social costs and the damage to our democratic political system.

Proposal 6: That the country's citizens, corporations and governments utilize the decreasing cost of computer memory and processing to gather more data which can be used to deter and sanction crime.

In early November 2014, the power of computer technology showed what can be done for law enforcement. On Sunday, November 2, Carlesha Freeland-Gaither was kidnapped in Philadelphia. Fortunately, a witness saw the crime and reported it to police, who then discovered that a security surveillance camera had recorded the abduction.

During the next two days, a surveillance camera recorded a man using Freeland-Gaither's ATM card and another camera caught him walking through a gas station minimart in Maryland.

A traffic monitoring camera captured an image of the car, and a careful viewing of the video then found the name of the seller of the car. Fortunately, the seller of the car had a practice of attaching GPS devices to cars which might need to be repossessed. It's estimated that two million cars in the U.S. are similarly tagged.[15] Using that GPS,

15. "Miss a Payment? Good Luck Moving That Car," by Michael Corkery and Jessica Silver-Greenberg. *New York Times*, September 24, 2014, at

the police were able to find the car within five minutes of learning that information. The alleged kidnapper and Freeland-Gaither were found inside the car on Wednesday, November 4.[16]

A news account reported that Freeland-Gaither had dropped or left her cell phone at the site of the kidnapping, which the police said helped them identify the person seen kidnapped on the video recording. On the other hand, if she had kept the phone with her, and if it had an app to monitor location, it could have assisted in her liberation in another way.

Installing a GPS tracking device on a car typically costs about $100, but it can be done at much less cost by manufacturers. In the interest of reducing crime, including car theft and kidnapping and other crimes where automobiles were involved, it should be a national goal to install GPS tracking on all automobiles.

However, in the interest of privacy, only law enforcement should have access to the factory-installed GPS devices, and that utility could be used only with the permission of the owner or with a court order.

The reduction of car-related thefts, and the quicker resolution of others would help reduce wrongful convictions in several ways. First, the reduction in the total amount of crime will liberate law enforcement resources to more effectively solve other crimes. Second, the quick resolution of some crimes will reduce the chances for mistaken

http://dealbook.nytimes.com/2014/09/24/miss-a-payment-good-luck-moving-that-car/

16. "Used-Car GPS Helps Police Find Abducted Woman," by Sean Carlin and Larry O'Dell. Associated Press, November 6, 2014, at http://abcnews.go.com/US/wireStory/abducted-philadelphia-woman-rescued-man-arrested-26724277?singlePage=true

eyewitness identifications. In the case of Ms. Freeland-Gaither, the alleged perpetrator was arrested while in Freeland-Gaither's car. Without that technology and quick capture, and the passage of some time, a different man might have been arrested for the crime and convicted because he had a similar appearance to the actual perpetrator and happened to be nearby during the crime. Third, the electronic devices made the identification of the suspect more accurate, as his images were captured on several video devices.

Proposal 7: That every prosecutor's office have a "conviction integrity unit" to give that office a first review opportunity to detect or prevent wrongful convictions, and to review post-conviction claims of innocence.

Craig Watkins was elected District Attorney for Dallas County, Texas in 2007. Six months later, after considering the allegations of many wrongful convictions prosecuted by his predecessors, Watkins established the country's first Conviction Integrity Unit. The goals of the unit were to re-investigate claims of wrongful conviction and, where appropriate, prosecute alternative defendants.

Such units operate in the same spirit as internal auditors in businesses and Inspectors General in government and the military. Their goals are to ensure adherence to the goals and standards of the organization. In the case of conviction integrity units, the goal is the delivery of justice.

Since then, the unit has exonerated more than 20 people, including Michael Phillips who in 2014 became the first person exonerated on the initiative of a prosecutor's office. Phillips who had spent 12 years in prison for a rape, was still suffering as an ex-convict and registered sex offender when he learned that he had been exonerated through the work of the Dallas Conviction Integrity Unit. Said the *USA Today* article about his case, he "had long ago given up trying to clear his name. At 57, he was a registered sex offender, living in a nursing home, wheelchair-bound from severe sickle cell anemia."[17]

The Dallas example has been emulated by several jurisdictions, including New York City and Brooklyn, New York, Pima County, Arizona, Yolo County, California, Cuyahoga County, Ohio and in 2012 the first Federal Conviction Integrity unit in Washington, D.C. In New York, the Conviction Integrity Program, begun in 2010, has reviewed 160 cases and vacated four convictions.[18] Despite the Dallas success, Watkins was defeated in his bid for re-election in 2014.

A hybrid conviction integrity office structure has emerged in New Orleans where the Orleans Parish District Attorney's Office and the Innocence Project of New Orleans have established a "joint conviction review project." With an annual budget of $630,000 staff and lawyers from each group will work together to correct and avoid wrongful convictions.[19]

17. "Man exonerated by DNA – and he didn't even request it," by Yamiche Alcindor. *USA Today*. July 24, 2014, at http://www.usatoday.com/story/news/nation/2014/07/24/dallas-mans-exoneration-makes-national-history/13040299/
18. "Cyrus Vance, Jr.'s 'Moneyball' Approach to Crime," by Chip Brown. *New York Times*, December 3, 2014, at http://www.nytimes.com/2014/12/07/magazine/cyrus-vance-jrs-moneyball-approach-to-crime.html
19. "DA, Innocence Project reveal more about wrongful conviction initiative," by Helen Freund, *Times-Picayune*. August 28, 2014, at

Daniel Medwed recommends that prosecutor offices have "review committees" or "review structures" to review major prosecutorial decisions such as indictment and plea bargaining.[20]

In December, 2014, the Center for Prosecutorial Integrity published a survey of the 19 conviction integrity units which have been established since 2007. The nine units which were established by the end of 2013, reviewed about 7,000 cases which led to 61 exonerations.[21] Using a crude extrapolation from the nine units to the 2,000 prosecutor offices, it might be predicted that conviction units in every office could detect 12,000 exonerations.

While the initial goal was to correct previous wrongful convictions, another logical outcome will be that every prosecutor's office with a Conviction Integrity Unit will know how to avoid a wrongful conviction. Every prosecutor and assistant prosecutor will want to avoid having his or her cases brought before such a unit.

The movement toward the establishment of Conviction Integrity Units in every prosecutor's and Attorney General's office was boosted by the first annual Conviction Integrity Conference in Chicago in October 2014. It was sponsored by the Center on Wrongful Convictions.

As Phil Locke of the Wrongful Convictions blog has noted, an internal system designed to correct errors in an office has a potential conflict of

http://www.nola.com/crime/index.ssf/2014/08/program_aimed_at_wrongful_conv.html.

20. *Prosecution Complex – America's Race to Convict and Its impact on the Innocent*, by Daniel S. Medwed. New York University Press. 2012. See Index at page 227.

21. At http://www.prosecutorintegrity.org/wp-content/uploads/2014/12/Conviction-Integrity-Units.pdf

interest.[22] However, many non-criminal justice organizations have successful internal auditors, ombudsmen and inspectors general. Further, the conviction integrity units in prosecutors' offices should not be intended to be the only reviewing agency. Every state should also have a commission like the North Carolina Innocence Inquiry Commission which carefully reviews claims of innocence and votes on whether to refer cases to the judiciary for exoneration. (See Proposal 9.)

Nonetheless, with more than a thousand district attorneys, 50 Attorney's General and 91 U.S. Attorneys, for a total of about 2,000 separate offices of prosecutors,[23] the goal of universal usage of Conviction Integrity Units is far from achieved. The 16 units established to date constitute .8 percent of all the prosecutor offices, but it's a promising start. When every jurisdiction with a prosecutor also has a Conviction Integrity Unit, the likelihood of wrongful convictions will be greatly reduced.

Proposal 8: That every state, and the Federal Government, have within it at least one Innocence Project, or equivalent organization, which works on behalf of those claiming innocence.

By the end of 2014, there were 58 Innocence Network member organizations, but 11 states had no such organization within their borders. While several organizations covered more than one state,

22. "A Word About Conviction Integrity Units," by Phil Locke. December 12, 2014, Wrongful Convictions Blog, at http://wrongfulconvictionsblog.org/2014/12/12/a-word-about-conviction-integrity-units/
23. *Prosecution Complex*, Page 5. op cit., Fn 20.

there is no substitute for having a state-based organization, linked to the nearest law school and state bar association, which works to prevent and correct wrongful convictions.

There is no Innocence Network member organization devoted entirely to those claiming innocence from Federal Government convictions.

Proposal 9: That every state have a statewide commission which reviews claims of wrongful conviction and makes recommendations to the judicial branch for exoneration based on innocence.

The North Carolina Innocence Inquiry Commission was established in 2007 and is a model for others to follow, but with one powerful caveat. That is, its exoneration standards are too strict. As of December, 2014, it had considered a total of 1,601 claims of innocence.[24] The North Carolina prison population in December, 2014 was approximately 37,800 and the number of probationers was 95,000, but with an annual number of admissions and exits approximating 20,000, the number of people eligible for filing claims since the Commission's inception is hard to estimate, in part because many of the annual admissions are repeat offenders or violators of probation or parole. If the total number of felons eligible to file a claim in North Carolina since 2007 was approximately 200,000, the 1,601 claims represent .8 percent. If the count of total eligible population was 100,000, the percentage would be

24. North Carolina Innocence Inquiry Commission, at http://www.innocencecommission-nc.gov

1.6, which is closer to the wrongful conviction rate assumed in this book of two percent.

Of course, not all claimants of innocence actually are innocent, so it could have been expected that the percentage of inmates (and some claimants were no longer inmates) asking for Innocence Commission help would be larger than 1.6 percent.

Of the 1,601, there were 7 exonerations. The 2007 case of Henry Reeves was the first referred by a majority vote of the five person commission to a three-judge panel. The commissioners made several findings of fact before concluding that "there was sufficient evidence of factual innocence to merit judicial review."[25] Thus, the Commission's level of certainty was beyond the reasonable doubt standard of legal innocence, but at the higher standard of factual innocence.

However, the three-judge panel denied relief to Reeves, saying that he had "failed to prove by clear and convincing evidence that he is innocent of the charge."[26] Perhaps the judges were influenced by the polygraph examination result which found that Reeves was being deceptive when he denied sexual contact with his daughter. The polygraph examiner reported that the exam was conducted at the request of the Commission.[27]

25. State v. Reeves, Commissioners' opinion. December 18, 2007, North Carolina Innocence Inquiry Commission, at http://www.innocencecommission-nc.gov/Forms/pdf/Reeves/NCIIC%20Opinion%20-%20Reeves.pdf
26. State v. Reeves, Three Judge Panel Decision, September 3, 2008, at http://www.innocencecommission-nc.gov/Forms/pdf/Reeves/OpinionReeves.pdf
27. See report of Charles Slupski, in "Handouts provided to the commission during hearing," at http://www.innocencecommission-nc.gov/Forms/pdf/Reeves/ReevesHandouts.pdf

The charge for which he was convicted in 2001 was taking indecent liberties with his young daughter. He was released from prison in 2002, so there was less pressure on the decision makers to overturn the conviction.

However, the standard given to the judges by the legislature should not have been that Reeves had to prove his innocence with clear and convincing evidence, as it's not clear whether the legislature or judges meant actual/factual innocence or legal innocence. Instead, the standard for the judges should have been whether Reeves should be declared legally innocent, i.e. whether there was now reasonable doubt as to his guilt, or whether the prosecution could again prove his guilt beyond a reasonable doubt. With that standard, the three judges more likely would have granted his claim.

Of the approximately 1590 claims which have been denied by the commission, more than half failed for lack of evidence of innocence. The three subcategories were: "no reliable evidence, 9 percent", "no way to prove, 20 percent" and "no new evidence, 28 percent" for a total of 57 percent.[28] It's not known the extent to which the commission urged claimants, in addition to Reeves, to submit to polygraphs, but it's likely that such an approach did not occur for most of them. That left more than half of the claimants with no further recourse, even though some or many of them are certainly innocent.

Perhaps it was the lack of evidence that led many claimants of actual or legal innocence to

28. "Reasons for Rejection," North Carolina Innocence Inquiry Commission, at http://www.innocencecommission-nc.gov/stats.html

simply not apply for relief at all. Without a follow-up survey, that theory will never be tested.

Since the 2007 establishment of the North Carolina Commission, no state has created a similar commission. Eleven states have created commissions to study wrongful convictions, in general, and to make recommendations on how to avoid such errors, but none of those commissions was empowered to make recommendations regarding individual claims of innocence.[29]

Proposal 10: That the subject of wrongful conviction be taught at every law school and police academy and that every continuing legal and professional education program for police, lawyers and judges provide further education about wrongful conviction. .

This proposal is close to recommending the eating of apple pie, as there is considerable agreement. The differences in quantity and quality of such education are usually a matter of degree rather than existential.

Professor Stephanie Roberts Hartung wrote in a 2012 law review article about the utility of using a claim of wrongful conviction as the core of an upper level legal writing course.[30] This is what she has done at Suffolk University Law School where her classes have considered the claims of innocence of

29. "Criminal Justice Reform Commissions," the Innocence Project, at http://www.innocenceproject.org/Content/Criminal_Justice_Reform_Commissions_Case_Studies.php

30. "Legal Education in the Age of Innocence: Integrating Wrongful Conviction Advocacy into the Legal Writing Curriculum," by Stephanie Roberts Hartung. *Boston University Public Interest Law Journal*. Winter 2013.

Alfred Trenkler[31] and Raymond Tempest,[32] among others. She reported that many law schools are now teaching about wrongful convictions, albeit from different perspectives.

Nancy Petro, co-author of a leading book about wrongful conviction, *False Justice – Eight Myths That Convict The Innocent,*[33] wrote an excellent blog about including wrongful convictions in law school curricula. She observed, "When I have asked law professors and deans of law schools if their curriculum includes wrongful conviction, the answer has been no. Some have said that wrongful conviction is sometimes included in legal ethics discussions, which is extremely important... perhaps the most critical issue of all."

Petro concluded with a call to action: "For all law graduates who aspire to become defense attorneys, prosecutors, judges, or legislators, the lessons of DNA-proven wrongful conviction are among the most important to be considered. They get to the very core of our overarching American commitment to provide justice for all, and they certainly should be in the core curriculum of every law school."[34]

The same arguments for professional education and further continuing education apply for police and other law enforcement professionals. Among the topics that must be taught should be "tunnel

31. See www.alfredtrenklerinnocent.org, and the book, Perfectly Innocent – The Wrongful Conviction of Alfred Trenkler.
32. See "DNA evidence being used to get 1992 murder conviction overturned," by Katie Mulvaney. *Providence Journal.* March 24, 2014.
33. Co-Author, Jim Petro. Kaplan Publishing, 2011.
34. "Law Schools: Add Wrongful Conviction to Core Curriculum," by Nancy Petro. Posted on April 19, 2012 at http://wrongfulconvictionsblog.org/2012/04/19/

vision: how it works and how to avoid it." Tunnel vision among the police and prosecutors causes them to focus on an early suspect and, consciously or unconsciously, to accept and encourage incriminating information and ignore information exculpatory to the person in the tunnel.

Proposal 11: That forensic science standards utilized in all jurisdictions be consistent with those recommended by the National Commission on Forensic Science.

No more should the U.S. tolerate convictions based on outdated or bogus science. There should never be another Cameron Todd Willingham[35] who was convicted of arson where there where was likely no arson.

No more should there be a Michael Hansen[36] convicted of murder, when there is no murder.

Simply, it should be the goal of the National Forensic Science Agency, as proposed below, to seek nationwide implementation of the standards proposed by the National Commission on Forensic Science.

35. For the most comprehensive review of the Willingham case, see "Fresh Doubts over a Texas execution – New evidence revives concerns that a man was wrongly put to death in 2004," by Maurice Possley. *Washington Post*, August 3, 2014 at http://www.washingtonpost.com/sf/national/2014/08/03/fresh-doubts-over-a-texas-execution/

36. "Michael Hansen" at National Registry of Exonerations at http://www.law.umich.edu/special/exoneration/Pages/casedetail.aspx?caseid=3885

Proposal 12: That a National Forensic Science Agency be established within the Department of Justice.

Below are excerpts from the recommendations of the Innocence Project for such an agency:

> Federal Support for Research and National Standards/Enforcement
>
> A national forensic science agency with comparable authority to the Food and Drug Administration (FDA) can scrutinize the forensic devices and assays that are both in use and in development. The Innocence Project believes that a national forensic science agency should focus on three main areas that will most improve the quality of forensics used in the criminal justice system: research; assessment of validity and reliability; and quality assurance, accreditation and certification of laboratories and practitioners. Each area is described below:
>
> Research: A national forensic science agency would identify research needs, establish priorities, and design criteria for reviewing forensic disciplines. Funding should also exist for expanded basic and applied research in order to test the validity of extant forensic methods, devices, and assays; and help develop new technologies to solve crime.
>
> Assessment of Validity and Reliability: This agency would also be responsible for reviewing both existing and new research data to determine whether a

technique, device or assay is scientifically valid and reliable for use in casework, and what the parameters of the assay should include. Furthermore, the agency should ensure the discontinuation of any invalid or unreliable methods, and support others only to the extent their practitioners present and interpret data within scientifically acceptable parameters.

Quality Assurance, Accreditation and Certification: A national forensic science agency would set and oversee enforcement of standards for public and private laboratories, as well as for individuals conducting forensic tests and examinations with intended use in U.S. federal and state courts. Quality controls and quality assurance programs must secure the integrity of the ultimate forensic product in the laboratory and in the courthouse. Forensic oversight should be obligatory, and non-compliance with accreditation and certification should allow for a loss of accreditation or individual certification and a cessation of business.

State Oversight Commissions or Advisory Boards:
Independent panels should be created in each state to help secure adequate resources for forensic work. These independent panels should include a wide range of experts who understand the needs of the forensic community and the criminal justice system alike.

Several states have already created commissions or advisory boards; they vary in many ways, but they are independent, expert panels committed to ensuring quality forensics.[37]

Proposal 13: That spending for indigent defense be increased to a level whereby judges and juries cannot easily determine by the availability of expertise or the quality of the work performed and testimony given whether a defendant's case is privately or publicly funded.

In 2012, the 50 States spent $2.3 billion for indigent defense services. This amount was approximately 10 percent of total State expenditure for judicial/legal systems.[38] The amount can be unfavorably compared to the cost of a single B-2 stealth bomber, which cost $2.2 billion or a Virginia class attack submarine at approximately $2.7 billion. In short, the $2.3 billion shows an insufficient commitment to justice for the indigent.

The 1963 U.S. Supreme Court decision of Gideon v. Wainwright guaranteed criminal defendants in felony cases the right to counsel. That constitutional requirement was later extended to misdemeanor cases and to juveniles facing imprisonment.

However, stating a constitutional requirement is not the same as dealing with the raw reality of the country's criminal courts. The *New York Times*

37. The Innocence Project, at http://www.innocenceproject.org/fix/Crime-Lab-Oversight.php
38. "State Government Indigent Defense Expenditures, FY 2008-2012, by Erinn Herbermann and Tracey Kyckelhahn, Bureau of Justice Statistics, Dept. of Justice. July 2014, at www.bjs.gov/content/pub/pdf/sgide0812.pdf.

noted at the 50th anniversary of the Gideon case that approximately 80 percent of criminal defendants do not have sufficient money to pay for their own attorneys.[39]

In Kentucky, 68 percent of indigent defendants are not represented by counsel in misdemeanor cases. In one-third of Florida's counties in 2010, 70 percent of defendants in misdemeanor cases pleaded no contest or guilty during arraignments which averaged less than three minutes. In the Miami public defender office, caseloads per lawyer have risen to 500 felonies per year, despite the American Bar Association recommendations that such caseloads not exceed 150 felonies.[40]

It's hard to calculate the precise sums which would be needed to bring the level of legal representation for indigent defendants to a level comparable to that of self-funded, but a doubling of the current $2.3 billion would be a start.

Even conservatives and conservative organizations are seeing that it's important that indigent people not be sent to prison just because they are poor. In October 2014, Koch Industries, led by Charles and David Koch, contributed several hundred thousand dollars to the National Association of Criminal Defense Lawyers (NACDL) to support the defense of indigent defendants.[41]

39. "The Right to Counsel: Badly Battered at 50," Editorial, *New York Times*, March 9, 2013 at http://www.nytimes.com/2013/03/10/opinion/sunday/the-right-to-counsel-badly-battered-at-50.html
40. ibid.
41. "Koch Industries gives grant to NACDL 'to address the nation's profound indigent defense crisis'" by Orin Kerr. *Washington Post*, October 21, 2014, at http://www.washingtonpost.com/news/volokh-conspiracy/wp/2014/10/21/koch-industries-gives-grant-to-nacdl-to-address-the-nations-profound-indigent-defense-crisis/

Proposal 14: That all states abandon the practice of appointing private counsel for indigent defendants and move to the practice of universal state funding of public defender offices.

Only 24 states fund statewide public defender systems.[42] The other states have either locally funded systems or systems for appointing private counsel or a combination. It's estimated that approximately 15 percent of indigent criminal cases are represented by appointed counsel.[43]

The system of appointing private counsel leads to less justice for the poor, according to two studies.[44]

Since 1983, Philadelphia had adopted a unique method of assigning attorneys to defendants in murder cases, which was to designate one out of every five to an appointed counsel and the remaining four to public defenders. This practice provided an excellent sample for research the results of such allocations.

Authors James Anderson and Paul Heaton summarized their findings:

42. "The Right to Counsel: Badly Battered at 50," op cit., Fn 39.

43. "Who's Better at Defending Criminals? Does Type of Defense Attorney Matter in Terms of Producing Favorable Case Outcomes," by Thomas H. Cohen, Administrative Office of the U.S. Courts: Office of Probation. 2011, at http://papers.ssrn.com/sol3/papers.cfm?abstract_id=1876474.

44. "Who's better..." ibid., and "Measuring the Effect of Defense Counsel on Homicide Case Outcomes," by James M. Anderson and Paul Heaton. *Yale Law Journal*, December, 2012.

> The differences in outcomes are striking. Compared to appointed counsel, public defenders in Philadelphia reduce their clients' murder conviction rate by 19%. They reduce the probability that their clients receive a life sentence by 62%. Public defenders reduce overall expected time served in prison by 24%.[45]

The Philadelphia sample showed that assigned counsel, often without significant criminal justice experience, were not providing effective assistance of counsel as is required by the Eight Amendment to the Constitution through the Gideon v. Wainwright case and its progeny.

Proposal 15: That the Innocence Movement participate in the election and judicial nomination processes at every governmental level to promote the goals of preventing and correcting wrongful convictions.

Many non-profit organizations participate in the political process by providing information to voters about candidates and elected and appointed public officials and by direct contributions to candidates and campaigns. The activities of these organizations are regulated by Sections 501(c) and 527 of the IRS Code.

For example, the League of Conservation Voters and Planned Parenthood raise money for local and state political activity. They issue "report cards" on the views and votes of candidates.

Currently, there is no such group or political action committee whose mission is to stop or even reduce wrongful convictions. The effort coming

45. "Who's better..." ibid. Introduction.

closest to that goal is the November 2014 announcement by the American Civil Liberties Union (ACLU) that it is launching a $50 million political campaign to "make a change of criminal justice policies a key issue in local, state and national elections."[46] A key goal of the campaign is to reduce mass incarceration in the U.S. within eight years. The funding came primarily from the Open Society Foundation of George Soros.

As Jim and Nancy Petro have stated in their book, *Failed Justice*, "...the voting public holds the ultimate power to change and improve the system, whether we recognize it or not..."[47] Further, they write, "...significant institutional change usually cannot change before conventional wisdom changes."[48] This is why the political landscape must be fertilized for the issue of reducing wrongful convictions.

Funding for legal representation and investigation for those who claim wrongful conviction is so scarce that it's unrealistic to expect the Innocence Movement to establish a political action committee, or PAC, which could raise funds to influence elections. However, with a relatively modest budget, an Innocence Movement Action Fund could present to its members and to the public information about how candidates for prosecutor offices and for elected judgeships and nominees for appointment to those offices view the wrongful conviction issue.

46. "A.C.L.U. in $50 Million Push to Reduce Jail Sentences," by Erik Eckholm. *New York Times*, November 6, 2014, at http://www.nytimes.com/2014/11/07/us/aclu-in-dollar50-million-push-to-reduce-jail-sentences.html?_r=0 .
47. *Failed Justice – Eight Myths that Convict the Innocent*, by Jim and Nancy Petro. Kaplan Publishing, 2010. Page ix
48. ibid. p. viii

In Maine, Assistant Attorney General William Stokes was nominated in 2014 to be a judge. For several years, he had been responsible for the state's efforts to block a new trial for Dennis Dechaine, a client of the Innocence Project since 1993. While arguing to sustain a jury verdict is nominally appropriate work for a prosecutor, Dechaine's supporters believed that Stokes' efforts seemed excessive and to be motivated more by the institutional desire to preserve a guilty verdict than by a desire for justice. A new trial where all the evidence is presented is what Dechaine has requested since his 1989 conviction.

At Stokes' nomination hearings, there were no objections by Dechaine supporters because they felt that if Stokes became a judge, he would no longer be the primary prosecutor blocking justice for Dechaine. Thus, in that case, the politics of justice played out in a distorted way.

When the issue of justice reform is presented to the voters, they have shown that they can respond affirmatively and eschew the stereotyped call to be tough on crime. In 2012, the voters in Culpepper County, Virginia elected Megan Frederick as its first woman district attorney, a position called the "Commonwealth Attorney." Her campaign successfully tied her opponent to the wrongful conviction of Michael Hash in 2001 and the stiff prosecutorial opposition to his exoneration which finally came in Federal Court in 2012. During the campaign, Michael Hash noted that no prosecutor had apologized to him for his wrongful conviction and eleven years of wrongful imprisonment.

In Brooklyn (Kings County), New York, in 2013, Ken Thompson defeated veteran District Attorney Charles Hynes in the Democratic Primary and went on to win the election in November. During the past several years, Brooklyn had seen more than its share of exonerations from wrongful convictions, and that record was part of Thompson's campaign. Compensation claims against New York City for compensation for those wrongful convictions now total more than $200 million, and more claims are being investigated.

In Massachusetts in 2014, the Democratic candidate for governor was Martha Coakley, who had been Attorney General since 2007. She lost. In 2010, she lost her bid for the U.S. Senate for the remaining three years of Senator Edward Kennedy's term. While not featured by the media as a primary issue, there were many votes against her from people who disapproved of her lead prosecuting role in the flawed conviction of Louise Woodward for murder in her shaken baby case.[49] Others remembered Coakley's support for the hysteria-hyped wrongful convictions of the Amiraults in the 1986-87 Fells Acres day care abuse case.[50] Coakley has never apologized for her involvement in either case.

Whether voters are motivated by the losses suffered by the wrongly convicted and the resulting failure to convict the actual criminals or by the monetary costs to the taxpayers, the results in these two elections show that the elimination of wrongful convictions can be an effective election issue.

The Innocence Movement needs to expand its role in the nominating election processes for prosecutors and judges. No longer should the conventional wisdom be thought to be that the

49. See Wikipedia entry for "Louise Woodward Case," at http://en.wikipedia.org/wiki/Louise_Woodward_case.
50. See Wikipedia entry for "Fells Acres Day Care Center preschool trial," at http://en.wikipedia.org/wiki/Fells_Acres_Day_Care_Center_preschool_trial.

public supports tough criminal justice policies without sufficient respect for justice. One organization fighting that view, www.justice-not-politics.com actually incorporates that theme in its name.

Proposal 16: That biometric software be developed that will standardize and render more accurate eyewitness recollections, including generic photo arrays.

Involved in approximately 35 percent of exonerations, mistaken eyewitness identification is one of the largest sources of wrongful convictions. As software now exists to assist the creation of police sketches of offenders and to show age-predicted changes in a person's appearance over time, there must be software that can be developed to standardize elements of the photo array lineup process.

With improvements, a computerized photo array system would become the standard replacement for the traditional human lineups. Figures in the computerized lineup could be clothed with the same clothing as was described by the witness.

Such software could standardize the incremental variations from a computerized police composite sketch, using techniques similar to the "aging" software.

By measuring the strength of the witness's recollection to the graded variations of the image, police can obtain a better understanding of the accuracy of the witness's recollection.

Proposal 17: That the goals be established that the annual level of crime be reduced to the levels of 1960 and/or the levels of crime for men be reduced to those of women and/or that the levels of crime be reduced to those of the United Kingdom.

This awkwardly phrased proposal aims at the same goal of reducing crime in the United States. It can be done, just as the country has reduced cigarette smoking. The proposal gives three vantage points: time, gender and geography.

The violent crime rate in the U.S. in1960 was 161 crimes per 100,000 people. That rate increased to a peak of 758 in 1991 and has fallen since then to 387 in 2012, which is still 240 percent of the 1960 rate. The numbers for property crimes show a similar trend from 1,726 per 100,000 to 5,264 in 1981 to 2,858 in 2012.[51] The 2012 rate is 165 percent of the 1960 rate.

The point of presenting these numbers is that we are basically the same people we were in 1960. Whatever has changed since then can be reversed. Adoption of the earlier proposals in this chapter may achieve this goal, but putting the goal into numerical form may help.

Another perspective is to look at gender. Approximately 20 percent of crimes are committed by women, sometimes with large variations by crime, but that's an average.[52] In 2012, there were 113,000 women in state and federal prisons,[53] or

51. "Crime in the United States," Wikipedia, at http://en.wikipedia.org/wiki/Crime_in_the_United_States
52. "Women and Girls in the Justice System," National Criminal Justice Reference Service, at https://www.ncjrs.gov/spotlight/wgcjs/facts.html
53. "Women in the Justice Sys.," The Sentencing Project, at http://www.sentencingproject.org/template/page.cfm?id=138

approximately 8 percent of the 1.4 million male inmate population. The incarceration percentage is substantially less than the crime rate because a primary function of prisons is to isolate violent people, and male crimes are more frequently violent than those of women.

The female:male ratio for those executed in Texas since 1819 has been 9:1,273, or .7 percent.[54] Since the resumption of executions in Texas in 1982, following the lull caused by the 1972 U.S. Supreme Court case, Furman v. Georgia, Texas has executed 518 people. Included were six women, or 1.2 percent.[55]

In any case, in a country where gender equality counts for a lot when measuring income and workplace representation, the 1:5 female:male ratio for crimes and the 1:12 ratio for incarceration and 1:85 for execution cry out for analysis and policy changes. How is our country educating men to be far more violent and criminal than women?

If we can have transform the gender representation of students in college to a majority female college population, we can reduce the over-representation of men in our criminal institutions.

The third perspective from which to examine and compare the U.S. crime rates is to look internationally. All countries in Europe have lower crime rates than the United States, but the United Kingdom is presented briefly here for comparison.

54. "Capital Punishment in Texas," *Wikipedia*, at http://en.wikipedia.org/wiki/Capital_punishment_in_Texas
55. "Executed Offenders," Texas Department of Criminal Justice, at http://www.tdcj.state.tx.us/death_row/dr_executed_offenders.html and "Lisa Coleman Becomes The Sixth Woman Executed By Texas Since 1982," *Buzzfeed*, September 14, 2014, at http://www.buzzfeed.com/tasneemnashrulla/lisa-coleman-could-become-the-sixth-woman-executed-by-texas

In 2013, with a total population of 64 million, there were approximately 550 homicides. That gives a rate of .9 per 100,000.[56] The rate in the U.S. with 14,196 homicide is 4.5 per 100,000. That's 39 per day, and five times of the U.K. rate. The United States needs to study the differences and similarities with the U.K. and learn how to bring the U.S. crime rates far closer to those of the U.K.

56. "Historic Crime Data," Government of the United Kingdom, at https://www.gov.uk/government/uploads/system/uploads/attachment_data/file/329801/rec-crime-2003-2014.ods

Chapter 4: Reduce Crime and Prison Populations.

The context of the plague of wrongful convictions is a vast criminal justice system that is overburdened. That overburdening diminishes the ability of the system to produce justice, just as the overburdening of any system would impair its functioning.

The *New York Times* editorialized in October 2014, "Multiple studies have shown that crime has gone down faster in states that have reduced their prison populations."[1]

Supplementing the staggering statistics in Chapter 1, Phil Locke, of the Wrongful Convictions Blog, has written that the United States has about 4.5 percent of the world's population, but it has 23-25 percent of the world's prisoners, when the U.S. jail population is included.[2] The U.S. incarceration rate in the United States is five times the global average. At an incarceration rate of 750 per 100,000, one out of every 133 adults in the US is in prison/jail. As most incarcerated adults are men, this means that approximately one out of 75 men is in prison. The incarceration rate in the US is 6-10 times that of other industrialized countries.

Locke noted that the U.S. incarceration "started to skyrocket" in the 1980s from the 500,000 level

1. "California Leads on Justice Reform," editorial, *New York Times*, October 30, 2014 at http://www.nytimes.com/2014/10/30/opinion/prop-47-could-take-the-state-a-step-further-in-reducing-overcrowding.html?_r=0
2. "Convictions by the numbers," by Phil Locke, Wrongful Convictions Blog, July 19, 2012, at http://wrongfulconvictionsblog.org/2012/07/19/convictions-by-the-numbers/ Locke asked rhetorically, "Does anybody else find these to be staggering statistics?"

in 1980 to 2.3 million by 2006.[3] That's an increase over 26 years of 460 percent or 17.7 percent a year. The increases came not because U.S. citizens became more inclined to breaking laws, but because more laws were enacted to criminalize more behavior and sentences were increased in length. Also, in the frenzy to prosecute and convict, despite the purported safeguards of Miranda warnings and Brady protections, it's likely that a higher percentage of people were being wrongly convicted.

Proposal 18: That all recreational drugs be legalized and regulated.

Fifty one percent, or 98,200, of the 192,500 Federal prisoners at the end of 2013 were serving sentences for drug offenses, e.g. possession, trafficking or other drug crimes.[4] At the state level, 16 percent, or 210,200, of the 1.3 million state inmates were incarcerated for drug crimes. The percentages for men and women were 15 percent and 25 percent, respectively.[5] The rounded totals are approximately .3 million out of 1.5 million, or 20 percent. Further, a substantial number of the other inmates were convicted of crimes which were often related to illegal drugs, such as burglary, robbery, and murder.

Simply, if the resources used to investigate, arrest, convict and imprison these inmates could have been devoted to the same activities with other

3. Locke, ibid.
4. "Prisoners in 2013," by E. Ann Carson, Bureau of Justice Statistics, U.S. Dept. of Justice, page 16, at http://www.bjs.gov/content/pub/pdf/p13.pdf#sthash.eYOPRay1.4zOo2zja.dpuf.
5. ibid, page 15.

crimes, many wrongful convictions could have been avoided. At the very least, the wrongful convictions for drug crimes would have been totally avoided. That would mean 6,000 fewer wrongfully convicted inmates (2 percent of .3 million) and 4000 fewer annual wrongful convictions for drug offenses.[6]

What would a country look like where drug possession is not a crime and where manufacturing and distribution is regulated? Fortunately, that question no longer needs to be answered as a hypothetical. While the Netherlands has the reputation for being the most liberated country regarding drugs, Portugal actually has led the way.

On July 1, 2001, Portugal decriminalized the personal possession of the most popular recreational drugs, including cocaine, heroin and marijuana.[7] Individuals were permitted to possess or purchase about one gram of heroin, two grams of cocaine, and 25 grams of marijuana leaves or five grams of hashish without a threat of imprisonment. Individuals who are found to abuse the use of such drugs or to be addicted are referred to treatment options rather than to courts and prisons.

By 2011, it was estimated that the number of drug addicts or abusers in Portugal declined from 100,000 to 40,000.[8]

6. This calculation multiplies the estimate from Chapter 1 of 1 million felony convictions per year multiplied by the 20 percent share for drug offenses multiplied by the two percent wrongful conviction rate.
7. For a thorough discussion of the law see the 2009 article "Drug Decriminalization in Portugal," by Glenn Greenwald. Cato Institute, at www.cato.org/pubs/wtpapers/greenwald_whitepaper.pdf.
8. "Ten Years after Decriminalization, Drug Use Down by Half in Portugal," *Forbes*, July 5, 2011, at http://www.forbes.com/sites/erikkain/2011/07/05/ten-

It will take a long time before the rest of the world catches up to Portugal's example, and even longer before the manufacturing and distribution of drugs will be regulated in ways similar to those now used for prescription drugs and alcohol.

In 1996, California became the first state to legalize marijuana for medical purposes. Several states followed, and opened the way to overall decriminalization.

In 2012, Colorado legalized the personal growing of marijuana for personal use and the production and sale of marijuana by licensed organizations. The sales of marijuana are taxed at the rate of 27 percent which has provided millions of dollars for school construction, even if not at the predicted $70 million annual rate. Washington state passed a similar measure the same year, but its implementation is slower and smaller.

In 2014, Alaska, Oregon and Washington, D.C. all passed marijuana legalization initiatives as did many municipalities.

In November, 2014, New York City announced that it would no longer arrest people for simple possession of small amounts of marijuana. Instead, it would issue a civil summons which would usually mean a fine. It's been estimated that the city has been making 20,000 such arrests a year, or 54 a day or about two every hour.[9] The city will, however, continue to arrest people for smoking marijuana in public. This small operational change will release thousands of police hours annually for other crime-related work.

years-after-decriminalization-drug-abuse-down-by-half-in-portugal/

9. "NYC to Stop Many Small-time Marijuana Arrests," by Jennifer Peltz. *Associated Press*, November 11, 2014. *Forensic Magazine.*

The momentum for marijuana legalization is likely to continue until the U.S. has something closer to Portugal's model for sensible drug regulation and treatment.

Proposal 19: That other victimless crimes, including prostitution and gambling, be legalized and regulated.

The primary problem with the criminalization of victimless "crimes" is that valuable law enforcement and judicial resources are diverted from the protection of society from serious crimes. Gradually, the U.S. has been decriminalizing victimless crimes as it has legalized homosexuality and gradually is legalizing several forms of gambling.

The primary concept behind the description of purported crimes as victimless is that the activities are performed by consenting adults, whether alone or with others.

The major remaining victimless crime in the U.S. is prostitution, as it is legal in only some counties in one state: Nevada. Prostitution is legal in about half the countries of the world. Some of those countries allow brothels and some allow pimping.[10]

Suicide can be considered a victimless crime as it's performed by a consenting adult. Often, the friends and relatives left behind feel victimized by a suicide, but the harm is the passive withdrawal of financial or emotional support rather than the active infliction of financial or physical harm.

10. "100 Countries and their Prostitution Policies," at ProCon.org at http://prostitution.procon.org/view.resource.php?resourceID=000772

Together with the crime of suicide is the crime of assisted suicide. Again, if a consenting adult wants to commit suicide and requests the assistance of another person, usually a doctor, there should be a legal way to do so. The states of Montana, Oregon, Vermont and Washington permit doctor-assisted suicide for people who are terminally ill. The countries of Luxembourg, the Netherlands, and Switzerland have similar or more liberal laws. Switzerland is home to the best known organization with provides assisted suicide services, Dignitas.[11]

While such issues are seemingly distant from the world of wrongful convictions, the purpose of this proposal is the same as for the legalization of drugs – to reduce the sheer scope of our criminal justice systems to a size where adequate resources can be devoted to the correct investigation and prosecution of genuine crime. With the appropriate allocation of such resources, the risks of wrongful convictions will be reduced. Behavior that is risky to people can be intelligently regulated, rather than being criminalized and prohibited.

Proposal 20: That the length of prison sentences be adjusted to reasonable levels, approximating those in Europe.

Prison sentences in the United States are the longest in the world. A 2011 report by the Justice Policy Institute found that the United States had the longest average criminal sentences, at 63 months of any of the countries studied: Australia, Canada, Finland, Germany, U.K., and the U.S.

11. See the "Dignitas" website at http://www.dignitas.ch/ and Wikipedia article http://en.wikipedia.org/wiki/Dignitas_(assisted_dying_organisation)

The next highest average was Australia with 36 months for comparable crimes.[12]

One of the most notorious and arbitrary methods of lengthening sentences was California's 1994 "three-strikes" law which required a minimum sentence of 25 years in prison with a third criminal conviction, even if that last conviction was for a minor offense. The ridiculous and obscene result was that thousands of people were incarcerated for long periods of time after a conviction for such offenses as shoplifting. In many cases the "3rd strike" resulted in a life sentence.

In a 2012 referendum, California voters reduced the severity of the three-strikes law. By October, 2014, more than 1,900 inmates had been released from their life sentences. Wrote the *New York Times* Editorial Board, "Dire warnings that crime would go up as a result were unfounded. Over two years, the recidivism rate of former three-strikes inmates is 3.4 percent, or less than one-tenth of the state's average."[13]

In November 2014 California voters again challenged the conventional wisdom that being "tough on crime" is the best politics by passing Proposition 47 with a 58 percent majority. Instead, the new mantra is "smart on crime." That ballot initiative "de-felonized," or reclassified as misdemeanors, several crimes including personal drug possession, e.g. heroin and methamphetamines, and several types of theft where the value of items stolen is less than $950. The new law operates retroactively with a provision

12. "Finding Direction- Expanding Criminal Justice Options By Considering Policies of Other Nations" by the Justice Policy Institute, April 2011, at www.justicepolicy.org/uploads/.../finding_direction-full_report.pdf
13. "California Leads on Justice Reform," op cit., Fn 1, above.

for re-sentencing inmates convicted of these crimes, unless they have serious criminal histories. It was expected that 10,000 California inmates became eligible for re-sentencing.[14] Also, it went into effect immediately, with dozens of inmates being released quickly from jail, as the crimes for which they were being detained were no longer punishable by incarceration.[15]

In April 2014, through a prosecutorial discretion initiative, the Department of Justice has launched a program to do what the Fair Sentencing Act of 2010 failed to do, which is retroactively re-sentence inmates who were sentenced by unfair drug laws. This refers primarily to the laws which punished users and sellers of crack cocaine far more harshly, and irrationally, with much longer sentences than for powder cocaine.

The six eligibility criteria are for inmates who:

(1) are currently serving a federal sentence in prison and, by operation of law, likely would have received a substantially lower sentence if convicted of the same offense today;

(2) are non-violent, low-level offenders without significant ties to large-scale criminal organizations, gangs, or cartels;

(3) have served at least 10 years of their sentence;

14. "California Proposition 47, Reduced Penalties for Some Crimes Initiative (2014), Ballotpedia at http://ballotpedia.org/California_Proposition_47,_Reduced_Penalties_for_Some_Crimes_Initiative_(2014)

15. "Prisoners freed quickly after voters OK measure," by Don Thompson. November 7, 2014. Associated Press in *Seattle Press-Intelligencer*, at http://www.seattlepi.com/news/us/article/Prisoners-freed-quickly-after-voters-OK-measure-5878960.php

(4) do not have a significant criminal history;
(5) have demonstrated good conduct in prison; and
(6) have no history of violence prior to or during their current term of imprisonment.[16]

As of July 2014, over 20,000 Federal inmates had applied for the program.[17] It's been estimated that 46,000 inmates, about 20 percent of all Federal inmates, are eligible for sentence reduction pursuant to this program. By late 2014, it was estimated that the average sentence reduction will be 25 months, but that no inmates will be released through the program until November 1, 2015. Each of the affected sentences is being reviewed for eligibility by the respective sentencing U.S. District Court.[18]

16. "Justice Dept. lays out criteria for clemency release of thousands of federal drug offenders," *Daily Kos*, April 23, 2014, at http://www.dailykos.com/story/2014/04/23/1294062/-Justice-Dept-lays-out-criteria-for-clemency-release-of-thousands-of-federal-drug-offenders#
17. "Defender hiccup or major headache for Clemency Project 2014?" Sentencing Law and Policy Blog from the Law Professor Blogs Network, at http://sentencing.typepad.com/sentencing_law_and_policy/criminal-justice-in-the-obama-administration/
18. "Courts, Defenders Brace for Petitions," by Zoe Tillman. *National Law Journal*, November 17, 2014. At http://www.nationallawjournal.com/id=1202676496775/Courts-Defenders-Brace-for-Petitions?slreturn=20141019120351

Proposal 21: That mandatory prison sentencing, and mandatory minimums[19] be eliminated.

Mandatory sentences, in general, should be eliminated. Sentencing guidelines should be sufficient to provide judges with the information they need for reasonable sentencing. Judges should be compared to each other on their variations from the guidelines.

Mandatory sentences have resulted in thousands of absurd results. For example, a woman in Florida, Stephanie George, was sentenced to life in prison in 1997 for being part of a conspiracy to distribute cocaine. Her then partner, and father of her daughter, was the leader of the conspiracy but he provided assistance to the prosecution and his sentence was fifteen years, as were the sentences of the other conspirators. The judge, Roger Vinson, has stated publicly that he regrets the life sentence that he was required by statute to impose on Ms. George, and she remains in prison.[20]

Some states are moving in the right direction. In 2002, Michigan dropped the mandatory minimum sentence requirements for most minor drug offenses.[21] In November 2014, a special commission in Massachusetts established to study the criminal justice system recommended the

19. "minima" would be more correct, but "minimums" has far more common usage.
20. "For Lesser Crimes, Rethinking Life Behind Bars," by John Tierney. *New York Times*. December 11, 2012. At http://www.nytimes.com/2012/12/12/science/mandatory-prison-sentences-face-growing-skepticism.html?pagewanted=all&_r=0
21. "Michigan to Drop Minimum Sentence Rules for Drug Crimes," Associated Press. *New York Times*, Dec. 26, 2002, at http://www.nytimes.com/2002/12/26/national/26MICH.html

abolition of mandatory minimum sentences for drug offenses.[22]

Proposal 22: That the bail process be changed from a money-based system to a risk-based system.

The Eighth Amendment to the U.S. Constitution, as applied to the States by the 14th Amdt., provides that "Excessive bail shall not be required," with the intent that people accused of crimes should not be unfairly detained before trial because of a lack of money.

The connection of this requirement to the problem of wrongful conviction is that innocent people who are in jail are more likely to plead guilty, at least to lower level crimes, because they cannot afford to be out of work. They are more likely to be found guilty at a trial by jury or judge than people who are released on bail. Further, the people who are in jails prior to trial are mostly those who are unable to pay for bail and poverty cuts across the lines of those who committed crimes and those who did not.

In 2012, the *Christian Science Monitor* reported that on any given day there were approximately 750,000 people in U.S. jails. Among that number were 500,000 who were awaiting trial and of those, 80 percent were there because they could not afford bail.[23] The article cited the case of a New

22. "Mass panel: Eliminate mandatory minimum drug sentences," by Matt Murphy, Statehouse News Service. November 18, 2014, *Worcester Telegram and Gazette*, at http://www.telegram.com/article/20141118/NEWS/311189572/1052
23. "Jailed without conviction: Behind bars for lack of money," by Katy Reckdahl, *Christian Science Monitor.*

Orleans high school girl who stole an I-phone from a neighbor's car. She spent 51 days in jail because her family could not afford the $200 bail.[24]

It costs the United States approximately $9 billion a year to detain defendants before trial.[25]

On Election Day, 2014, New Jersey voters endorsed part of a bail reform package that the Legislature had initiated. The first part was to make the issuance of bail more a function of the likelihood of the arrestee to come to his/her trial, and less a function of his/her ability to pay. The second part was a constitutional amendment which allowed judges to evaluate applicants for bail on the basis of their propensity for violence.

These new laws were passed after a New Jersey study found that 40 percent of defendants remaining in jail before trial were there only because they were poor, and not because they were deemed dangerous.[26] The Pretrial Justice Institute reported that the nationwide percentage of jailing for those charged with felonies is 53 percent.[27]

December 16, 2012, at http://www.csmonitor.com/USA/Justice/2012/1216/Jailed-without-conviction-Behind-bars-for-lack-of-money
24. ibid.
25. "Laura and John Arnold Foundation Announces New Pilot Sites for Court Risk Assessment Tool," Press Release, February 20, 2014, at http://www.arnoldfoundation.org/laura-and-john-arnold-foundation-announces-new-pilot-sites-court-risk-assessment-tool
26. "New Jersey Jail Population Analysis: Identifying Opportunities to Safely and Responsibly Reduce the Jail Population," by Marie VanNostrand, Luminosity and the Drug Policy Alliance, 2013, at http://www.drugpolicy.org/sites/default/files/New_Jersey_Jail_Population_Analysis_March_2013.pdf.
27. "In America, Innocent Until Proven Guilty? Not For Most People Who Are Stuck in Jail," by April M. Short. *Alternet*, December 29, 2013. At http://www.alternet.org/civil-

A typical case was of a Raul Hernandez who was arrested for drug possession in New York in 2013. Because he claimed innocence, he declined a plea bargain which would have meant seven days in jail, but it would have added to his criminal record which was already too long. His trial date was set for the ninth day and the complainant policeman did not appear, so the case was continued. Rather than wait in jail for the next trial date, Hernandez plead guilty, probably without the niceties of an Alford plea, and was sentenced to time already served, and he went home.[28] This was one more possible or probable instance of wrongful conviction.

In Chicago, Sheriff Tom Dart estimated that about a third of his 10,000 inmates, mostly pre-trial, are mentally ill and non-violent and don't belong in a jail. Another 2-3,000 could be released, Dart said, without any danger to society.[29]

One promising development is a program developed by the Laura and John Arnold Foundation to measure risk of flight or risk of violence pre-trial defendants. Called "PSA-Court," for Public Safety Assessment, the system is being used in Kentucky and several other jurisdictions.

The "PSA-Court" analyzes nine factors which have been determined to be the most likely predictors of risk that an arrestee will either

liberties/america-innocent-until-proven-guilty-not-most-people-who-are-stuck-jail

28. ibid.

29. "It's time to stop packing the jail," by Mick Dumke. *Chicago Reader*, December 22, 2014, at http://www.chicagoreader.com/Bleader/archives/2014/12/22/sheriff-dart-its-time-to-stop-packing-the-jail

commit a new crime or will not appear at trial.[30] The result is a lower rate of pre-trial incarceration.

Proposal 23: That parole, and/or other processes of early release be established or re-established in those states which do not have them.

Parole is the system through which an inmate is released subject to monitoring conditions prior to serving his/her full sentence. It was first used in the United States in New York's Elmira Reformatory in the late 19th century, and then spread to the rest of the country. If a paroled inmate violated the parole conditions, s/he could be returned to prison.

Ironically for inmates claiming wrongful conviction, one requirement for parole is remorse for crimes committed. Thus, an innocent inmate who continued to insist on innocence would serve an entire maximum sentence where a guilty inmate would be released earlier. As with false guilty pleas where innocent people plead guilty to lesser offenses to avoid risking draconian longer sentences for more severe crimes, the effect was to encourage innocent people to lie by stating involvement in a crime in order to achieve release.

In 1984, as part of the trend to be "tougher" on crime, the Federal Government eliminated parole with the Comprehensive Crime Control Act of 1984. Instead, good behavior by Federal inmates was encouraged by a system of awarding up to 54 days per year of "good time" which would be applied to the reduction of a sentence. Thus, for every six years of good behavior, an inmate could expect a

30. "Laura and John Arnold Foundation Announces...." op cit., Fn. 25, above.

sentence to be reduced by a year. The effective result of the new system was to lengthen the time inmates actually spent in prison.

Similarly, by 2000 about one-quarter of the states abolished parole, depending upon the definition of particular early release programs. The political problem with parole was that it was inevitable that at least one inmate who was released early would commit a serious crime, and the political pressure for abolition would start or increase.

In 2007 in Connecticut a parolee, Joshua Komisarjevsky, was one of two participants in a horrendous home invasion, which involved the murder of a mother and her two daughters. In response, the governor abolished parole for those convicted of violent crimes. Before 2007, Connecticut had abolished parole for everyone, but had then reinstated it due to the pressures of prison overcrowding.

Similarly, for many voters, it is now the cost of incarceration which is driving renewed interest in parole in the 2010s, and it remains one tool to help reduce the actual lengths of U.S. prison terms.

Proposal 24: That a claim of innocence during parole hearings not be an absolute bar to granting such parole.

For some exonerees, there came a time during their imprisonment that they were eligible for parole, but were denied parole due to their claims of innocence. That's because it's almost always required that inmates show remorse for their crimes, before parole can be granted. Perhaps the best known inmate denied parole for that reason is Jeffrey R. MacDonald, who is serving two life sentences for murdering his wife and two daughters at Fort Bragg, North Carolina in 1970. At his 2005 parole hearing, he refused to admit guilt or show remorse and told the parole board that he is "factually innocent."[31] His next scheduled parole hearing will be in 2020.

This proposal to allow parole despite claims of innocence is supported by retired Utah Federal judge Paul Cassell who wrote:

> One way to create a safety valve is to change our parole rules so that a refusal to admit guilt is not an absolute bar to obtaining parole. But at the same time, we should require that a prisoner refusing to admit guilt must provide a compelling reason for his failure to do so. We could require, for instance, that a prisoner sign a statement under penalty of perjury that he is asserting a claim of actual innocence.[32]

In October 2014, Freddie Cox was paroled from prison in New York after 28 years in prison for a murder he always denied committing. In 2011 the co-defendant, who admitted his role in the murder, but denied Cox's role, was paroled. At Cox's 2014 parole hearing, as he had done at three previous parole hearings, Cox claimed innocence.

31. "Jeffrey R. MacDonald," *Wikipedia* at http://en.wikipedia.org/wiki/Jeffrey_R._MacDonald
32. "The Parole System Needs a Small Safety Valve for the Innocent," by Paul Cassell. *New York Times*, (The Opinion Pages: Room for Debate), November 13, 2013, at http://www.nytimes.com/roomfordebate/2014/11/13/parole-when-innocence-is-claimed/the-parole-system-needs-a-small-safety-valve-for-the-innocent

Fortunately, the parole board was finally persuaded that Cox's claim might have merit.[33]

New York may the leader among the states in this opening the door to inmates for parole even when they claim innocence. Since 2011, three men, and probably more, had been paroled in New York while claiming innocence. Said the lawyer representing one of them, "Parole commissioners, like the rest of society, have come to recognize that there are far more innocent people in prison than we had ever imagined, so they're more receptive to that argument."[34]

Proposal 25: That the number and lethality of guns be reduced through taxation and regulation.

The United States has the largest prison population in the world and the highest rate of gun ownership. Surely, there is more to the correlation than coincidence.

Americans own 250 million, or 38 percent, of the approximately 650 million small arm weapons owned by civilians worldwide.[35] These numbers must be compared with the 4.3 percent U.S. share of the global human population, with 313 million people out of the world's 7.23 billion. Thus,

33. "A Claim of Innocence is No Longer a Roadblock to Parole," by Stephanie Clifford. *New York Times*, November 12, 2014, at http://www.nytimes.com/2014/11/13/nyregion/a-claim-of-innocence-is-no-longer-a-roadblock-to-parole.html?src=recg
34. ibid. Derrick Hamilton(2011), Sundhe Moses(2013) and Robert Hill(2014). Moses actually lied at his 2011 parole hearing and expressed guilt and remorse and parole was denied. At his 2013 hearing he claimed innocence.
35. Wikipedia, "Gun Control," at http://en.wikipedia.org/wiki/Gun_control

Americans are eight times as likely to own a gun as the rest of the people in the world and five times as likely to be incarcerated. For those who believe that the U.S. is an "exceptional" nation that holds a beacon of light to the rest of the world, these numbers should be disconcerting.

With so much gun ownership, it's inevitable that guns are used in crimes. Conversely, the reduction in gun ownership will lead to fewer crimes and a reduction of the overall burden of the criminal justice system. Again, a less-burdened criminal justice system will be better able to apprehend the guilty and protect the innocent from wrongful conviction.

Proposal 26: That the death penalty be abolished.

There are many reasons, discussed in many books, to discard the death penalty, including the facts that most countries of the world prohibit it and that number is increasing. Putting it in the alternative, the count of the 193 U.N. members which still execute their citizens for any crime has dropped to 92 or less. The last two countries to abolish capital punishment were Cameroon and Chad in 2014.

Here in this volume about wrongful convictions, the death penalty is a symbolic relic of the misguided legal fiction that justice in a death penalty case can be certain enough so as to preclude the possibility of error. Sometimes lawyers refer to a "legal fiction" which is a non-truth that lawyers adopt as truth just to make the system work. One example was the former practice in divorce law of using the legal fiction that the husband was an adulterer, because fault was required by the divorce statutes. In paternity law, the legal fiction was often the presumption that the husband in a relationship was the father of the child borne by the wife. Now, there is no need for such fictions as divorce is accepted as a normal practice and there are scientific methods for determining paternity.

Even with this book's goal of 99.9 percent conviction accuracy, that is enough certainty to preclude the possibility of error and the execution of an innocent person. The legal fiction of certainty in death penalty cases must be exposed.

In 2003, Governor Mitt Romney of Massachusetts appointed a commission to recommend the reinstitution of the death penalty. In 2004 the Governor's Council on Capital Punishment proposed such resumption of executions, but only upon a finding of "no doubt" of guilt for the most heinous crimes.[36] The recommendations were not adopted, and Massachusetts has not executed an inmate since 1947, a not-so-obscure fact which was not mentioned in the Council's report.

Opponents of the death penalty have sought to prove that an innocent person has been executed in modern times, knowing that the public has no stomach for such an injustice. It's not enough to know, for example, that William Jackson Marion was hanged in Nebraska in 1887 for the murder of a man who returned to the state very much alive four years later.[37] More contemporary, but not recent enough was the 1939 execution in the Colorado gas chamber of Joseph Arridy, a man who was so certainly innocent that Colorado issued him

36. Report of the Governor's Council on Capital Punishment, May 3, 2004, at www.lawlib.state.ma.us/docs/5-3-04governorsreportcapitalpunishment.pdf.
37. "William Jackson Marion," in Wikipedia at http://en.wikipedia.org/wiki/William_Jackson_Marion

a posthumous pardon in 2011.[38] In 1944, a 14-year old boy, George Stinney, Jr., was executed by electrocution for the murders of two girls in South Carolina. In December, 2014, a state court judge vacated Stinney's convictions on the grounds of prosecutorial misconduct or error and ineffective assistance of defense counsel.[39] Thus, he was declared legally innocent.

Most recently, but not with the requisite certainty, opponents of the death penalty have focused on the 2004 execution in Texas of Cameron Todd Willingham for the arson murder of his children. Several experts have concluded that there was no arson at all, and the inmate informant who claimed at trial Willingham's admissions to him has recanted.[40]

Another example from Texas is Carlos de Luna who was executed in 1989, but who was almost certainly mistaken for another man with the same name and similar physical appearance.[41] While in

38. "Joe Arridy," Wikipedia, at http://en.wikipedia.org/wiki/Joe_Arridy
39. "South Carolina Judge Vacates Conviction of George Stinney in 1944 Execution," by Campbell Robertson. December 17, 2014, *New York Times*, at http://www.nytimes.com/2014/12/18/us/judge-vacates-conviction-in-1944-execution.htm
40. "The Prosecutor and the Snitch," by Maurice Possley. August 3, 2014 by the Marshall Project, at https://www.themarshallproject.org/2014/08/03/did-texas-execute-an-innocent-man-willingham/, Also in the *Washington Post*, August 3, at http://www.washingtonpost.com/sf/national/2014/08/03/fresh-doubts-over-a-texas-execution.
41. See "Yes, America, We Have Executed an Innocent Man," by Andrew Cohen. May 14, 2012, *The Atlantic*, at http://www.theatlantic.com/national/archive/2012/05/yes-america-we-have-executed-an-innocent-man/257106/. Also see the book, *The Wrong Carlos: Anatomy of a Wrongful Execution*, by James Liebman and Shawn Crowley. Columbia

prison, De Luna had requested a polygraph examination, but the request was denied.

Because of the obvious severity and finality of the death penalty, a substantial portion of the resources of the Innocence Movement has been devoted to the prevention of the execution of the wrongly convicted. Since 1989, 150 inmates have been exonerated while on death row, with the most recent being two men in North Carolina in September 2014,[42] and three in Ohio who were on death row during their wrongful imprisonments.[43] Those five were among the seven death row inmates exonerated in 2014, the most since 2009.[44] By comparison, there were 35 people executed in seven of the United States in 2014.[45] That's the lowest count since the count of 31 in 1994.[46]

With the abolition of the death penalty in Illinois in 2011, Connecticut in 2012 and Maryland

University Press, 2014. At http://www.amazon.com/The-Wrong-Carlos-Wrongful-Execution/dp/0231167237

42. "List of Those Freed From Death Row," the Death Penalty Information Center, at http://www.deathpenaltyinfo.org/innocence-list-those-freed-death-row.

43. "Ohio Men Wrongly Convicted of Murder After 39 Years Released," by Cynthia McFadden, Erik Ortiz and Elisha Fieldstadt. *NBC News*, November 21, 2014, at http://www.nbcnews.com/news/crime-courts/ohio-men-wrongly-convicted-murder-after-39-years-released-n253356

44. "Number of Death Sentences and Executions at 20-Year Lows," December 18, 2014, *NBC News*, at http://www.nbcnews.com/storyline/lethal-injection/number-death-sentences-executions-20-year-lows-n269356

45. "DPIC Releases Year End Report: Executions and Death Sentence[s] Fall to Historic Lows," Death Penalty Information Center. December 18, 2014, at http://www.deathpenaltyinfo.org/node/5989.

46. "Executions by Year," Death Penalty Information Center, at http://www.deathpenaltyinfo.org/executions-year

in 2013, the count of states without a death penalty has risen to 18.[47]

Another substantial portion of resources has been devoted to exoneration of those sentenced to life in prison. Since 1989, 387 inmates have been exonerated from life sentences, not including those sentences for a term of years up to a maximum of life.[48]

So much of the Innocence Movement's scarce resources have been devoted to claims of innocence from those sentenced to death or life in prison, that the Movement and related scholars know very little about the level of wrongful convictions for lesser crimes which result in shorter prison terms. Eve Primus argued in a 2013 article that the rate of wrongful conviction is higher in misdemeanor cases. She wrote, "when procedural fairness and evidentiary accuracy are no longer relevant considerations, the frequency of wrongful convictions skyrockets."[49]

The elimination of the death penalty will help reallocate Innocence Movement resources to lower level crimes, including misdemeanors.

47. "States with and without the death penalty," Death Penalty Information Center, at http://www.deathpenaltyinfo.org/states-and-without-death-penalty.
48. See detailed listing at the Nat'l Registry of Exonerations at http://www.law.umich.edu/special/exoneration/Pages/detaillist.aspx.
49. "Our Broken Misdemeanor Justice System: Its Problems and Some Potential Solutions." by Eve Brensike Primus. A review of "Misedemeanors." A. Natapoff. *S. Cal. L. Rev.* 85, no. 5 (2013); 1313-75. *S. Cal. L. Rev.* Postscript 86 (2013): 80-7, at http://repository.law.umich.edu/reviews/62/

Chapter 5: Investigation Process

Every step of the criminal justice process is important, but the investigation stage is where the die is often incorrectly set. It is at this stage where incorrect police assumptions and theories too often guide investigative actions with tunnel vision past the evidence and filter the perceptions of others, including witnesses, informants and victims.

Proposal 27: That all interviews and interrogations be recorded, preferably video recorded. Further, that no confession be admissible in court without a recording, preferably video, of the confession and the interview(s) preceding the confession.

The proposal is near the top of the various Innocence Movement lists of remedies for wrongful convictions. Too often, prosecutors have claimed that defendants confessed to crimes without judges and juries having the opportunity to see how such confessions were extracted. Incredibly, false confessions have led to wrongful convictions for 13 percent of the exonerees in the National Registry of Exonerations.[1]

On the morning of Martin Tankleff's first day of senior year in high school on Long Island, New York in 1988, he discovered the bodies of his dead mother and nearly dead father. By the end of that day, his police interrogators had written Tankleff's "confession." Despite Tankleff's refusal to sign the

1. "% Exonerations by Contributing Factor," National Registry of Exonerations, at http://www.law.umich.edu/special/exoneration/Pages/ExonerationsContribFactorsByCrime.aspx#

claimed confession, prosecutors were allowed to present it to the jury. Tankleff was convicted and it took 17 years of struggle, and a little luck, to finally achieve his exoneration in 2008.[2]

The claim of confession can be so persuasive, that such evidence should no longer be allowed in a courtroom without an electronic recording.

Proposal 28: That in every criminal case there be full open file disclosure to the defense of everything in the files of the prosecution and police and their experts related to the case against the defendant, except information which may jeopardize the safety of one or more people.

The Brady v. Maryland (1963) line of cases requires that prosecutors provide to defense counsel all potentially exculpatory materials. However, in the U.S. v. Ruiz case in 2002, the Supreme Court did not apply that requirement as a matter of constitutional law to the plea bargaining stage of a criminal proceeding.

Nonetheless the proposal for full open file disclosure is here in the Investigations chapter because justice is best served when information is shared as early as possible. Too often, innocent people have pled guilty to crimes because they were misled by the prosecution about the amount of evidence against them. As the *New York Times* editorialized, "In both the federal and state court systems, it is essential that rules about disclosing

2. See *A Criminal Injustice: A True Crime, a False Confession, and the Fight to Free Marty Tankleff*, by Richard Firstman and Jay Salpeter. New York, 1990.

evidence be followed in ways that promote justice."[3] One of the causes of wrongful conviction is that the police and prosecution often establish a theory of a crime and then pursue that theory with tunnel vision to the exclusion of others. If the defense were to see police and prosecutor files earlier in the process, such tunnel vision might be avoided with contrary information from the defense.

The Registry of Prosecutorial Misconduct, sponsored by the Center for Prosecutorial Integrity, shows that Brady violations by Federal prosecutors are the largest cause of federal wrongful convictions.[4] The Center has proposed a Federal law to stop such violations, call the "Federal Prosecutor Integrity Act."[5]

Generally, however, the requirements for disclosure come later for those cases going to trial. Two other proposals to assure and emphasize the requirements of disclosure are mentioned here.

First is the proposal by Barry Scheck and Nancy Gertner that defense counsel file a motion for an order for prosecutor disclosure, pursuant to the local jurisdiction's equivalent of the American Bar Assn. Model Rule 3.8(d) ("Special Responsibilities of a Prosecutor").[6]

3. "Justice and Open Files," *New York Times*, February 26, 2012, at http://www.nytimes.com/2012/02/27/opinion/justice-and-open-files.html?_r=1&
4. Registry of Prosecutorial Misconduct at http://www.prosecutorintegrity.org/registry/database/
5. See the draft of the proposed law at http://www.prosecutorintegrity.org/legislation/fpia/
6. "Combatting Brady Violations With An 'Ethical Rule' Order for the Disclosure of Favorable Evidence," by Barry Scheck and Nancy Gertner. In *The Champion*, a journal of the National Assn. of Criminal Defense Lawyers. May 2013, page 40, and at http://www.nacdl.org/Champion.aspx?id=28478

The motion could track the rule by asking the judge for an order that the prosecutor search his/her file and disclose all information that "tends to negate the guilt of the accused or mitigates the offense." Such an "ethical rule" order would go slightly beyond the requirements of Brady v. Maryland, and it would put the prosecution clearly on notice that the judge stands behind the rule. The sanction for failure to disclose information to the defense would be contempt of court, as well as the usual bar association penalties.

Another proposal, "The Brady Colloquoy" by Jason Kreag, is that judges engage prosecutors in a colloquoy (discussion at the bench) about the requirements of disclosure.[7] Such a colloquoy could be requested by the defense.

The article recommends:

> ...five questions judges could use in most jurisdictions. The first four questions are designed to be asked during a pretrial hearing or before accepting a guilty plea. Judges should ask the fifth question after the prosecution's case in chief or after the defense's opening statement.
>
> 1. Have you reviewed your file, and the notes and file of any prosecutors who handled this case before you, to determine if these materials include information that is favorable to the defense?
> 2. Have you requested and reviewed the information law enforcement possesses, including information that may not have been reduced to a formal written report, to

7. "The Brady Colloquoy," by Jason Kreag. *67 Stanford Law Review*. Online 47, Sept. 2, 2014. At http://www.stanfordlawreview.org/online/brady-colloquy

determine if it contains information that is favorable to the defense?

3. Have you identified information that is favorable to the defense, but nonetheless elected not to disclose this information because you believe that the defense is already aware of the information or the information is not material?

4. Are you aware that this state's rules of professional conduct require you to disclose all information known to the prosecutor that tends to be favorable to the defense regardless of whether the material meets the Brady materiality standard?

5. Now that you have heard the lines of cross-examination used by the defense and have a more complete understanding of the theory of defense, have you reviewed your file to determine if any additional information must be disclosed?

Finally, in addition to these questions, the judge should remind prosecutors throughout the proceedings that she is prepared to conduct an in camera review of any information that the prosecutor is on the fence about disclosing.

Even though prosecutors are required to provide exculpatory information to the defense before trial, these two approaches, "Ethical Rule Order," and "Brady Colloquoy," would bring additional emphasis of the importance of the obligation.

Often forgotten in the struggles over police and prosecutor disclosure is that one of the goals in the criminal justice system is to present the truth, and a time-tested way to test truth is to present it to others for review.

Second, the information in the police and prosecutor files belongs to the people of that jurisdiction and not just to the law enforcement agency. The people have a greater interest in disclosure of information and truth than they do in the win/lose status of the players of the legal system game.

Proposal 29: That the Office of the Coroner or Medical Examiner in each state be placed within that state's Health or Public Health Department.

A primary role for the Coroner or Medical Examiner ("Medical Examiner") is to determine the cause of death where there is doubt or where a criminal act may be suspected. In most states, the Medical Examiner reports to a law enforcement person, such as the Attorney General or a Deputy or Assistant Attorney General.

The problem with that alignment is that the Medical Examiner may be influenced, explicitly or implicitly, to make a determination of cause of death that is consistent with law enforcement's theories of the case, i.e. not only that a crime occurred, but perhaps a certain kind of crime at a certain time.

The institutional temptation for Medical Examiners in such offices is to determine that deaths were criminal when they were not.

In Iowa in 1997, Medical Examiner Dr. Thomas Bennett declared the death of the three-month old son of Teresa Engberg-Lehmer and her husband Joel Lehmer to be a homicide due to shaken baby syndrome (SBS). Faced with such scientific "proof" the couple pled guilty to involuntary manslaughter and were each sentenced to 15 years in prison. Their "luck" was that the same medical examiner had misdiagnosed another child death as SBS only a few months earlier and a babysitter was finally acquitted at a third trial in that case. Teresa Engberg-Lehmer contacted the attorney in that babysitter case and she and her husband were ultimately released. The Medical Examiner resigned.[8]

In Florida in 1998, John Peel and his girlfriend woke up to find their son dead on the floor near the bed. The Medical Examiner, Dr. Joan Wood, declared the death a homicide, caused by "closed head injury – child abuse." Faced with such proof, Peel pled guilty to involuntary manslaughter and was sentenced to ten years in prison. Again, his "luck" was that Dr. Wood had made several other mistaken death determinations, including a death by pneumonia as SBS. She was forced to resign in 2000. Peel was released in 2002.[9]

Of course, medical examiners can make errors wherever their offices are located, but the closeness to law enforcement can increase the chances of a pro-crime pathology determination.

In New Hampshire in 2000, Chad Evans was the man friend of Amanda Bortner, whose 21-month old daughter, Kassidy, had died at the Maine home of her male babysitter.[10] Because Evans had pled guilty to domestic violence the year

8. "Terry Engberg-Lehmer," National Registry of Exonerations, at http://www.law.umich.edu/special/exoneration/Pages/casedetail.aspx?caseid=3952

9. "John Peel," National Registry of Exonerations, at http://www.law.umich.edu/special/exoneration/Pages/casedetail.aspx?caseid=3813

10. For more information about the Chad Evans case, see www.chadevanswronglyconvicted.org.

before, the police quickly developed the theory that he had abused and killed Kassidy. The police ignored the police and court records showing threats to women and assaults by the babysitter.

In this case where the Maine Medical Examiner, Dr. Margaret Greenwald, learned that either of the two men were close enough to Kassidy to have been responsible for murder, it was surely tempting to conclude that the multiple bruises on Kassidy's body were caused by abuse. The signs from the autopsy that Kassidy suffered from pre-existing heart problems were ignored. Even though Dr. Greenwald did not report to the New Hampshire Attorney General, her reporting relationship to the Maine Attorney General was sufficient to make the point here. It should also be noted that Evans's medical expert, Dr. Michael Baden, also concluded that there was abuse and murder, but his perspective may have been affected by the defense theory that the babysitter was the perpetrator.

In any case, the medical examiner's neutrality would have been more assured if she were part of the Maine Department of Public Health rather than the Office of the Attorney General.

Proposal 30: That DNA be collected at all crime scenes where the deposit of the perpetrator's DNA is probable.

This proposal goes together with the earlier Proposal 4 to expand the DNA database to include all individuals in the United States.

In most jurisdictions where DNA is collected, the methodology is restricted to the most serious or violent crimes, including rape. Felons and future felons commit misdemeanors, and the sooner that

DNA is collected and submitted to CODIS, the more effective will be law enforcement.

Although the time and laboratory costs of DNA collection at minor crime scenes have seemed large, the benefits will come from the future reduction of further crimes by the same perpetrators.

To maximize the utility of a universal DNA database, the collection of DNA samples at crime scenes should be maximized. Currently, collection is limited in most jurisdictions to serious crimes, such as murder and rape and where there is an obvious DNA source immediately available, such as blood, semen or saliva.

Studies have been conducted to evaluate the effectiveness of collecting DNA at scenes of property crimes, such as burglary. In a 2007 study of five cities conducted by the National Institute of Justice, it was found that the "clear" rate, i.e. solving of a crime, was twice as high for burglaries, 24 percent vs. 12 percent, when DNA was gathered at the crime scenes.[11]

In a more recent experiment, 2009-2011 Palm Beach County in Florida launched an intensive effort to collect DNA samples from scenes of property crimes. Knowing that habitual burglars commit approximately 230 crimes annually, the County found that the increased efforts raised the "clear" rate for burglaries, reduced the frequency of property crimes and led to the "clearing" of non-property crimes for which DNA matches were not yet available. As a result, the experiment was

11. "DNA Solves Property Crimes (But Are We Ready for That?)" by Nancy Ritter. *NIJ Journal*, Issue 261, October 2008, at http://www.nij.gov/journals/261/Pages/dna-solves-property-crimes.aspx

transformed into an ongoing process of increased DNA collection.[12]

As the cost of DNA collection and processing continues to decline, and the value-added of increased DNA collection becomes more apparent, police across the country should be collecting DNA wherever it can be found for all crimes.

Proposal 31: That for every investigation where there is an eyewitness identification, the witness's verbal description of all relevant aspects of the perpetrator be written and signed by the witness, and a drawing or other visual representation be created. And that these steps be taken before there is any lineup or other actual effort to have the eyewitness identify the perpetrator.

By having the victim either commit to writing or an audio or visual recording his/her description of the perpetrator, the police can prevent the contamination of the eyewitness account from subsequent pressure to make the witness's memory become synchronized with the information in a photograph or lineup of possible suspects.

Such a procedure is not a guarantee against wrongful conviction, but it helps, and it also helps when other evidence pointing away from the wrongly accused person is found.

12. "Evaluating the Effectiveness of DNA Analysis on Property Crimes and Identifying a New Model for Outsourcing" by Cecelia Crouse and others. *Forensic Magazine*, October/November 2014 at http://www.forensicmag.com/articles/2012/12/evaluating-effectiveness-dna-analysis-property-crimes-and-identifying-new-model-outsourcing

One case where not enough was done to confirm the initial description in order to prevent a wrongful conviction in 1983 for rape was that of Warith Habib Abdal of New York. The summary of his case at the National Registry of Exonerations states that the victim, "described her attacker as [a] black man between five feet eight and five feet ten with a space between his upper front teeth and a "tenor-type" voice." The man who was later convicted of the crime, Warith Habib Abdal, "did not fit this description. He was six feet two inches tall, there was no gap between his teeth, and he had a deep voice. Nonetheless, he was picked up for questioning about the crime four and a half months after it occurred."[13] It was only the advent of DNA testing, and perseverance of the Innocence Project that brought Abdal's release in 1999.

In the case of exoneree John Vera, the store robbery victims in New York City described one of their attackers as five feet, eight inches tall with dark skin. Vera was 5' 4" and had light skin. Nonetheless, he was identified when he visited a barbershop next to the robbed store, and later convicted. Subsequently, several of the actual participants in the crime told police that Vera was not involved, and one of those participants bore a resemblance to Vera. He was exonerated a year after his conviction.[14]

In each case, it would have helped to secure a more detail description of the culprits, together with a hand-drawn or software-created sketch.

13. "Warith Habib Abdal," National Registry of Exonerations: http://www.law.umich.edu/special/exoneration/Pages/casedetail.aspx?caseid=2978. Abdal died in 2005 of cancer.
14. "John Vera," National Registry of Exonerations: http://www.law.umich.edu/special/exoneration/Pages/casedetail.aspx?caseid=3940

Proposal 32: That subsequent use of a physical lineup or photo-array process be conducted without any suggestion or hint regarding the possible perpetrator.

As eyewitness error is the major source of error leading to wrongful convictions, lineup and photo array procedures have received much scrutiny in recent years. Where a live lineup is held, these recommendations[15] of the Innocence Project should be heeded:

Blind administration: Research and experience have shown that the risk of misidentification is sharply reduced if the police officer administering a photo or live lineup is not aware of who the suspect is.

Lineup composition: "Fillers" (the non-suspects included in a lineup) should resemble the eyewitness' description of the perpetrator. The suspect should not stand out (for example, he should not be the only member of his race in the lineup, or the only one with facial hair). Eyewitnesses should not view multiple lineups with the same suspect.

Instructions: The person viewing a lineup should be told that the perpetrator may not be in the lineup and that the investigation will continue regardless of the lineup result. They

15. The Innocence Project, "Eyewitness Identification," at http://www.innocenceproject.org/fix/Eyewitness-Identification.php

should also be told not to look to the administrator for guidance.

Confidence statements: Immediately following the lineup procedure, the eyewitness should provide a statement, in his[/her] own words, articulating his[/her] level of confidence in the identification.

Recording: Identification procedures should be videotaped whenever possible – this protects innocent suspects from any misconduct by the lineup administrator, and it helps the prosecution by showing a jury that the procedure was legitimate.

The equivalent procedures should be applied to photo-array identifications.[16]

Proposal 33: That checklists be used by law enforcement, prosecutors, defense attorneys and others to ensure that best practices are followed.

As has been famously recorded by Atul Gawande, the use of checklists is a powerful method of ensuring that participants in a complicated process remember each step. Gawande wrote in *The New Yorker* in 2007, and in the 2011 book *The Checklist Manifesto: How to Get Things Right*, about how hospitals had used checklists to reduce infection and increase survival rates. He

16. See "Supreme Judicial Court Study Group on Eyewitness Evidence: Report and Recommendations," Massachusetts, July 25, 2013, at http://www.mass.gov/courts/sjc/docs/eyewitness-evidence-report-2013.pdf

wrote about the prototype for the B-17 bomber which crashed in 1943 for the lack of performance by the experienced pilot of a critical step during takeoff. The plane's development was almost canceled but a checklist was developed to prevent future similar errors, and the plane proceeded to massive production and massive destruction of enemy targets.[17]

Defense lawyers can be reminded in checklists to ask about an alibi, or other witnesses. Prosecutors can be reminded about turning evidence over to defense attorneys and deadlines for speedy trials.

As doctors in hospitals, and pilots in planes, have found, it is much better to take the time to ensure that all the required steps are taken, than to suffer later the consequences, such as a wrongful conviction, of a missed step.

Proposal 34: That polygraph examinations be made available to all defendants and witnesses on an ability-to-pay basis, with public funding paying the balance. And that if an exam result is not acceptable to the defendant, s/he may request a peer review of that exam, and/or another exam with a different examiner.

A polygraph is a forensic tool, like fingerprints and DNA collection. Although it is not as reliable as those two tools, it still has an accuracy rate of approximately 80 percent. That level makes it arguably more reliable than eyewitness testimony.

17. "The Checklist." by Atul Gawande. December 10, 2007, *The New Yorker*, at http://www.newyorker.com/magazine/2007/12/10/the-checklist and *The Checklist Manifesto: How to Get Things Right*, by Atul Gawande. Picador, 2011.

Some polygraph examiners claim an accuracy rate of 90 percent or more, but it's difficult to verify such claims. In 2013, the author wrote the article "Polygraphs and 215 Wrongful Conviction Exonerations,"[18] which concluded that when polygraphs were used in cases of wrongful conviction and subsequent exoneration, they had an accuracy rate of 80 percent. The information about polygraph usage came from media reports of the cases, or the summaries from the National Registry of Exonerations or directly from the exonerees or their lawyers.

The polygraphs from those cases were those of the exonerees or of co-defendants or witnesses. The accuracy of the polygraph examinations was measured before and after trial. If the subsequently exonerated examinee passed a polygraph, it was said to be accurate and inaccurate if the exoneree was found to be deceptive. If a witness or inmate informant claiming the exoneree's direct involvement in the crime passed his/her polygraph, it was said to be inaccurate. If s/he failed, it was said to be accurate.

Later in 2013, the article was updated for online publication with 250 cases, and the accuracy percentage improved very slightly.[19]

Innocence Projects sometimes use polygraphs to corroborate the claims of innocence of applicants. In Texas, the University of Texas at Arlington Innocence Project administered

18. "Polygraphs and 215 Wrongful Conviction Exonerations," by Morrison Bonpasse. *Polygraph*, A Journal of the American Polygraph Association, Vol. 42, Summer 2013. At http://www.bonpasseexonerationservices.com/about.html
19. See "Polygraphs and 250 Wrongful Conviction Exonerations," by Morrison Bonpasse. November 2013 at http://www.bonpasseexonerationservices.com/about.html

polygraphs to its two clients, Christopher Scott and Claude Simmons, and they passed. Another test was administered for that same case to Alonzo Hardy who had admitted that he was the actual murderer and the polygraph exam corroborated that admission.

In New York, Martin Tankleff had written hundreds of letters to lawyers and investigators asking for their help in his claim of wrongful conviction for the murders of his parents in 1988. Finally, he reached private investigator Jay Salpeter who agreed to take Marty's case if he passed a polygraph – which he did.

For the author's "215" and "250" articles, there were no controls on the quality of the examination or for who performed the polygraph examinations. While the polygraphs given before trials were performed by a mixture of police and private examiners, those performed after trial were nearly all performed by private examiners. In the "250" article, 114 exonerees passed their polygraphs, with 51 before trial and 63 after trial. All the 25 exonerees who failed polygraphs had their examinations performed before trial and by the police. Conversely, none failed after trial.

Even with an 80 percent accuracy rate, defense attorneys and prosecutors are generally reluctant to use polygraphs. Of the 171 exonerees who took polygraphs in the "250" article, 136 are listed in the National Registry of Exonerations. Most of the remaining 35 were exonerated before the Registry's 1989 start date. At the time of publishing the article, there were 1,250 exonerations, giving an 11 percent polygraph usage rate. The fear of failure through an inaccurate or unwelcome result (either a defense client failing or from the prosecution's viewpoint, a defendant passing) seems to be the primary source of reluctance.

The fear of an inaccurate result can be substantially overcome by a simple recourse, which is to take a second exam, or to have the exam peer-reviewed or both. With an 80 percent accuracy rate, and a corresponding 20 percent failure rate, the risk of an inaccurate result in two successive examinations is 4 percent (.2 X .2 = .04).

Of course, for polygraphs to be useful, the results must be believed. In 1975, Clarence Chance and Benny Powell were convicted in California of murdering a policeman, in some part because of the allegations of an incriminating informant. However, when the informant failed his polygraph exam, the prosecutor did the right thing and the informant was given another exam, which he failed. Then the prosecutor erred on two counts. First, he ignored the results of the polygraph exams and second, he failed to inform the defense of those exams. Chance and Powell remained in prison until their 1992 exonerations.[20]

In the murder case in Ohio of Clarence Elkins, the prosecutor did understand the power of multiple polygraph examinations, but only after the alternate suspect failed five successive exams. Those failures, plus exculpatory DNA, led to Elkins's release from prison after six years. The chance of the polygraph results being incorrect on five successive tests is .032 percent, or $.20^5$

Polygraphs are not perfect, but they are an underutilized tool, and should be used more often in the pursuit of truth in the criminal justice process. In the coming years, the competing claims of other truth verification tools, such as computer

20. "Clarence Chance," National Registry of Exonerations, at http://www.law.umich.edu/special/exoneration/Pages/casedetail.aspx?caseid=3097 and "Clarence Chance and Benny Powell," Death Penalty Focus at http://www.deathpenalty.org/article.php?id=407

voice stress analysis and FMRI (functional magnetic resonance imaging) will be tested and if their actual accuracy performance meets or exceeds the 80 percent standard, those tools should be utilized more frequently as well.

Proposal 35: That where internal and external experts are used by the police and prosecution to prove guilt, an amount of money equivalent to the costs of those experts should be made available to the defense for expert consulting and witnesses. And that if such funding is not made available, the evidence from the government's experts should not be allowed at trial.

Often trials are battles of experts, but only if the defendant has the ability to pay for them.

In approximately 22 percent of the National Registry of Exonerations cases, "false or misleading forensic evidence" is a contributing cause.[21]

It's not known how many of those cases involved the absence of adequate information from defense experts.

In the literature of the pre-1989 wrongful convictions, there were several convictions for check forgery where the defendant was not able to pay for a handwriting expert. In 1956, Eugene Tucker was wrongly convicted of forging a check for $96.23. He was convicted despite a polygraph examiner's opinion that Tucker was telling the truth during his inconclusive polygraph. Two years later, thanks to a prosecutor devoted to justice, Tucker was freed. The prosecutor did not realize

21. "% Exonerations by Contributing Factor," Nat'l Reg. of Exonerations,http://www.law.umich.edu/special/exoneration/Pages/ExonerationsContribFactorsByCrime.aspx#

that a police handwriting expert had been unable to determine that the signature was a forgery.[22] A defense expert would surely have helped Tucker's defense.

More recently, James Hebshie was convicted in 2001 in Massachusetts Federal court of arson, by setting fire to the building where his business was a tenant. His attorneys had no expert to challenge the prosecution's claims of arson with the use of an accelerant. Later, on appeal, a defense expert said that the fire had started in another unit of the building. Hebshie was exonerated in 2006.[23] A defense expert at trial likely would have prevented five years of wrongful imprisonment for Hebshie.

More tragically was the 1992 conviction in Texas of Cameron Todd Willingham for the arson murder of his children.[24] The Texas Fire Marshal testified that an accelerant caused the fire to burn in areas not usually burned in such a fire. Willingham was executed in 2004 a few minutes after his final declaration of innocence, "I am an innocent man – convicted of a crime I didn't commit."[25] Over the next ten years, several arson experts have disputed the finding of arson. A competent expert at Willingham's trial could have saved his life.

22. *The Innocents*, by Edward D. Radin. Tower Publications, 1964, pp. 50-53.
23. James Hebshie, Exoneree summary, National Registry of Exonerations, at http://www.law.umich.edu/special/exoneration/Pages/casedetail.aspx?caseid=3857
24. "Cameron Todd Willingham," *Wikipedia*, at http://en.wikipedia.org/wiki/Cameron_Todd_Willingham, and the recent article by Maurice Possley presenting Willingham's innocence, "The prosecutor and the Snitch," op cit (Fn 40, Chapter 4).
25. "Offender Information," Texas Dept. of Criminal Justice, at http://www.tdcj.state.tx.us/death_row/dr_info/willinghamcameronlast.html

Chapter 6: Grand Jury/Preliminary Hearing for Indictment

Proposal 36: That prospective defendants be invited to give testimony to grand juries or to prosecutors who are considering indictments.

The objective of the criminal justice system is to provide justice for the victims and perpetrators of crime. The necessary corollary to that objective is to determine the truth of what happened.

The Fifth Amendment to the U.S. Constitution requires that "No person shall be held to answer for a capital, or otherwise infamous crime, unless on a presentment or indictment of a Grand Jury,..." That requirement has been determined to include Federal felonies. “Targets” or suspects of federal grand juries do not have the right to testify, but the U.S. Attorney Manual provides for that possibility, upon request.[1] Usually, however, “targets” are not invited to testify.

The requirement for Grand Jury indictment has not been held applicable to the states by the Fourteenth Amendment.

All the states have laws or constitutional requirements for grand juries, but only about half of the states regularly use them to prepare indictments. The other states use preliminary hearings before judges.[2] Generally, defense attorneys are reluctant to have their clients testify before these proceedings, fearing that they will

1. U.S. Attorney Manual, Title 9, “Criminal Division,” 9-11.00 Grand Jury, at http://www.justice.gov/usao/eousa/foia_reading_room/usam/title9/11mcrm.htm#9-11.010
2. “Grand juries in the United States,” *Wikipedia*, at http://en.wikipedia.org/wiki/Grand_juries_in_the_United_States

preempt a more valuable defense strategy at trial or that their clients will make incriminating admissions to the grand jury.

However, in order to reduce wrongful convictions, the better practice is for "targets," suspects or defendants to be invited to testify. Too often, wrongful convictions occur because the defendants did not get the opportunity, and not early enough, to present the truth of an event as they saw it, or perhaps to deny all knowledge of that event.

The New York experience with grand juries is instructive. The state gives "targets" of grand juries the right to appear before them, and through a 1978 law, they were permitted to be bring their attorneys. The result in New York City was an increase in the number of "targets" appearing before grand juries. In Brooklyn in 2004, 14 percent of "targets" testified, and of those, less than half were actually indicted. Further, the *New York Times* reported, "At the Legal Aid Society, which represents tens of thousands of defendants every year, some lawyers have aggressively allowed their clients to testify before grand juries. In some years, they said, grand jurors in some boroughs voted not to indict in more than 60 percent of cases in which Legal Aid clients testified."[3]

In the Federal system, where "targets" are not encouraged to testify, the indictment rate is greater than 99 percent.[4]

3. "New Trend Before Grand Juries: Meet the Accused," by William Glaberson. *New York Times*, June 20, 2004, at http://www.nytimes.com/2004/06/20/nyregion/new-trend-before-grand-juries-meet-the-accused.html

4. "Grand Juries Almost Never Fail to Indict, But They Did in Ferguson," by Anthony L Fisher. *Reason.com*, November 25, 2014 at http://reason.com/blog/2014/11/25/grand-juries-almost-never-fail-to-indict. Using data from *2010 Federal*

Professor Sara Beale of Duke University, an expert on grand juries, has suggested that other states should consider adopting the New York procedures for encouraging "target" testimony.[5]

Of the cases in the National Registry of Exonerations, very few exonerees were given the opportunity to testify, or actually testified, before a grand jury or preliminary hearing officer.

Justice Statistics at http://www.bjs.gov/content/pub/pdf/fjs10st.pdf. [Table 2.2 "193,021 minus 15.9% declined, and Table 2.3 "No True Bill Returned"]
5. ibid.

Chapter 7: Pleas and Plea Bargaining

Ideally, all parties to a crime would agree on the identity of the perpetrator of the crime and the proper punishment. That's what the plea bargaining system accomplishes. Plea bargaining occurs on different levels. In return for a guilty plea, a prosecutor can offer any of the following:

- a conviction of a lesser charge than was originally charged, or even overcharged, and/or
- a reduction in the sentence to be proposed, and/or
- a change in the facts reported to a judge which would reduce the judge's sentencing options or lead to a lesser sentence.

About 95 percent of criminal cases are resolved by guilty pleas, with or without plea bargaining. In fact, this is the ideal way to complete a cycle of criminal justice:

Criminal commits crime.
Criminal admits to crime.
Criminal suffers appropriate punishment.
Criminal is returned to society.

One might ask, "why is plea bargaining a part of the wrongful conviction problem?" Astonishingly, approximately 12.3%[1] of all exonerees pled guilty to their alleged crimes. They plead guilty because they were fearful that they would be found guilty by a judge or jury if they went to trial and then would be subjected to much greater punishment. This harsher punishment for those who contest the charges against them is called the "trial penalty."

1. 187 of 1,520 exonerations in the National Registry of Exonerations (www.exonerationregistry.org) as of December 31, 2014.

One example is the case of Wesley Tuley in Texas. In 1997 he went to trial on the charge that he had raped the 12 year old daughter of his girlfriend. The jury deadlocked at 10-2 for acquittal and a mistrial was declared. The prosecutor offered Tuley a sentence of 10 years of supervised release, and time in jail already served, in return for a guilty plea. Not knowing that his jury voted 10-2 in his favor, and thus a probability that a second jury might find him not guilty, Tuley accepted the offer. He had already served 10 months in pre-trial detention and did not want to return to prison.

Unfortunately, his supervised release was revoked due to a drug violation and he was sent to prison. Three years later, he learned that his accuser had recanted, and he filed for a writ of habeas corpus. The judge granted the writ, saying that "no rational jury would convict" Tuley at a new trial.[2]

Proposal 37: That a prosecutor not proceed, nor continue, with a charge against a defendant unless s/he believes beyond a reasonable doubt that the defendant committed the crime, and that s/he believes that s/he could persuade a jury of the defendant's guilt beyond a reasonable doubt; and that the prosecutor sign a nationally standardized form affirming those beliefs.

Little has been written and published about the standard of review or proof that an ethical

2. "Wesley Tuley," National Registry of Exonerations, at http://www.law.umich.edu/special/exoneration/Pages/casedetail.aspx?caseid=3700

prosecutor must have before going forward to obtain an indictment. An exception is Bennet Gershman's view that "responsible prosecutors should be morally certain that the defendant is guilty."[3] Even less has been written about the continuing need for the prosecutor to reconsider the charges against that standard at each further step in the prosecution process.

American Bar Association Model Rule 3.8, "Special Responsibilities of a Prosecutor" begins with subsection "The prosecutor in a criminal case shall: (a) refrain from prosecuting a charge that the prosecutor knows is not supported by probable cause;"[4]

The standard of "probable cause" is the same as it used to obtain a search warrant or make an arrest. Effectively, this standard means that a prosecutor can initiate and continue to prosecute a case even if s/he doesn't believe a person to be truly guilty of the crime, or guilty beyond a reasonable doubt.

In the movie, "The Thin Blue Line," about the wrongful conviction of Randall Dale Adams,[5] his appellate attorney said, "Prosecutors in Dallas have said for years, 'any prosecutor can convict a guilty man, but it takes a great prosecutor to convict an

3. *Prosecution Complex* by Daniel Medwed. Op cit (Fn 23, Introduction) at p. 19, quoting from "A Moral Standard for the Prosecutor's Exercise of the Charging Discretion," by Bennett Gershman, 20 *Fordham Urban Law Journal* 513, 524 (1993).
4. Rule 3.8 Model Rules for Professional Conduct – Special Responsiblities of a Prosecutor, American Bar Assn., at http://www.americanbar.org/groups/professional_responsibility/publications/model_rules_of_professional_conduct/rule_3_8_special_responsibilities_of_a_prosecutor.html
5. "Randall D. Adams," National Registry of Exonerations at www.law.umich.edu/special/exoneration/Pages/casedetail.aspx?caseid=2984

innocent man.' "[6] This caricature is of a prosecutor willing to pursue the victory of a conviction without a sincere belief in the guilt of the defendant. Such prosecutors believe that it is their job to present a case to a jury and see if it sticks rather than using their own professional judgment to make an evaluation of guilt or innocence.

It is often said that prosecutors and defense lawyers are "officers of the court," with the prosecutors being the more obvious, as they are paid by the government. Comment 1 to Model Rule 3.8 states, "A prosecutor has the responsibility of a minister of justice and not simply that of an advocate."[7] A minister of justice must do more than see if a jury will buy his/her presentation of a case. The jury should have full confidence that the prosecutor believes beyond a reasonable doubt that the charges are true.

The 3.8 (a) standard should require that a prosecutor only prosecute a case if s/he believes the person to be guilty. Further, it should state that the prosecutor has a continuing obligation to stop such prosecution if his/her belief in that guilt wavers below that standard of beyond a reasonable doubt.

Proposal 38: That a judge participate in the plea bargaining process and hear evidence, if necessary, to ensure fairness, and to protect where applicable a defendant's claim of innocence.

6. "The Thin Blue Line." by Errol Morris 1988.
7. Rule 3.8. op cit., Fn 4, above.

This proposal is borrowed from New York Federal Judge Jed Rakoff, who presented the idea at a lecture in 2014:

> "What I have in mind is a magistrate judge or a junior judge would get involved," Rakoff said. "He would take offers from the prosecutor and the defense. ... He would evaluate the case and propose a plea bargain if he thought that was appropriate, and he might, in appropriate cases, say to the prosecutor, 'You don't have a case and you should drop it.' This would be very difficult for the judiciary; it's not something I come to lightly, but I can't think of any better solution to this problem."[8]

Whatever the details of the recommended or permitted judicial involvement, it will prevent or severely limit prosecutorial bullying which has led many innocent people to plead guilty.

In the *New York Daily News* coverage of Judge Rakoff's idea, was the story of Rodney Roberts who was exonerated in 2014 of a rape he did not commit. He spent 17 years in prison after pleading guilty.

> I knew I didn't do it, but I didn't want to be in prison for the rest of my life," Roberts said. "They made me believe they were ready to enforce a life sentence."[9]

8. "Why Innocent People Plead Guilty – Federal judge says thousands are in prison after taking deals," by Gilien Silsby. *USC News*, April 18, 2014 at https://news.usc.edu/61662/why-innocent-people-plead-guilty/

9. "EXCLUSIVE: Judge Jed Rakoff says plea-deal process is broken, offers solution," by Daniel Beekman, *New York Daily News*. May 27, 2014, at http://www.nydailynews.com/news/crime/judge-plea-deal-process-fixed-article-1.1806358

Proposal 39: That prosecutors meet with defendants, together with counsel for at least one hour in order that prosecutors understand that they will be prosecuting a human being with a life story. And that questions which prosecutors may ask would come from a national standardized list.

From the Sixth Amendment to the U.S. Constitution and similar provisions in most state constitutions, a defendant has a constitutional right "to be confronted with the witnesses against him."[10]

What is missing, and this is more of a human relations issue than a constitutional law issue, is a requirement that prosecutors meet with the defendants they plan to prosecute. The reason for this proposal is simple: people tend to dehumanize others whom they do not know, especially those who can be characterized as evil in some way.

Face-to-face meetings have often made a substantial difference in the relationships of adversaries. The 1986 Reykavik Summit Meeting between Ronald Reagan and Mikhail Gorbachev brought the two men very close, on the spot, to a groundbreaking disarmament agreement. Despite the failure to finalize that agreement, their meeting nevertheless led to better relations and more modest disarmament agreements. In 1983 before meeting Gorbachev, Reagan had described the Soviet Union as the "evil empire."[11]

10. U.S. Constitution, 6th Amendment, which says, in part, that "in all criminal prosecutions, the accused shall enjoy the right...to be confronted with the witnesses against him."
11. "Evil Empire Speech," by President Ronal Reagan. March 8, 1983. To the National Association of Evangelicals, in

In New Hampshire in 2001, Assistant Attorneys General N. William Delker and Simon Brown prosecuted Chad Evans for the alleged murder of Kassidy Bortner, the 21-month old daughter of Evans's woman friend, Amanda Bortner.[12] As with most prosecutions, the prosecutors never had or took the opportunity to meet Chad Evans and get to know him. The current "rules of the game" don't encourage such meetings, but the system loses for that omission.

At the defendant's option the proposed meeting could include discussion of the alleged crime, or it could just be limited to the defendant's life before the alleged crime. If Chad's prosecutors had heard from Chad directly about his life with Amanda and Kassidy Bortner, it's hard to see how they could have claimed in Brown's closing argument, "That was Kassidy living with the defendant. A living hell."[13]

It's easier to say something like that about another person if there is no personal contact with that other person. Of course, a pre-trial meeting might not have made any difference in that final characterization by the prosecutor, but it would have reduced likelihood or severity of such a statement.

Orlando, Florida. At http://millercenter.org/president/speeches/speech-3409

12. For more information about this case, see the website, www.chadevanswronglyconvicted.org. See also the book, *EYE CONTACT – The Mysterious Death in 2000 of Kassidy Bortner and the Wrongful Convictions of Chad Evans and Amanda Bortner.*

13. Transcript, State v. Evans. Closing Arguments, December 18, 2001, at http://www.chadevanswronglyconvicted.org/documents/011218ClosingArgumentsChadEvanstrial.pdf

Proposal 40: That the Alford plea, which allows a defendant to plead guilty even while claiming innocence, be eliminated. Alternatively, no plea bargaining should be permitted for a defendant who claims innocence.

The "Alford plea" doctrine began to be known by that name from the 1970 U.S. Supreme Court case of North Carolina vs. Henry C. Alford.[14] The decision was split 6-3, with Justice White writing the opinion for the Court and Justices Brennan, Douglas and Marshall dissenting. Alford had claimed his innocence of the murder of Nathaniel Young on or about November 22, 1963 – otherwise an important day in American history.

Justice White summarized the circumstances of Alford's plea,

> After the summary presentation of the State's case, Alford took the stand and testified that he had not committed the murder but that he was pleading guilty because he faced the threat of the death penalty if he did not do so. In response to the questions of his counsel, he acknowledged that his counsel had informed him of the difference between second- and first-degree murder and of his rights in case he chose to go to trial. The trial court then asked appellee if, in light of his denial of guilt, he still desired to plead guilty to second-degree murder and appellee answered, "Yes, sir. I plead

14. 400 U.S. 25 (1970), at http://www.law.cornell.edu/supremecourt/text/400/25

> guilty on—from the circumstances that he (Alford's attorney) told me."[15] [The court's footnotes omitted]

One of the factors leading Alford to plead guilty was to avoid the risk of execution if he had gone to trial and been found guilty of first degree murder. He was convicted by his plea in 1963 and he died in prison in 1975.

Since 1970, the use of Alford pleas has grown, but the frequency of a "pure" Alfred plea, i.e. with an explicit claim of innocence, has not been measured. The term, "Alford plea," is often used interchangeably with "no contest" and "nolo contendre" pleas, but they are not exactly the same and the latter two categories are not considered here.

Of the 1,520 exonerees in the National Registry of Exonerations as of December 31, 2014, at least nine involved Alford pleas, where the exoneree bargained for going to prison for a shorter period time than s/he faced with the "trial penalty" of a guilty verdict.

The use of the Alford plea has been criticized as being unfair to defendants who claim innocence. Wrote Professor Albert Altschuler in 2003, "Alford pleas are awful. There could hardly be a clearer violation of due process than sending someone to prison who has neither been found guilty nor admitted his guilt. If anything short of torture can shock your conscience, Alford pleas should."[16]

In the same law review volume, Professor Stephanos Silbas wrote with feeling,

15. ibid.
16. "Straining at gnats and swallowing camels: The selective morality of Professor Bibas," by Alan Alschuler, *Cornell Law Review*, Vol 88, pp. 1412–1424 (2003).

Alford and nolo contendere pleas, I contend, are unwise and should be abolished. These procedures may be constitutional and efficient, but they undermine key values served by admissions of guilt in open court. They undermine the procedural values of accuracy and public confidence in accuracy and fairness, by convicting innocent defendants and creating the perception that innocent defendants are being pressured into pleading guilty. More basically, they allow guilty defendants to avoid accepting responsibility for their wrongs. Guilty defendants' refusals to admit guilt impede their repentance, education, and reform, as well as healing of victims. In addition, pleas without confessions muddy the criminal law's moral message. Both kinds of pleas, but especially Alford pleas, equivocate: one might call them guilty-but-not-guilty pleas. They permit equivocation and ambiguity where clarity is essential. This equivocation undermines denunciation of the defendant and vindication of the victim and the community's moral norms. Sacrificing these substantive goals of the criminal law is too high a price for an efficient plea procedure.[17]

17. "Harmonizing Substantive Criminal Law Values and Criminal Procedure: The Case of Alford and Nolo Contendre Pleas," by Stephanos Bibas. *Cornell Law Review*, Vol 88, No. 6, July 2003, at http://www.pbs.org/wgbh/pages/frontline/shows/plea/four/nolo.html

Essentially, Sibas argues that the criminal justice system should not settle for anything other guilty or not-guilty. Anything less is not justice.

The best known recent example of an Alford plea was for the West Memphis [Arkansas] Three, (Damien Echols, Jessie Misskelley, Jr. and Jason Baldwin) who agreed to Alford pleas in 2011 in order to leave their prison cells after 18 years of wrongful imprisonment. Instead of being exonerated, and eligible for compensation, the three pled guilty and were sentenced to the time in prison already served, plus ten additional years, suspended unless they committed crimes in the future.

When announcing the Alford plea and overall agreement, the prosecutor, Scott Ellington, said that the state (and presumably he as well) believed that the three men were guilty, but Ellington acknowledged that it was not likely that a new jury at retrial could be persuaded of their guilt.[18] By that standard, and by Proposal 37 at the beginning of this chapter, the prosecutor should have abandoned the prosecution because a jury was not likely to be persuaded. Insisting, as the state of Arkansas did, on an Alford plea and the abandonment of the right to claim compensation for wrongful conviction, was an act more of governmental bullying than justice.

One of the Memphis Three, Jason Baldwin, said it best, "This is not justice."[19]

The Proposal to abandon Alford pleas is made here in the context of reducing wrongful convictions. Put simply, wrongful convictions

18. "Deal Frees 'West Memphis Three' in Arkansas," by Campbell Robertson, *New York Times*. August 19, 2011, at http://www.nytimes.com/2011/08/20/us/20arkansas.html
19. ibid.

cannot be stopped if the criminal justice system permits a person to plead guilty to something s/he claims that s/he did not do, and then be punished for it. Alternatively, in the interest of stopping wrongful convictions, prosecutors should not browbeat defendants claiming innocence into accepting prison time for something they deny. It's really asking the defendant to lie or commit perjury to a court.

When defendants claim innocence, they should be encouraged to bring those claims to a full trial, with full rights of discovery and access to expert witnesses. Such defendants should be encouraged to take a polygraph or other methods of truth verification such as FMRI exams and voice stress analysis tests.

In Henry Alford's case, he could have taken a polygraph as could his claimed alibi witnesses and as could the two witnesses who claimed that Alford told them of his intent to kill the victim and that afterwards told them that he had done so.

Of course, if a person claims innocence and goes to trial and is found guilty beyond a reasonable doubt, s/he may still claim innocence. The difference between that scenario and an Alford plea is that the defendant's claims have been heard in open court by a jury of his/her peers, and not just by a prosecutor who appears to have immense powers to send defendants to prison for long periods of time.

Chapter 8: Trials

As noted in the previous chapter, the pressures to avoid the expense of trials and the risk of an unjust trial outcome, have resulted in an extraordinary 95 percent of criminal cases being resolved by guilty pleas, with or without plea bargaining. This is not your "Perry Mason" criminal justice system where the innocent are always actually found not guilty. There is enormous pressure on innocent defendants to plead guilty so as to avoid the risk, among others, of a wrongful conviction and much more punishment. One part of the solution, therefore, is to make trials more reliable adjudicators of guilt beyond a reasonable doubt and the absence of such guilt. The goal of this book is to make them 99.9 percent accurate, and the proposals below are presented to help achieve that goal.

Proposal 41: That jury training be at least one day in duration and include nationally produced videos, with emphasis on the meaning of "beyond a reasonable doubt" and the risks and causes of wrongful conviction.

While the legal fiction is that common citizens can come to a trial and talk with each other in a room and come up with justice, the reality is that decisions about guilt beyond a reasonable doubt require considerable sophistication and subtlety.

Since 1997, New York has used a 23 minute film, "Your Turn" which begins with "a costumed re-enactment of the medieval judicial process known as trial by ordeal: Accused parties are thrown into a lake. Those who float are deemed guilty. Those who drown are vindicated."[1] The remainder of the film discusses the current American system.

While such a film may have been a good start, jurors deserve better training for their momentous task. One possibility is an updated version of "Twelve Angry Men," the 1957 film which showed how eleven jurors were ready to convict an innocent man before Jimmy Stewart's character persuaded them to look at the facts more closely. There was a 1997 update, with Jack Lemmon, but that version also presented twelve male jurors. A future remake might be called, "Twelve thoughtful jurors," and include a diverse jury.

However, such a film would still be entertainment rather than training. What jurors really need is at least a full day of instruction about how they can best do their work, and achieve justice and avoid injustice. (Proposal 51 deals with structured guidelines for deliberations.)

Proposal 42: That no witness or victim be asked to identify the defendant at trial.

It's sometimes called the "Perry Mason moment," when a witness, usually a victim, is asked at a trial, "Is the person who attacked you in this courtroom?" The witness then responds, "Yes, that's him over there," and points at the man sitting at the defendant's table with his lawyer.

1. "Ted Steeg, Who Found Big Audience With Jury Duty Films, Dies at 84," by Margalit Fox. *New York Times*, July 11, 2014, at http://www.nytimes.com/2014/07/11/nyregion/ted-steeg-documentarian-who-produced-jury-duty-films-dies-at-84.html

As an exercise in revealing truth, the exercise is pointless. At a trial several months, even years, after a crime, the defendant is very likely to be wearing different clothes and have different hair than at the time of the crime. The key for such a witness's identification of a suspect is that it occurred as soon as possible after the crime.

A classic eyewitness error is when a witness or complainant identifies is asked to identify at trial the person who committed the crime. Despite the presence of the defendant at the defense table with his/her lawyer, witnesses have sometimes identified jurors or trial observers or even a judge as the culprit.[2]

While there will always be a degree of theatre about a public trial, the pursuit of truth must trump the pursuit of drama, and this one small symbolic scene could be easily deleted from a fair trial, and that's the request to a witness to identify the defendant.

Proposal 43: That the testimony of defendants be encouraged, and that if a defendant is reluctant to testify the trial judge (in a jury trial, or other judge in a bench trial) intervene to negotiate the terms or boundaries of the defendant's testimony.

It is often said that juries or fact-finding judges want to hear from the defendant, but that message

2. See, for example, the case of exoneree Alfredo Vargas at the National Registry of Exonerations at http://www.law.umich.edu/special/exoneration/Pages/casedetail.aspx?caseid=4220. In that case, the victim identified a juror as her abuser, but Vargas was convicted anyway.

is not explicitly given. It is not thought to be stated in any court cases.

Instead of explicit encouragement, the drift of U.S. criminal law has been to protect a defendant's right not to testify, as guaranteed by the 5th Amendment to the Constitution, which states that defendants, among other protections, shall not "...be compelled in any criminal case to be a witness against himself,..." This right against self-incrimination was inserted into the 5th Amendment as a way of allowing defense counsel to test the prosecution's case, without forcing the defendant to testify. The theory was that if the prosecution's case could not stand on its own feet without the defendant's testimony, then it should fail. The purpose of the protection also was to prevent law enforcement officials from using mental or physical force to extract testimony and confessions from defendants.

This shield against the testimony of defendants was not always thought to be necessary. Prior to the rise of the role of defense counsels in the late 18th century and the rise of the adversarial trial system, it was the obligation of defendants to speak at their own trials in order to defend themselves.[3]

The summaries of most (926, 72 percent) of the 1,284 exonerees at the National Registry of Exoneration as of January 10, 2014, did not reflect whether they testified at their own trials. Ten percent (122) pled guilty, and 16 percent (201) testified. The summaries of only three percent (35) indicated that the defendants did not testify.[4]

3. See John Langbein, "The Historical Origins of the Privilege Against Self-Incrimination at Common Law," *92 Michigan Law Review 1047* (1994) at http://digitalcommons.law.yale.edu/fss_papers/550/n
4. "To Testify or Not to Testify – Is the Choice Unfair to the Innocent?" by Morrison Bonpasse. Unpublished draft,

An ad hoc survey by the author of exonerees attending the 2013 Innocence Network conference in Charlotte, North Carolina indicated that the split was that half testified and half did not testify, among those who went to trial.

The issue of the decision of exonerees on whether to testify is different from the general question about defendants, because these people were later found to be innocent. Thus, for these exoneree defendants who did not testify, their reason for not testifying was not because of guilt, but for other reasons. The most frequently mentioned other reason is the fear or expectation that the jury can be told of a defendant's previous criminal record.

Such was the case for John Thompson who was indicted in Louisiana for the crimes of carjacking and murder, arising from separate incidents in 1984. The District Attorney, Harry Connick, Sr., tried Thompon first on the carjacking charge knowing that if Thompson testified at the murder trial, the prosecutor could tell the jury about the carjacking conviction.

Thompson chose not to testify at the murder trial and was therefore unable to tell the jury that the reason he was in possession of the murder weapon was because the prosecution's primary witness, and co-defendant, Kevin Freeman, had sold it to him after the murder. Thompson was convicted and sentenced to death, but was exonerated in 1999 after an investigator discovered DNA evidence from the carjacking that had been

January 14, 2014, at http://www.bonpasseexonerationservices.com/documents/ArticleIschoicetotestifyunfairtoinnocentswspreadsheets.pdf suppressed by the prosecutors.[5] Thompson had come within two weeks of execution in 1999 for a crime he didn't commit.

The rule that would have allowed the prosecutor to tell the jury about Thompson's carjacking conviction, and presumably other crimes, should be repealed and replaced with rules that encourage defendants to testify.

The idea of encouraging defendants to testify was incorporated into the utopian novel, *2121*, which described a "mid-21st century reform in the U.S. criminal justice system, which culminated in the 31st Amendment[6] to the U.S. Constitution, which became law in 2030."[7]

The purported 31st Amendment restored the obligation of defendants to speak in the interest of presenting the truth to the fact finder in a trial, whether it be a judge or jury. This change reduced the risk that a jury or fact-finding judge would not have the benefit of hearing the defendant's side of the story, if his/her defense counsel had a trial strategy which did not include the defendant's testimony.

Whether such a Constitutional amendment will be needed will depend upon public perceptions of the U.S. criminal justice system, as it responds to the wrongful conviction disaster.

5. "John Thompson," National Registry of Exonerations at http://www.law.umich.edu/special/exoneration/Pages/casedetail.aspx?caseid=3685
6. The fictional 31st Amendment reads, "Defendants in criminal cases shall testify as to what they know about the facts of the case against them, unless a disinterested judge shall determine, after an appropriate hearing, that the risk of prejudice outweighs the prospective value of the defendant's testimony."
7. *2121*, by Morrison Bonpasse. *CreateSpace Publishing*, 2014, pp. 125-26, at http://www.amazon.com/2121-Morrison-Bonpasse-ebook/dp/B00MBXW17Y

Proposal 44: That when a defendant testifies, the jury be instructed during the post-evidence charge to the jury that if it is leaning toward a guilty finding beyond a reasonable doubt, it must also find the defendant guilty of perjury and make specific findings that specific statements by the defendant were lies beyond a reasonable doubt.

As noted earlier, an informal survey of exonerees by the author indicated that about half testified at their own trials. That means that their fact-finding judge or jury determined that the defendant's testimony was not believed and was intentionally false. However, it is not currently the practice to bring any additional sanction upon a convicted defendant for lying. None of the exonerees who testified at their own trials where they were convicted, were also convicted, or even charged, with perjury.

It's not the goal of this proposal to increase punishment upon convicted defendants, whether actually guilty or not, as sentences in this country are already too long. Instead, the goal is to force the jury to focus more closely on what it is doing. It's one thing for members of a jury to say during deliberations, "I don't believe the defendant," but it's another to say that "I'm confident beyond a reasonable doubt that the defendant lied on these specific statements...."

Note that while this proposal focuses on the defendant, there could also be a requirement that if a defendant is found innocent, a jury should consider specific statements by witnesses which it found to be lies or perjury. (Alibi witnesses are covered in the next proposal.) Such a requirement would be cumbersome, as there are usually many witnesses at a trial. Also the differences between a Guilty and a Not-Guilty verdict do not force a parallel structure for such perjury charges. That is, to find guilt beyond a reasonable doubt, a jury must believe certain facts beyond a reasonable doubt. However, to reach a finding of Not Guilty, a jury is simply stating that it doesn't know with enough certainty what happened. A Not Guilty verdict is not a finding of innocence beyond a reasonable doubt; it's a finding of something NOT beyond a reasonable doubt.

Proposal 45: That when witnesses testified for an alibi defense, the jury be instructed during the post-evidence charge to the jury that if it is leaning toward a guilty finding beyond a reasonable doubt, it must also make specific findings that specific statements by the alibi witnesses were false beyond a reasonable doubt.

Such a determination of false testimony by an alibi witness would leave it to the prosecutor to consider whether to indict the witnesses for perjury. The key issue would be whether the incorrect testimony was intentionally or unintentionally false.

Alibis were a factor in about 180, or 12 percent, of the 1,520 exonerations in the National Registry of Exonerations as of December 31, 2014. Of those, about 60 percent involved multiple witnesses whose testimonies were disbelieved. In another 10 percent, the defense lawyers expected so little from the alibi witnesses that they were not called to testify.

In 1997 in Louisiana, Nathan Brown was convicted despite his own testimony that he was at home at the time of a sexual assault. Further, he had four alibi witnesses: his mother and her man friend, and Brown's two nephews. The police arrived at his home an hour after the assault, so there was little question about the uncertainty of recollection of time. Still, the jury chose to convict Brown and he spent the next 17 years in prison before his exoneration.[8]

It is one thing for a member of a jury to disbelieve an alibi witness, but it's another to specifically declare what was false and to state that belief beyond a reasonable doubt. Requiring such a statement by a jury might make its disbelief of an alibi witness or of multiple witnesses more difficult, and it might make it more difficult to find a defendant guilty beyond a reasonable doubt. In Brown's case it would have meant charges of perjury against five people, including Brown himself.

Proposal 46: That jurors be authorized by statute or court rule to ask questions during trials, but before deliberations.

Jurors are a unique set of temporary workers who are brought together for a very short period of time to decide a very important question: whether a person has committed one or more crimes and whether s/he should be deprived of his/her freedom, and sometimes even of his/her life.

8. "Nathan Brown," National Registry of Exonerations, at http://www.law.umich.edu/special/exoneration/Pages/casedetail.aspx?caseid=4457

During the performance of that role, jurors are usually asked to be passive observers and listeners.

However, there is a growing trend to permit and encourage jurors to ask questions of witnesses. Some judges support the practice on their own initiative. Washington, D.C. Federal Judge Reggie Walton has become a national advocate for the practice of encouraging juror questions. During the 2007 trial of I. Lewis "Scooter" Libby for obstruction of justice and perjury, Judge Walton permitted jurors to ask questions which he then presented to the jury. He did the same in the 2012 perjury trial of baseball star, Roger Clemens.

Judge Walton's practice is to have the jurors write the questions and then he discusses those questions with the prosecution and defense attorneys. If a question is deemed satisfactory and not in conflict with the rules of evidence, the judge then puts the question to the witness.

Since 2003, Indiana has permitted juror questions in its Rules of Court, Jury Rule 20(a)(7) which provides "that jurors, including alternates, may seek to ask questions of the witnesses by submission of questions in writing."[9]

On the other side, Arkansas specifically prohibited the practice in its Rule of Court 33.8 which was established in 2007. It states, "Questions by Jurors: Jurors shall not be permitted to pose questions to witnesses, either directly or through written questions submitted to the judge or to the parties." The notes to the change indicate that "Permitting jurors to question witnesses may cause delay, prejudice, or error."[10]

9. Indiana Rules of Court – Jury Rules, at http://www.in.gov/judiciary/rules/jury/index.html#_Toc243295750
10. Court Rules: Rule 33.8 "Questions by Jurors" at https://courts.arkansas.gov/rules-and-administrative-orders/court-rules/rule-338-questions-jurors

Of course, that's true of all questions in a trial, but it is through questions that information, and hopefully, truth, is presented to the fact finder, whether it be a judge or jury. The Arkansas law does not seem aimed at assisting jurors with their pursuit of the truth.

Since the beginning of Western culture, as exemplified in Plato's *Republic*, the presentation of information through the answering of questions has been a favored method. The "Socratic Method" of questioning is a favored method of teaching in law schools.

In the interest of preventing wrongful convictions, it is obvious that the practice of jurors asking questions is more likely to generate truth than not asking questions. Thus, all states and the Federal Government should authorize and welcome the practice.

Proposal 47: That jurors be authorized by statute or court rule to ask questions after deliberations have begun which may require the reopening of the evidentiary portion of the trial including the recalling of witnesses for providing additional testimony and/or the production of documents.

Currently, the practice is that when the testimony is over and the opposing sides have given their closing statements and the judge has given his/her charge to the jury, there can be no further questions of witnesses or production of documents.

To illustrate, if an alibi witness testified that s/he was with the defendant from noon to 3:00 p.m. on a certain day and it was determined through subsequent testimony at the trial that the crime occurred at 5:00 p.m. instead of the previously thought time of 2:00 p.m., jurors might want to hear the witness's testimony about the later time period. This example presumes that the defense attorney didn't think of recalling the witness during trial and the jurors didn't think of the question at the time, assuming they were able to ask.

In today's courts throughout the U.S., the judge's answer to a request for a recall of the witness for more testimony would be denied. However, with the proposed change it would be approved.

The normal practice in decision-making outside the courtroom is that a person or group may come to a point where more information is needed. For example, if a group is meeting to decide where to position a new building in a coastal town or city, it would be important to know the predicted amount of sea rise over the next hundred or thousand years. In such a circumstance, the meeting would be adjourned until the information was obtained. In our cyber-world, that might not take long, but the principle of not moving forward with a decision without critical information is the same.

In the criminal justice system, there is a legal fiction, or myth, that the trial has generated all the information that is available and sufficient for a jury to make a just decision. Despite that limitation, if the defendant is to be found guilty, that decision would have to be beyond a reasonable doubt.

The reluctance to give jurors more information, or even the ability to sort out the information they already have heard or seen is systematic. For example, judges have been reluctant to give juries copies of transcripts of evidence they already heard or written copies of their own charge to the jury. The jury request described below is typical:

> [a]fter receiving the case and deliberating for approximately an hour, the jury requested further instructions. The foreman stated that the jury would like to have in writing [the] definition of the four degrees of homicide included in the indictment for first degree murder as stated in the court's oral charge. The judge informed the jury such information could not be supplied in written form. He proceeded to orally re-state the elements of each included offense.[11]

No reason was given for declining to give the jury the definitions in writing. In normal business transactions, a refusal by one party to give the other a statement in writing would indicate a fear that the requesting party might actually see and remember what was said. That's not an encouraging sign for a jury.

No record was found of a judge reopening a trial as proposed here, in response to a jury request for more information from a witness. Without a change in a law or court rule, as proposed here, such a reopening would not be permitted.

Proposal 48: That inmate informants not be utilized to present allegations at trial that during conversations in jail or prison a defendant admitted guilt or said anything else to the informant which was incriminating.

11. Owens v. State, 302 So. 2d 240 (1974)(Court of Criminal Appeals, Alabama) at http://leagle.com/decision/1974542302So2d240_1527.xml

Inmate informants are a notorious source of wrongful convictions. Of 1,520 exonerees as of December 31, 2014, 39 of their wrongful convictions were caused in part by inmate informants, who are also called "jailhouse snitches." Another 54 wrongful convictions came with the assistance of police informants.[12]

The primary problem with informants is that they have an interest in providing incriminating evidence for the government. If their information helps to convict someone, it's valuable to the Government, and the informant can anticipate a reduction in sentence or other assistance. If not valuable, and/or the government's prosecution in the case is unsuccessful, there will be less of a reward for the informant.

In California in 1980, Thomas Lee Goldstein was convicted of murder, due in part to the claim by a jailhouse snitch, Edward Fink, that Goldstein had confessed to him. During the hearings leading to Goldstein eventual exoneration 24 years later, in 2004, the truth about Fink's ten years of fictionalizing cellmates' confessions became known.[13]

12. These numbers are likely underestimates, as they were calculated by searching for the word "informant" among the 1,520 summaries of the exonerees registered in the National Registry of Exonerations, on December 31, 2014 and then reading those 151 summaries to extract the inmate informant cases. Other studies and articles have found a higher percentage. See "See No Evil: Wrongful Convictions and the Prosecutorial Ethics of Offering Testimony by Jailhouse Informants and Dishonest Experts," by Myrna S. Raeder. *Fordham Law Review*, Vol. 76, Issue 3, pp. 1413-1452. See also articles listed at Fn 1, on page 1413 of that article. At http://papers.ssrn.com/sol3/papers.cfm?abstract_id=1016244

13. "Thomas Lee Goldstein," National Registry of Exonerations, at http://www.law.umich.edu/special/exoneration/Pages/casedetail.aspx?caseid=3244

In the Alfred Trenkler case in Massachusetts, a convicted drug dealer, W. David Lindholm, testified that he had heard Trenkler admit to incriminating facts about the bomb that later killed a Boston policeman. As a reward for his testimony, even though he testified that he would not look for favorable treatment for it, Lindholm's eight year sentence was reduced to four and a half years.[14]

In the Chad Evans case in New Hampshire, a jailhouse informant, Cory Merrill, was permitted to testify about Evans's alleged admissions. However, defense objections led to the end of his testimony, but before cross-examination. Thus, the jury heard his claims without challenge, except for the cautions of the judge to the jury, to ignore Merrill's testimony. That a jury can ignore what it has heard is a legal fiction and the equivalent of the unringing of a bell. Such unexplained instructions to a jury contribute to cynicism about the mantra that the goal of a trial is to present the truth.

The appropriate response to such egregious behavior is to forbid the testimony of inmate informants. If police and prosecutors receive such claims of jailhouse confessions and they lead to other evidence which is admissible, so be it, but those claims should not be used in court.

Rule 35(b) of the Federal Rules of Criminal Procedure allows a judge to reduce a defendant's sentence if the defendant provides "substantial assistance in investigating or prosecuting another person."[15] The rule should apply only for

14. For more information about the Trenkler case, see www.alfredtrenklerinnocent.org and/or the book, *PERFECTLY INNOCENT - The Wrongful Conviction of Alfred Trenkler* by Morrison Bonpasse.
15. Rule 35, Federal Rules of Criminal Procedure. Cornell Legal Information Institute, at http://www.law.cornell.edu/rules/frcrmp/rule_35

information known by the defendant before his/her incarceration and should not be used for defendants to become inmate informants about what they heard in prison. The rule should be amended with such a restriction as sub-paragraph 35(e).

One alternative to the proposal here is to permit such testimony if the inmate informant passed a polygraph examination with "no deception indicated."

Proposal 49: That when potentially exculpatory evidence which was in the possession of the police or prosecution disappears or is destroyed, that evidence be construed to be favorable to the defendant.

Many inmates claiming innocence have sought to have DNA testing on evidence collected at the scene. Their efforts to have that evidence tested are often frustrated by the disappearance of such evidence.

Sometimes such evidence is miraculously found by a lucky search of police files. This happened in the Dennis Maher case in Massachusetts. Convicted in 1984, Maher wrote to the Innocence Project in 1993 for help, but the Innocence Project was told that the evidence was lost. In 2000, the case was transferred to the New England Innocence Project and in 2001, a law student found two boxes of evidence in the Middlesex County Courthouse. That evidence was tested and he was exonerated in

2003. He would still be in prison if the law student had not found that evidence.[16]

More often, the lost evidence is never found. In the Dennis Dechaine case in Maine, there was an unidentified fingerprint found on a door where 12-year old Sarah Cherry was babysitting and abducted. That fingerprint did not belong to Dechaine, but it has disappeared and is thus no longer available to be matched with alternate suspects.

Even worse, after Dechaine was convicted in 1989 of sexual assault and murder, evidence in the case was intentionally destroyed by the State Police at the request of the Attorney General's Office. The evidence was destroyed purportedly to save space in the evidence rooms. Included in that destruction was hair found on the victim's body that was, to the naked eye, apparently not hers. It likely did not appear to belong to Dechaine either, or the prosecution would have presented it at trial. Now it is gone.[17]

Because the hairs were destroyed, they were not eligible for the DNA testing which was subsequently ordered by the Superior Court for other items which had not been destroyed.

With such a proposed rule, the hairs would be legally presumed to belong to someone other than the victim and other than Dennis Dechaine.

If Maine had a rule as proposed here, and the lost evidence was construed to be exculpatory, he would have won a new trial. Further, if Maine had

16. See summary of Dennis Maher's case at the Registry of Exonerations at http://www.law.umich.edu/special/exoneration/Pages/casedetail.aspx?caseid=3404.
17. See "Summary of Evidence" by James Moore, at http://www.trialanderrordennis.org/summary-of-evidence/

such a rule, the evidence might not have been lost or destroyed in the first place.[18]

Proposal 50: That where evidence of "consciousness of guilt" is allowed into a trial, the defendant be permitted to introduce evidence of "consciousness of innocence," or that in the alternative, the concept of "consciousness of guilt" be disallowed as evidence.

Several states allow testimony and prosecutor argument about a state of mind of defendants called "consciousness of guilt."

The concept was used by prosecutors in the Chad Evans case in New Hampshire. They persuaded the judge that Evans's contact, in violation of his bail conditions, with the mother of the girl he was charged with murdering was an indication of "consciousness of guilt."[19] Also, the prosecution claimed that Evans's lies to the police during his initial interview showed "consciousness of guilt."[20]

However, there are equally reasonable explanations for the alleged "consciousness of guilt," i.e. that Evans loved Amanda Bortner and that his lies were aimed at protecting Amanda not himself. His contact with Amanda was an indication of his love and concern for her well-being after the loss of her daughter.

18. For more information about the Dennis Dechaine case, see his website, www.trialanderrordennis.org and the book, *Human Sacrifice*, by retired ATF agent, James Moore.
19. *EYE CONTACT*, op cit., (Fn 12, Ch 7) page 363.
20. *EYE CONTACT*, op cit., (Fn 12, Ch 7) See pages 363, 477, 507, 529, 530, 569 and 620.

There was no offer by the defense of evidence of "consciousness of innocence," at least not by that name. For example, the agreement by Evans, as relayed to the police by his woman friend and mother of the victim, to take a polygraph was not presented by his lawyers as an indication of his "consciousness of innocence."

The 1995 Massachusetts case of Commonwealth v. Oeun Lam is instructive. The prosecution was allowed to present evidence of Lam's escape attempt as showing "consciousness of guilt."[21] However, just as prisoners of war are encouraged in their pre-combat training to try to escape possible future capture and imprisonment, wrongly convicted people also have a good reason to try to escape from prison. In fact, such escapes or escape attempts could just as well show "consciousness of innocence" as of guilt. Aren't the innocent more likely to feel that they shouldn't be in prison?

One of Canada's most notorious or celebrated wrongful conviction cases was that of David Milgaard. In 1970, at the age of 17, he was sentenced to life in prison for rape and murder.[22] In 1973, Milgaard escaped from prison and was quickly recaptured. In 1980, he did not return from a day pass, and was captured again 77 days later, and shot in the back. In 1992, a month after testifying of his innocence before a special tribunal, Milgaard did not return to his halfway house. He was recaptured and returned to prison. Later in 1992, his conviction was overturned and in 1999,

21. Commonwealth v. Oeun Lam, 420 Mass. 615 (1995) at www.masscases.com/cases/sjc/420/420mass615.html
22. "David Milgaard," *Wikipedia*, at http://en.wikipedia.org/wiki/David_Milgaard

the Saskatchewan government awarded Milgaard and his family $10 million compensation.[23] His three escapes could not now be said by any court to have shown a "consciousness of guilt."

Jerome and Barbara Frank wrote in their 1957 classic, *Not Guilty*, of a case of presumed consciousness of guilt:

> Yet not only the guilty show signs of apparent guilt. Lemuel Shaw [1781-1861], a great Massachusetts judge, remarked that 'an innocent man, when placed in circumstances in a condition of suspicion and danger, may resort to deception in the hope of avoiding arrest and conviction'; he may be 'stunned under the mere imputation of guilt.' Shaw went on to tell of the famous old English case of Graham, tried for murder of his young niece. Graham, at his trial, attempted to deceive the jury by presenting another girl as his niece. The prosecution's exposure of this deception led to Graham's conviction. He was executed by hanging. Some seven years later his niece turned up, alive.[24]

In 2014, a Federal District Court judge in New York allowed a motion to permit a defendant to argue that his return from Brazil to the U.S. after indictment was an indication of "consciousness of innocence." Defendant Rengan stated in his memorandum supporting the motion:

23. "Timeline - David Milgaard Inquiry," by Injustice Busters, at http://injusticebusters.org/05/Milgaard_Inquiry1.shtml
24. *Not Guilty*, by Jerome and Barbara Frank. Popular Library Edition, 1962. p. 114.

In United States v. Biaggi, 909 F.2d 662 (2d Cir. 1990). . . the defendant sought to prove that the government had offered him immunity in return for information about wrongdoing by others, and that the defendant "denied knowledge of any such wrongdoing, thereby 'rejecting' immunity." Biaggi, 909 F.2d at 690. The district court excluded this evidence, primarily on relevance grounds. The Second Circuit reversed, holding that "the probative force of a rejected immunity offer is clearly strong enough to render it relevant." Id. at 691....

In support of its holding, the Biaggi Court quoted extensively from Dean Wigmore: Let the accused's whole conduct come in; and whether it tells for consciousness of guilt or for consciousness of innocence, let us take it for what it is worth . . . . Let us not deprive an innocent person, falsely accused, of the inference which common sense draws from a consciousness of innocence and its natural manifestations. Id. (citing 2 *Wigmore on Evidence* § 293, at 232 (J. Chadbourn rev. ed. 1979)).[25]

Proposal 51: That jury deliberations be structured by written guidelines from the court, with explicit provisions for voting procedures.

25. "Fugitive's Return to U.S. Upon Indictment Admissible to Show 'Consciousness of Innocence,' " by Robert Connolly, June 16, 2014 in blog CartelCapers at http://cartelcapers.com/blog/fugitves-return-us-upon-indictment-admissible-show-consciousness-innocence/

There appears to be a reverence for the jury process which borders on worship of the magical, and that the jury process is a black box from which justice magically appears. That is, barring clear evidence of illegal juror activity, such as bribery during jury deliberations, the courts leave the members of the jury, usually 12, to themselves.

However, group decision-making is a difficult process in any context, and especially difficult for people who do not know one another beforehand.

In 2013, James "Whitey" Bulger was sentenced in Boston to Federal prison for life after being convicted of racketeering and multiple murder charges. In November 2014, the jury foreman, Terry Fife, wrote about his jury experience. The essay makes the verdicts seem more about interpersonal dynamics than about justice. He clearly lacked guidance from the court on how the jury could perform its work, especially in such a complex case.[26]

There need to be explicit guidelines for how discussions of the case should be conducted, how to select a foreperson and how and when to conduct votes.

Some states use guidelines in a 1999 51 page booklet, *Behind Closed Doors*, by the American Judicature Society.[27] Wisconsin condensed its

26. "Confessions of a Jury Foreman," by Terry Fife. *Boston Magazine*, November 2014, at http://www.bostonmagazine.com/news/article/2014/10/28/whitey-bulger-trial-confessions

27. *Behind Closed Doors*, American Judicature Society, 1999, at http://www.amazon.com/Behind-closed-doors-resource-deliberations/dp/0938870955. On November 15, 2014, the author purchased the last copy available at that time on Amazon. This book is not to be confused with the 45+ other books available on Amazon with titles beginning with the suggestive "Behind Closed Doors."

version, "Behind Closed Doors: A Guide for Jury Deliberation," to two pages.[28]

Instead of recommending time-tested procedures for reaching sound verdicts, the Wisconsin guide struggles with the concepts of citizens' freedom and the need for disciplined discussion. It begins with "You are free to deliberate any way you wish," and proceeds in a Q[uestion] and A[nswer] format, e.g.

> Q. Are there any set rules to tell us how to deliberate?
>
> A. No.

Then the guide gives suggestions, such as "Go around the table, one by one, to talk about the case," and "Have jurors speak up anytime, when they have something to say."

The guide misses the opportunity to encourage disciplined analysis, such as "Begin by discussing the evidence presented in support of the prosecution's perspective on the facts relating to the first count, and then the evidence of facts supporting that of the defendant. Which seem more believable? If the prosecution's evidence is more believable, is it believable beyond a reasonable doubt? Alternatively, does the defense's version of the facts introduce reasonable doubt about the prosecution's version?"

A critical point for a jury is voting, and here, too, the guide is equivocal.

> Q. When should we take the first vote?
>
> A. There is no best time. But, if you spend a reasonable amount of time considering the evidence and the law and

28. "Behind Closed Doors - A guide for jury deliberations," Wisconsin Court System, at https://www.wicourts.gov/services/juror/docs/deliberate.pdf The U.S. District Court for Maine uses the same two page guide. See www.med.uscourts.gov/pdf/SegJryDelb.pdf

> listening to each other's opinions, you will probably feel more confident and satisfied with your eventual verdict than if you rush things.

Instead, guides should be quite specific that no votes should be taken on any counts in the indictment until there has been at least some discussion of each count. By delaying the votes, a juror will tend to be more influenced by the evidence than by whether s/he is in the majority or minority in the early voting.

> Q. Is there any correct way to take the vote?
>
> A. No, any way is okay. You might vote by raising your hands, by a written ballot, or by a voice ballot. Eventually, a final vote in the jury room will have to be taken with each of you expressing your verdict openly to the other jurors.

Instead, there is likely to be group psychology research which indicates which method, on the first votes at least, is most likely to encourage honest, reasonable deliberation. It seems reasonable that jurors should be advised to vote by raising a hand, as they did when being sworn in as jurors. This allows each juror to publicly present his/her view, but it doesn't commit him/her to something in writing which is less amenable to change. Phrasing a jury guide with such affirmations gives reassurance that there IS a good way to proceed, as shown by thousands of juries in the past, in order to help achieve a correct verdict.

In North Carolina, jurors view a 15 minute video, which includes only the following segments related to deliberations:

> After closing arguments, the judge will instruct you on the law that applies to the case. There are different degrees of

proof required in civil and criminal cases.... However, in a criminal case, the state must prove the defendant's guilt "beyond a reasonable doubt." The judge will explain in detail what the burden of proof is in the case you will hear. Pay close attention. You must understand and apply the law as the judge gives it to you, not as you think it is or would like for it to be.

After the judge's instructions, you will be taken by the bailiff to the jury deliberation room. Your first job will be to choose a foreperson. This person will preside over discussions during your deliberations and speak for you in the courtroom. The foreperson should make sure that the discussion is free enough for ideas to be shared but orderly enough for each person to be heard. Give real consideration to the opinions of others because in North Carolina, a verdict requires a unanimous vote. This means that everyone must agree. In determining your verdict, consider all the evidence presented, the weight of the evidence, as well as opening and closing statements made by the attorneys, and the credibility of witnesses. Then make up your own mind....

Pay attention to the facts, use common sense and share opinions with your fellow jurors during the deliberation process.[29]

29. Transcript of video, "You the Jury," *The North Carolina Court System*, at http://www.nccourts.org/Citizens/JDuty/JDutyvideo.asp.

The above examples show that there is not much guidance provided to jurors on how to perform a task which may be the most important in some jurors' lives, and the effects of which may last longer than some jurors' lives.

Proposal 52: That the number of jury votes on any indictment count be limited to three and if a vote leaves only one or two jurors in the minority, that s/he/they must be advised of the right to request the cessation of deliberations on the count at issue.

Nowhere do the Wisconsin guidelines mention the critical concept of reasonable doubt. While the judge's instructions surely mention it, the guide says nothing about how to explore with other jurors what doubts are reasonable and what are not. The Wisconsin guide does, however, explicitly prohibit bullying, with "do not let yourself be bullied into changing your opinion, and do not bully anyone else."[30]

A wrenching problem for some juries is what to do when one or two jurors do not agree with the majority. Such jurors are called "holdouts." What often happens is that these jurors are persuaded by power and intimidation, usually short of "bullying," rather than by reason and evidence.

In several exoneration cases, there were holdout jurors for reasonable doubt and innocence. In the 1990 Illinois case of David Dowaliby, a holdout juror contacted Professor David Protess, after learning of his efforts on behalf of Dowaliby. The juror told Protess that she "caved in" from pressure

30. ibid.

from other jurors. Dowaliby was exonerated two years later.[31]

The day after the 1998 convictions of David Moreno and Justin Pacheco in California, several jurors called defense attorneys to report that they had been coerced by the majority jurors into agreeing with a guilty verdict. One juror stated that when the judge polled the jurors, her hand was held to her chair by a majority member juror. The two men were exonerated two years later.[32]

In the 1993 joint cases of Christopher McCrimmon and Andre Minnitt, the pressure on a holdout juror was administered by a judge. The two men were sentenced to death for murder, but the convictions were overturned when the Arizona Supreme Court ruled that the efforts by the trial judge to persuade the holdout juror to change his/her vote amounted to impermissible coercion.[33]

With a limit on the number of votes on a particular count, the majority members of a jury would see the procedural, and not entirely symbolic, restraint on their attempts to persuade the holdout(s) to change their views. In addition, the knowledge that the holdout(s) could assert their rights to cease the deliberations on a difficult count would further restrain efforts to force agreement.

31. "David Dowaliby," National Registry of Exonerations at http://www.law.umich.edu/special/exoneration/Pages/casedetail.aspx?caseid=3873.
32. "Justin Pacheco," National Registry of Exonerations at http://www.law.umich.edu/special/exoneration/Pages/casedetail.aspx?caseid=4185. Moreno's summary is identical.
33. "Christopher McCrimmon," National Registry of Exonerations at http://www.law.umich.edu/special/exoneration/Pages/casedetail.aspx?caseid=4185. Minnitt's summary is identical.

Proposal 53: That when a mistrial is declared due to the failure of a jury to agree on a defendant's guilt, and the jurors' positions are determined to be reasonable, that such mistrial be deemed to be a trial with a Not Guilty verdict and not subject to retrial.

About half of the declared mistrials are for a procedural reason such as misconduct of a juror or an erroneous presentation by a witness of a fact that was improper to present to the jury – regardless of its merits.

However, for those mistrials where jurors struggle for at least three votes on an issue and a mistrial is declared, and if the views of the minority jurors (usually one or two) are reasonable as might be later determined by a judge, that should be sufficient evidence of reasonable doubt to warrant a Not Guilty determination.

In the case of exoneree Eddie Andre, his first trial in 1988 ended in a mistrial with the jury deadlocked 11-1 in favor of acquittal. A retrial was ordered where he was found guilty of second degree murder and sentenced to 25 years to life. He was exonerated in 1994 after two witnesses recanted.[34]

In 1982, George Allen, Jr. faced trial for rape and murder in St. Louis, Missouri. A jury trial ended when the jury deadlocked for 10-2 in favor of acquittal. Allen was retried and convicted and remained in prison for 30 years until his 2013 exoneration.[35]

34. "Eddie Andre," National Registry of Exonerations, at http://www.law.umich.edu/special/exoneration/Pages/casedetail.aspx?caseid=4347

35. "George Allen, Jr.," National Registry of Exoneration, at http://www.law.umich.edu/special/exoneration/Pages/casedetail.aspx?caseid=4091

Of course, some hung juries are stuck in the other direction. At Clarence Brandley's first trial in 1980, there was one white juror who was not convinced beyond a reasonable doubt of Brandley's guilt of murder and rape. At the second trial in 1981, Brandley was found guilty and sentenced to death. It was not until 1990, with the assistance of Centurion Ministries that Brandley was able to convince a Texas appeals court that his conviction was wrongful.[36]

By this proposal, the first mistrials in each of these three cases should have been sufficient evidence of reasonable doubt to declare a verdict of Not Guilty.

Proposal 54: That jury deliberations be video-recorded and be open to review by either party for up to one year. And that if any irregularities which may have influenced the verdict are identified, they should be brought to the attention of the trial judge to ensure that the jury verdict was fairly and legally reached.

In 2011 in Portland, Maine, a juror in Federal Court wrote a letter to the judge saying that he or she misunderstood the need for a unanimous verdict. The juror wrote that he or she believed the defendant, Peter Enzinger, was innocent, but mistakenly thought that unanimity was required for either verdict, guilty or not guilty. Given the 11-1 votes for a guilty verdict, the juror gave up, and misunderstood that his/her single not guilty vote would have been enough to stop a guilty verdict.

36. "Clarence Brandley," National Registry of Exonerations, at http://www.law.umich.edu/special/exoneration/Pages/casedetail.aspx?caseid=3044.

Judge Brock Hornby denied the request for a new trial and stated that, generally, judges and lawyers must not inquire about jury deliberations. He noted that there were exceptions such as when racial bias is an overt factor in such deliberations.[37]

The denial was not unusual as judges have historically tried to avoid "piercing the veil" of jury deliberations. The difficulty is that such willful ignorance seemed reasonable in former times when citizens and participants in the criminal justice system had a reasonable faith that the system worked nearly all the time. Now, however, many informed citizens know that the system has worked with only about 98 percent accuracy, using our two percent estimated wrongful conviction rate.

With such a transformed understanding about the system, it's no longer acceptable for judges and others to argue that the jury deliberative process is too sacrosanct to examine.

It's been reported that 75 percent of people who have served as jurors do not understand that they should have voted for a verdict of "not guilty" if they had reasonable doubt about the prosecution's case, i.e. that the defendant committed the crime, as charged.[38]

In 1987 in the U.S. Supreme Court, Justice Sandra Day O'Connor wrote the majority opinion in

37. "Judge rejects businessman's new-trial plea," by Ann Kim, *Portland Press Herald*, at http://www.pressherald.com/2011/08/05/judge-rejects-businessmans-new-trial-plea_2011-08-05/

38. "What social science teaches us about the jury instruction process," by Joel D. Lieberman and Bruce Sales. *Psychology, Public Policy and Law*, 1997, pp. 589-644, at http://psycnet.apa.org/index.cfm?fa=buy.optionToBuy&id=1998-00175-002, as presented in "Helping Jurors Understand What Instructions Don't – The Law," by Jon May in "The Champion," Jan/Feb 2008.

a decision supporting a lower court's decision to not hear evidence about allegations of alcohol and drug abuse during jury deliberations. She stated,

> There is little doubt that post-verdict investigation into juror misconduct would in some instances lead to the invalidation of verdicts reached after irresponsible or improper juror behavior. It is not at all clear, however, that the jury system could survive such efforts to perfect it. Allegations of juror misconduct, incompetency, or inattentiveness, raised for the first time days, weeks, or months after the verdict, seriously disrupt the finality of the process. [citation omitted] Moreover, full and frank discussion in the jury room, jurors' willingness to return an unpopular verdict, and the community's trust in a system that relies on the decisions of laypeople would all be undermined by a barrage of post verdict scrutiny of juror conduct.[39]

The case was a challenge to Federal Rule of Evidence 606(b) which states,

> (b) During an Inquiry into the Validity of a Verdict or Indictment.
> (1) Prohibited Testimony or Other Evidence. During an inquiry into the validity of a verdict or indictment, a juror may not testify about any statement made or incident that occurred during the jury's deliberations; the effect of anything on that juror's or another juror's vote; or any juror's mental processes

39. Tanner v. United States, 483 U.S. 107, 121 (1987) (In this case there were allegations that a juror was drunk during deliberations.)

concerning the verdict or indictment. The court may not receive a juror's affidavit or evidence of a juror's statement on these matters.

(2) Exceptions. A juror may testify about whether:

(A) extraneous prejudicial information was improperly brought to the jury's attention;

(B) an outside influence was improperly brought to bear on any juror; or

(C) a mistake was made in entering the verdict on the verdict form.[40]

Justice O'Connor's admission that there is "little doubt" that looking more closely at jury deliberations would result in changed verdicts and her fear that "the jury system could [not] survive such efforts to perfect it," speak agonizingly loudly for themselves.

On December 8, 2014, the Supreme Court reaffirmed the stand-off position of the Federal Courts when hearing allegations of juror misconduct. In the Warner v. Shauers case, the court barred consideration of testimony by a juror that another juror made statements showing her bias in favor of the civil defendant. The allegedly offending juror denied making those statements.[41]

The irony of the reluctance of the justice system to examine its own processes is that that same legal system is very willing to examine the processes of everyone else, such as doctors and

40. "Federal Rules of Evidence," by Legal Information Institute, Cornell University, at http://www.law.cornell.edu/rules/fre/rule_606.

41. "Justices Reject Jurors' Testimony on Deliberations," by Adam Liptak. *New York Times*, December 9, 2014. At http://www.nytimes.com/2014/12/10/us/supreme-court-sotomayor-rejects-jurors-testimony-on-deliberations.html

corporations. If a recording was made of a nurse telling a surgeon that it appeared that a surgical pad was left inside a patient's body and the doctor replied, "Who would know?" we can be sure that the malpractice trial would have heard the entire recording.

We no longer need to rely upon the legal fiction that juries reach their verdicts fairly and rationally. We need not rely upon convenient presumptions when the means exist now to record all jury proceedings and verify that a jury has reached a verdict fairly.

One judge in San Diego expressed openly the views of many about jury deliberations, comparing them to the making of sausage. "You don't really want to know how it's made," he said.[42] By this proposal we do want to know how it's made.

It is time for the jury deliberation process to be opened to closer scrutiny. However, this doesn't have to mean that it is opened to the public without reservation. The proposal here is that the video recording be available to attorneys of both sides for only one year after the trial. After that point, or other to-be-determined period, it could be destroyed just as the records of some court proceedings if parties do not request them within a set period of time.

Proposal 55: That the standard of "beyond a reasonable doubt" be restored to its proper meaning by defining it mathematically as 99.9 percent certain. OR, if that proves unfeasible,

42. "Judge serves life in courtroom," by Jennifer Bruce. July 24, 2013, *San Diego News*, at http://www.utsandiego.com/news/2013/jul/24/judge-serves-life-in-courtroom/#

to change the standard of guilt to "beyond any doubt" or "no doubt."

The U.S. and most other countries with adversarial justice systems use the "beyond a reasonable doubt" standard to determine a defendant's guilt. The U.S. Supreme Court has been reluctant to precisely define that standard or to issue its view of what standard instructions to juries should say on that issue. However, it did state in the juvenile justice case of In Re Winship that a finding of guilty required "proof beyond a reasonable doubt of every fact necessary to constitute the crime with which he is charged."[43]

Given the large number of exonerations from wrongful convictions, it seems clear that either the "reasonable doubt" standard is not sufficient, or that it is not being correctly applied, or a combination of both.

Below is a line of a continuum about the standard of belief in a fact in the previously referenced Federal case in Boston in 1993, U.S. v. Trenkler. Alfred Trenkler was convicted of building a bomb that exploded when being examined by a Boston Bomb Squad officer, Jeremiah Hurley, Jr., who was mortally wounded.[44] The fact issue presented below is whether Trenkler built the bomb.

This is the continuum:

% 100---99.9---99---90---80---70---60---50---40---30---20---10---1---.1---0

|------------------------NOT GUILTY-------------------------| |Gty|

On the next page are explanations of the percentages:

43. In re Winship, 397 U.S. 358 (1970)

44. For more information about the Alfred Trenkler case, see www.alfredtrenklerinnocent.org.

Alfred Trenkler.....

Pct Fact Statment

100 - did not build the "Shay bomb" - absolutely not, with total certainty. NOT GUILTY

99.9- did not build the "Shay bomb" with much certainty. NOT GUILTY

99 - did not build the "Shay bomb" with some certainty. NOT GUILTY

90 - very likely did not build the "Shay bomb". NOT GUILTY

80 - probably did not build the "Shay bomb". NOT GUILTY

70 - might not have built the "Shay bomb". NOT GUILTY

60 - possibly did not build the "Shay bomb". NOT GUILTY

50 - Undecided. Don't have an opinion. NOT GUILTY

40 - possibly did build the "Shay bomb". NOT GUILTY

30 - might have built the "Shay bomb". NOT GUILTY

20 - probably did build the "Shay bomb". NOT GUILTY

10 - very likely did build the "Shay bomb". NOT GUILTY

1 - did build the "Shay bomb", with some certainty. NOT GUILTY

.1- did build the "Shay bomb", beyond a reasonable doubt. GUILTY

00- did build the "Shay bomb", absolutely, with total certainty. GUILTY

It's not known exactly how the jurors in Trenkler's case would have characterized their beliefs by this chart at the time of deliberations, but since then, five members have read the book about the case and have written the trial judge to recommend a new trial.[45]

45. Alfred Trenkler, ibid. The book is *Perfectly Innocent – The Wrongful Conviction of Alfred Trenkler.*

Unlike many aspects of life which can be characterized as being "shades of gray," there is an "all or nothing" aspect to criminal justice. The continuum above only describes changing beliefs, but the consequences are binary: on or off, and Not Guilty or Guilty. The possible punishments for a crime do not vary along with the degree of belief. For example, a person cannot be convicted with only a 20 percent belief in guilt, with a commitment that the punishment would be only 20 percent of the minimum. Instead, it's like riding in the first leg of a rollercoaster, in that there are no consequences until the tipping point is reached - and then zoom! However, in a criminal case the all-or-nothing result can be a disaster. The consequences of guilt are so severe, sometimes including death, that the system must take severe care that only the truly guilty are found guilty.

Apparently, in the cases of the 1,520 exonerees since 1989, the "reasonable doubt" standard was applied by many judges and juries as meaning something less than 99.9 percent certainty, and likely something closer to the 80 percent standard above, "probably did [it]."

In the article cited above by Jon May, he wrote about the concern that juries didn't understand the concept of "beyond a reasonable doubt." He suggested that

> One technique that has been demonstrated to increase juror comprehension involves translating abstract concepts into concrete examples. Expressing the burden of proof in a quantitative fashion has shown to increase understanding of reasonable doubt. Without instruction, jurors are likely to underestimate the quantum of proof required. Explaining the burden in

> terms of percentages, preponderance equals more than 51 percent, while reasonable doubt is greater than 90 percent or saying that it was 10 times worse to convict an innocent man than to acquit a guilty one, has a significant effect upon jurors' ability to understanding the government's burden in criminal cases.[46]

While the idea of quantifying the required standard of proof is supported here, it's astounding that an attorney wrote that "greater than 90 percent" was the equivalent of "beyond a reasonable doubt." If lawyers do not understand the concept, what hope is there for citizen jurors?

In 2004, the previously mentioned panel commissioned by Massachusetts Governor Mitt Romney to make recommendations regarding reinstating a death penalty recommended a higher standard of guilt at the sentencing stage as a requisite for imposing a death penalty. The panel stated,

> ...we propose to add a new and heightened burden of proof at the sentencing stage of a capital trial. Under this heightened burden of proof, even after the jury has found the defendant guilty of capital murder 'beyond a reasonable doubt' at the guilt-innocence stage of the trial, it would be required further to find at the sentencing stage, as a prerequisite for a death sentence, that there is "no doubt" about the defendant's guilt. In other words, before imposing the

46. "Helping Jurors Understand What Instructions Don't – The Law," op cit., Fn 38, above.

death penalty, the jury would be required to find the absence of any "residual" or "lingering" doubts about the defendant's guilt.[47]

The report stated that there were six states with capital punishment which required guilt at the sentencing stage without any "residual" or "lingering" doubt. It cited a U.S. Supreme Court case which acknowledged room for "residual" doubt which logically had to be located somewhere in between "beyond reasonable doubt" and "no doubt." The report cited another case which said that there could be "genuine doubt" even if there was no "reasonable doubt" of guilt. The court said of "genuine doubt," that "It may reflect a mere possibility; it may be the whimsy of one juror or several. Yet this whimsical doubt – this absence of absolute certainty – can be real."[48]

Thus, it seemed acceptable to that court, and to the writers of the 2004 report to the Massachusetts Governor Romney that it was permissible to sentence a person to prison, and even life in prison, even if there was "genuine doubt," "lingering doubt" or "residual doubt," but it was not permissible to execute that person if such doubt existed.

If jurors can be instructed and advised that the meaning of "beyond a reasonable doubt" means 99.9 percent, then the proposal here would be to stick with that existing standard. Otherwise, the country should move to a "no doubt" standard.

As noted in Chapter 1 the percentage of criminal convictions which are wrongful is not

47. *Report of the Massachusetts Governor's Council on Capital Punishment*, May, 2004, at www.lawlib.state.ma.us/docs/5-3-04governorsreportcapitalpunishment.pdf
48. Smith v. Balkcom, 660 F.2d 573 (5th Cir. 1981)

known. In the absence of contrary evidence, this book is using a compromise percentage estimate of two percent. That would mean that the current ad hoc or actual definition in the U.S. of "guilt beyond a reasonable doubt" is approximately 98 percent guilt.

Whatever the words that are used, i.e. "beyond a reasonable doubt," or "with no doubt" etc. the country needs to move the numerical standard to 99.9 percent and keep it there. Measuring compliance with that standard is the "devil" that is in the "details," but one after-the-fact measurement that can be used to monitor progress is the frequency of wrongful conviction. That is, when the frequency of wrongful conviction declines to .1 percent, it can be said that juries have correctly understood the meaning of "beyond a reasonable doubt" as being 99.9 percent certain.

Proposal 56: That juries be re-empaneled in the interest of justice when new evidence develops and that the available jurors be asked whether, for a Guilty verdict, the new evidence would have introduced sufficient reasonable doubt to prevent them from reaching a guilty verdict, or, for a Not Guilty verdict, whether the new evidence would have erased their previously expressed doubts.

This proposal is similar to Proposal 47, above, which urged that jurors be permitted to ask questions during deliberations which might require re-opening the trial. This proposal is about the re-empaneling the jury when new evidence appears.

In the "real world" when a group, such as a family, makes a decision and new information comes to the attention of the decision makers, the same group can revisit the decision. In government, a legislature can revise a statute when new information indicates that it can be improved.

In the criminal justice system, the jury is dismissed after rendering a verdict and their services are done. There is very little room for further factfinding. Until the current DNA exoneration era, the courts viewed "beyond a reasonable doubt" as sacrosanct and finality as more of a certainty than a belief.

This cut-off for the jury is enshrined in rules and court decisions. Federal Rule of Criminal Procedure 31(d) provides for polling a jury: "After a verdict is returned but before the jury is discharged, the court must on a party's request, or may on its own, poll the jurors individually." Thus, after a jury has left the courthouse, its members cannot be polled by a judge.

In New York in 2008, Nicholas Rojas was found guilty of several drug offenses. When announcing the verdict, the courtroom deputy left out the word "base" in the phrase "cocaine base" on two occasions. One of them was immediately corrected. To correct the other, after the jury had been discharged, the judge recalled the jury to the courtroom for the verdict to be re-read. Part of Rojas's appeal to the Second Circuit Court of Appeals was to claim that once the jury had been "discharged," it could not be recalled, even to correct a misreading of the verdict. The Second Circuit held that since the jury was still in the courthouse, it was still eligible for recall.[49]

In a civil case, the Hawaii Supreme Court upheld in 2012 a trial judge's recalling of the jury, because the jury was still within the courthouse. However, the unanimous court declined to overturn

49. U.S. v. Rojas, 617 F. 3d 669 (2010).

a verdict even after several jurors testified that they misunderstood the meaning of their special verdicts.[50]

In 2013, the U.S. Virgin Islands Supreme Court upheld a lower court's recalling the jury after the judge declared a mistrial and discharged the jury. Upon recall, the jurors clarified that they had found the defendant Not Guilty on some of the counts, but were deadlocked on others. The trial judge corrected the statement of mistrial, and the defendant was later retried only on the deadlocked charges.[51]

By their strong reluctance to revisit procedural questions, courts signal their reluctance to permit a jury to revisit the substance of what it decided.

An exception to the prohibition against recalling juries comes when there are allegations that the jury's deliberations were flawed in some way, such as by explicit racism exhibited by a juror during deliberations, which conduct was subsequently revealed by another juror.

Another typical reason for recalling a jury is to for a judge to inquire about allegations that a juror visited the crime scene on his or her own.

In 2014, a Federal judge in a Vermont habeas case overturned a murder conviction because one juror went to the scene of the crime to reinvestigate the case himself, and two other jurors had misrepresented their backgrounds in juror questionnaires.[52] Earlier in the year, Judge

50. Lahaina Fashions v. Bank of Hawaii, 131 Haw. 437, (January 7, 2014).
51. Adrian Benjamin v. People of the Virgin Islands, Sup.Ct. Crim No. 2012-0026, Sept. 6, 2013.
52. "U.S. Judge orders new trial for Donald Fell," by Jennifer Costa. *WCAX*, July 27, 2014, at http://www.wcax.com/story/26107306/us-judge-orders-new-trial-for-donald-fell

Sessions had recalled the jury for a several day hearing on those juror misconduct issues.

On the other hand, a Kansas judge declined to recall a jury to consider defense counsel allegations that a juror had inappropriately stated during deliberations that he had outside information about the case.[53]

However, there have been no cases found where a jury has been recalled to reopened a trial to hear additional evidence and to reconsider the verdict. That's a loss to the system and to justice, because jurors have already developed considerable knowledge about a case. If something developed shortly thereafter, such as new evidence, why not call the jury back and ask jurors to hear that new evidence and then reconsider their verdict?

In such a circumstance there would need to be some inquiry by the judge about what the jurors may have heard in the media about the case since the trial, and such an inquiry could insulate the case against improper influence.

53. "Judge denies request to recall jury," by Tim Hrenchir. *The Capital Journal*, Topeka, Kansas. March 24, 2004. At http://cjonline.com/stories/032404/bre_cook.shtml. The judge's decision was upheld on appeal in Kansas v. Kenneth Cook, Kansas Supreme Court, 2006 at http://www.kscourts.org/cases-and-opinions/opinions/supct/2006/20060609/92731.htm

Chapter 9: Post Trial

The primary emphasis in this book is to prevent wrongful convictions. However, it is inevitable that they will continue to occur. The next challenge, therefore, is to correct and cancel those wrongful convictions as soon as possible after conviction.

This means that there must be reforms in the rules and laws for new trials, and habeas corpus laws and post-conviction reviews.

Proposal 57: That judicial reviews of cases be permitted at any time, but at least every year, when claimants of innocence present new evidence or new interpretations of law, and that such reviews consider all the evidence in a case.

Among the best provisions for judicial reviews of claims of wrongful conviction is the Massachusetts Rule of Criminal Procedure 30(b), which provides:

> b) New Trial. The trial judge upon motion in writing may grant a new trial **at any time if it appears that justice may not have been done.** Upon the motion the trial judge shall make such findings of fact as are necessary to resolve the defendant's allegations of error of law. [emphasis added.]

The practical limit on such motions is no more than once a year, but the provision for "at any time" is outstanding. Most of the approximately 56 Massachusetts wrongly convicted felons exonerated since 1976 have been exonerated through the use of this rule.

There is no outside time limit and no restriction as to whether there is new evidence or not. Around the country, hundreds of petitions for relief from wrongful convictions are blocked through such limits at the state and Federal levels. In Maine, for example, a motion for a new trial on the basis of new evidence must be filed within two years of conviction.[1] After that, procedure trumps truth and justice. One exception to that time limit is the recently amended DNA testing statute, but that statute has been narrowly interpreted by a lower court in the Dennis Dechaine case to block reconsideration of new evidence or views of other related issues, such as the time of death of the victim.[2]

The Federal Antiterrorism and Effective Death Penalty Act of 1996 (AEDPA) is the best known of such laws restricting appeals. It was passed in the context of publicity about the burdens on the Federal courts from inmate appeals, but before the full impact of the Innocence Movement was understood in Washington. That is, in 1996, there was no National Registry of Exonerations and the media were still treating the DNA exonerations as one isolated miracle after another. By the end of 1992, the year that Barry Scheck and Peter Neufeld established the first Innocence Project, there had been only 16 DNA-based exonerations in the U.S.

The AEDPA passed by strong majorities in each house of Congress and was signed by President Bill Clinton. The law seemed to forbid inmates from filing petitions for habeas corpus with claims which

1. Rule 33, Maine Rules of Criminal Procedure, at http://www.courts.maine.gov/rules_adminorders/rules/text/mr_crim_p_only_2014-5-7.pdf
2. See Newsletter at the Dennis Dechaine website, at http://www.trialanderrordennis.org/2014/09/trial-error-newsletter-september-2014/

had been raised in previous petitions.[3] However, the law still requires lower courts to view the "evidence as a whole."[4] In the case of Jeffrey MacDonald, who was convicted in 1979 of murdering his wife and daughters at Fort Bragg, North Carolina, the Fourth Circuit Court of Appeals ordered in 2011 the U.S. District Court in his case to reconsider its denial of MacDonald's most recent habeas petition.[5] The lower court had denied MacDonald's previous habeas corpus motions by considering separately only the claims made in each motion.

As ordered by the Fourth Circuit, the District Court held an evidentiary hearing in September 2012 on the new evidence "as a whole," but in July, 2014 that court denied MacDonald's claims for relief.

This proposal would reduce the AEDPA restrictions, and their state-based equivalents, on post-conviction relief by inmates.

Proposal 58: That filing deadlines for motions for relief from wrongful convictions be waived in the interest of justice when the petitioner has presented a non-frivolous justification for the delay.

3. "Antiterrorism and Effective Death Penalty Act of 1996," in Wikipedia at http://en.wikipedia.org/wiki/Antiterrorism_and_Effective_Death_Penalty_Act_of_1996.
4. The subsection states, "the facts underlying the claim, if proven and viewed **in light of the evidence as a whole**, would be sufficient to establish by clear and convincing evidence that, but for constitutional error, no reasonable factfinder would have found the applicant guilty of the underlying offense." (emphasis added) 22 U.S.C. 2244(b)(2) at http://www.law.cornell.edu/uscode/text/28/2244
5. See "Jeffrey R. MacDonald," *Wikipedia* at http://en.wikipedia.org/wiki/Jeffrey_R._MacDonald

Lawyers learn in law school about the necessity of meeting filing deadlines, and some attorneys have suffered the indignity of having to tell a client that a case has been lost because of missed deadline.

More important than a civil client's discomfort, however, is the result that innocent people sometimes are kept in prison due to such missed deadlines.

In the effort to reduce the volume of habeas petitions, the AEDPA imposed a one-year filing deadline, from the date of the last direct appeal decision, on petitions for habeas relief. There is one exception to that deadline which is that when petitioners claim new evidence, they have one year to file from the date when they could have discovered that evidence when it "could not have been discovered previously through the exercise of due diligence."[6]

However, for a claimant of wrongful conviction, the standards must be different. The Supreme Court has taken several steps in that direction, but a sweeping waiver of filing time requirements for claimants of wrongful conviction has not been issued by that court or by other courts and legislatures. Indeed, many, including Justice Antonin Scalia, strongly oppose such relaxation.

His dissent came in the 2013 habeas petition of Floyd Perkins against his warden, Greg McQuiggin. Perkins was convicted of murder in Michigan and his conviction became final in 1997 after losing his direct appeals. He filed his federal habeas petition in 2008, 11 years later, claiming ineffective assistance of counsel and claiming innocence

6. 22 U.S.C. 2244(b)(1) at http://www.law.cornell.edu/uscode/text/28/2244

based on affidavits which had been prepared no more recently than 2002. Clearly, Perkins missed the one-year statute of limitations of the AEDPA statute. The U.S. District Court denied Perkins's petition because he had filed it too late.

The U.S. Supreme Court ruled that a pre-AEDPA exception to procedural rules for those claiming innocence survived after the enactment of AEDPA because Congress had not explicitly excluded it.[7]

That exception had been carved out in Schlup v Delo, a pre-AEDPA U.S. Supreme Court case which held that a valid claim of innocence enabled a petitioner to avoid a procedural limitation on filing a habeas petition. The devil in the details was that "validity" was defined by requiring that a petitioner "must show that it is more likely than not that no reasonable juror would have convicted him in the light of the new evidence."[8]

Lloyd Schlup had been convicted in 1985 in Missouri of murdering a fellow inmate and sentenced to be executed; and he had lost all his state appeals. A first habeas petition failed, and his second was dismissed in 1993 for filing too late and because his claim of innocence was not strong enough to meet the standard at the time. That standard came from Sawyer v. Whitley, 505 U.S. 333 (1992) which said that the denial of such claims of innocence must result in a fundamental miscarriage of justice.

In the Schlup case, Justice Stevens wrote for the Supreme Court that the case must go back to the District Court for an evidentiary hearing, and

7. McQuiggin v. Perkins, 569 U.S. ___, 133 S. Ct. 1924 (2013) at http://www.supremecourt.gov/opinions/12pdf/12-126_lkgn.pdf.

8. Schlup v. Delo, 513 U.S. 298, 327 (1995).

that the procedural barriers to bringing his claim must be set aside. Lloyd Schlup's claim of innocence trumped the court's concerns for the "threat to judicial resources, finality and comity."

The new standard for providing relief from procedural barriers was to be that, "it is more likely than not that no reasonable juror would have convicted him in light of the new evidence presented in habeas proceedings."[9]

In 1999, Schlup pled guilty to a lesser charge and remains in prison.[10]

Two years earlier, the Court had held that the claims of innocence by Leonel Herrera in Texas were not strong enough to warrant an order by the U.S. Supreme Court that the Texas courts reconsider his conviction. Four months after that decision, Herrera was executed after uttering his Final Statement, "I am an innocent man, and something very wrong is taking place tonight."[11] Perhaps in the subsequent Schlup case, the Supreme Court was trying, by its word-smithing, to reduce the chances of another execution of an innocent person.

The proposal here would widen and allow the "gateway" to court relief when the claims of innocence are non-frivolous, which is a lower standard than the Supreme Court has required to date. Such a new standard could be legislated by Congress or mandated by the Supreme Court as its evolving standards confront the reality that too many innocent people are in U.S. prisons, and that some have been executed.

9. ibid.
10. *St Louis Post-Dispatch*, March 25, 1999.
11. "Herrera v. Collins," *Wikipedia* at http://en.wikipedia.org/wiki/Herrera_v._Collins

In Alabama, William Kuenzel ran afoul of another requirement from AEDPA, which is that the one year timetable would be paused if the claimant had "properly filed" a claim in state court. Kuenzel had been convicted of murder in 1988, but new evidence was disclosed by the prosecution 22 years later, in 2010. His attorney had thought that a 1996 filing in state court paused the AEDPA one-year requirement, and allowed him more time for the habeas petition. However, a state circuit court ruled that the 1996 filing did not meet the "proper filing" standard. Thus, his habeas petition was three years late, and it was denied.[12] So far, he remains in prison with no judicial recourse.

Proposal 59: That the standard for the post-trial vacating of a previous verdict be: whether the jury, or fact-finding judge, would have been likely to have had "reasonable doubt" or "any doubt" if all the evidence now available had been presented at trial.

Too often, claims for relief in the state and federal appellate courts have failed because of a high standard for predicting what would have happened at the trial court if the newly available evidence or interpretations of law had been known at trial.

In July, 2014, as noted earlier in this chapter, the U.S. District Court judge in the Jeffrey

12. "Death by Deadline, Part One – How bad lawyering and an unforgiving law cost condemned men their last appeal," by Ken Armstrong. November 15, 2014, from the Marshall Project, at https://www.themarshallproject.org/2014/11/15/death-by-deadline-part-one

MacDonald case denied relief, saying, "The court finds that MacDonald has failed to establish, by clear and convincing evidence, that no reasonable factfinder would have found him guilty of the murder of his wife and two daughters.

Alternatively, the court finds that MacDonald has failed to adequately establish the merits of any of his claims."[13] That's too severe a standard. Instead of asking whether a single reasonable juror would have had "reasonable doubt," the judge required that MacDonald needed to prove that no juror would have voted to convict.

In 2012, the Connecticut Appeals Court granted a new trial for Richard Lapointe, and gave as its standard of review "that there is a reasonable probability that the result of his criminal trial would have been different" had the newly available evidence been made available at trial.[14] That's the equivalent of the standard proposed here, as a trial verdict would be different if a juror had reasonable doubt. The Supreme Court of Connecticut is now considering the State's appeal. Lapointe was originally convicted in 1992.

In parallel with the standards for a jury, an appeals court should reverse a conviction if it finds that there is reasonable doubt as to the guilt of the defendant.

In 2014, in Buffalo, New York a judge released Josue Ortiz from 10 years in prison for a murder he

13. "Judge rejects bid for new trial in 'Fatal Vision' case," *WRAL*, July 24, 2014 at http://www.wral.com/judge-rejects-bid-for-new-trial-in-fatal-vision-case/13839177/

14. "Connecticut Court Orders Retrial for Man Convicted in '87 Murder," by Liz Robbins. *New York Times*, October 12, 2012, at http://www.nytimes.com/2012/10/02/nyregion/connecticut-court-grants-retrial-for-richard-lapointe-in-1987-murder.html

did not commit. The current district attorney, Frank Sedita, wrote "Simply stated, I cannot, in good conscience, permit a man to remain in jail when I have a reasonable doubt concerning his guilt."[15] That is the standard that should be applied to all the inmate claims of wrongful conviction. That is, if the trial or appellate judges, or prosecutors, or even jurors come to have reasonable doubt as to the guilt of an inmate, those doubts should be presented in court and, if reasonable, the inmate should be released.

Proposal 60: That in appeals from Guilty trial verdicts, every split decision at the appellate court level be interpreted as a reversal of the lower court's decision on the issues raised, or of the entire verdict.

At trials, the judge actually has a vote on the jury, even if not commonly recognized. That is, a judge may decide not to submit a particular issue or even the entire case to a jury because of insufficient evidence or other reason. Also, the judge may issue a "directed verdict" in a case there the facts or the law are so overwhelming that there is no value in sending it to the jury.

If a judge, despite doubts about a case, sends it to a jury and hopes the jury decides the case correctly, s/he may be surprised by the jury's decision. In such a case, in most states, the judge has the power to issue a judgment NOV ("non-

15. "DA drops opposition to Ortiz's release in wrongful conviction," by Phil Fairbanks. *Buffalo News*, December 8, 2014. At http://www.buffalonews.com/city-region/erie-county-court/da-drops-opposition-to-ortizs-release-in-wrongful-conviction-20141208

obstante-veredicto"), which is a verdict opposite to the jury's.

In these senses, a trial judge has a vote on the guilt or innocence of a defendant, even if not on the "fact finding" jury. Thus, a jury trial can be considered to have a jury of 13.

When a case is appealed, appellate courts typically have panels of three or five and sometimes more judges. The proposal here is that each of those judges has a vote equal to the "13" judges at trial. If there is an appellate panel of three, then the total "jury" can be said to be 16.

The current practice is that if the appellate court votes 3-0 or 2-1 in support of a trial verdict, the conviction stands. The proposal here is that a 2-1 vote should be interpreted as showing a "holdout" of one the "16 jurors," i.e. an appellate judge, and thus the verdict should be reversed. It is true that an appellate judge does not have the opportunity to see and hear witnesses, but an appellate judge does have more experience than jurors in seeing the justice system at work.

In short, if an appellate judge votes, whether one out of three or five or nine, to reverse a guilty verdict that vote should show enough doubt about the validity of the verdict to cast it aside. If the appellate judge feels sufficiently strongly about a case to vote against his/her fellow judges, there must be enough doubt about a conviction to call that "reasonable doubt" which should nullify a conviction.

In the aforementioned Massachusetts Federal case of Alfred Trenkler, he lost his appeal at the Federal Court of Appeals for the First Circuit by a vote of 2-1.[16] In a sense, he has remained in

16. United States vs. Trenkler, 61 F.3d 45 (1st Circuit, 1995) at

prison since 1993 because of one vote of one judge, i.e. one of the members of the majority.

By the proposal here, the most important vote of the three should have been the minority vote of Chief Judge Juan Torruella. He described what was submitted to Alfred's jury as "otherwise weak circumstantial evidence of defendant's guilt." Below are some further excerpts from his dissenting opinion of what he wrote about the Trenkler verdict.

> First, it is clear to me that the district court relied on the improper EXIS[17] evidence in its decision to allow the government to present evidence of the Quincy incident to the jury to prove identity under Rule 404(b). The second reason that admission of the EXIS evidence cannot be considered harmless is that this type of "scientific" evidence is too misleading, too powerful, and has too great a potential impact on lay jurors, to be disregarded as harmless. The third reason that admission of the EXIS evidence is not harmless beyond a reasonable doubt is that the other evidence against Trenkler was not "overwhelming."
>
> The majority decision in this case not only defies common sense, it is also

http://www.alfredtrenklerinnocent.org/documents/950718FirstCircuitOpiniononappealWestlawat61F3d45.pdf

17. EXIS was the acronym for the EXplosives Incident System, as it was then called by the Bureau of Alcohol Tobacco and Firearms. In 1998, it was renamed the AEXIS for Arson and EXplosives Incident System. 2005 ATF Audit Report, at http://www.justice.gov/oig/reports/ATF/a0501/intro.htm [Footnote not in original opinion.]

> contrary to our precedent....
> Unfortunately, and with all due respect to my brethren, I believe the defendant's right to a fair trial was violated when the government was permitted to introduce the highly prejudicial evidence derived from the EXIS computer database. Because this error so severely violated defendant's Sixth Amendment right to confront the witnesses against him, and because the remainder of the evidence against him was not "overwhelming," I dissent.[18]

Yet the 2-1 vote in 1995 kept Trenkler in prison where he remains almost 20 years later. Shouldn't this articulate voice of an experienced judge have as much weight as would have a holdout juror at Trenkler's trial?

If the case had been sent back to the U.S. District Court, and had been retried, the prosecution would have had the opportunity to address the concerns of Judge Torruella when it sought to present evidence using the EXIS database. On the other hand, if those concerns were insurmountable, as they appeared to be, the prosecutors could have presented the case without that claimed evidence. Given the subsequently expressed views of five of his jurors, Trenkler would have been found Not Guilty at a retrial. In fact, an unbiased review of all the evidence in the case would come to the clear conclusion that he is factually innocent.

18. United States v. Trenkler, op cit., Fn 16, above. Also at http://www.alfredtrenklerinnocent.org/documents/DissentingOpinion1995ofChiefJudgeJuanTorruella.doc

Proposal 61: That when an appeals court or habeas court rules that a conviction must be reversed for reasons relating to the existence of reasonable doubt as to guilt, the case must be returned for the option of retrial without further appeal.

Again, the point is that an appellate judge's views about the actual guilt or innocence of a defendant should be worth as much as the views of a single juror at trial. If a judge has reasonable doubt as to guilt, the conviction should not stand. If a single juror can force a mistrial and therefore a retrial, then such power should also belong to a single judge.

One of the most heartbreaking types of wrongful conviction cases arises when a person claiming wrongful conviction is freed from prison on appeal or a habeas petition, but is returned to prison on further appeal.

Such a sequence has beset former Akron Police Department Captain Douglas Prade, who was convicted in 1998 of murdering his wife, Dr. Margo Prade. In January, 2013, after serving 15 years of a life sentence, Prade was released after Court of Common Pleas Judge Judy Hunter ruled that he was "actually innocent," after DNA test results were released.[19] His freedom was short-lived when an appeals court ruled that the exoneration was invalid and sent the case back to the lower court, but to a different judge because Judge Hunter had

19. "Former Akron police captain Douglas Prade cleared of murder, released from prison," by Rick Armon, Ed Meyer and Phil Trexler. *Akron Beacon Journal*, January 29, 2013 at http://www.ohio.com/news/break-news/former-akron-police-captain-douglas-prade-cleared-in-murder-released-from-prison-1.368825

retired. Prade was returned to prison on July 25, 2014, and awaits the lower court's next hearing.[20]

By this proposal, the first lower court finding of "actual innocence" should have been enough by itself to raise the necessary doubt to vacate the trial verdict and open the way to a retrial if the prosecutors chose to take that route. If the state wished to proceed, it could have convened a new trial instead of asking a higher court to overcome the lower court's doubt, which in this case was so large that she called Prade "actually innocent."

In Pennsylvania in October, 2011, the Third Circuit Court of Appeals vacated the 1995 conviction of Lorenzo Johnson for murder.[21] He was released in January, 2012, after 16 years in prison but in May of that year, the U.S. Supreme Court reversed the Third Circuit's opinion.[22] The result was that Johnson was returned to prison on June 4, after four and a half months of freedom. The Supreme Court reasoned that appellate courts should not overturn the factual determinations of trial courts. However, the proposal here would reverse that rule, because it recognizes that judges know a lot about criminal justice even if they were not at the trial to hear testimony. Johnson remains in prison waiting for the slow grind of appellate justice to address his claims.

20. "Appeals judges send Douglas Prade murder case back to Summit County judge," by Rich Armon, Ed Meyer and Phil Trexler, *Akron Beacon Journal*, January 29, 2013 at http://www.cleveland.com/akron/index.ssf/2014/08/appeals_judges_send_douglas_pr.html

21. Double Injustice: Lorenzo "Cat" Johnson, Innocence Project of Pennsylvania, at https://innocenceprojectpa.wordpress.com/2013/06/17/double-injustice-lorenzo-cat-johnson/

22. Coleman v. Johnson, 566 U.S. ___, 132 S. Ct. 2060 (2012) at http://www.supremecourt.gov/opinions/11pdf/11-1053.pdf

By the above proposal, the votes of the judges of the Third Circuit should have been enough to release Johnson permanently, or hold him long enough for the State of Pennsylvania to retry him or dismiss the charges.

Proposal 62: That no evidence be discarded or destroyed or returned to owners until the death of a defendant or the end of his/her judicial penalty. But that in severe circumstances where storage is expensive and/or where property needs to be returned to owners, such disposition be with approval of the defendant and his/her counsel which approval shall not be unreasonably withheld.

In too many cases of claims of wrongful conviction, there was evidence collected, but it has been destroyed. In Dennis Dechaine's case, as noted in the previous chapter, there were human hairs found on the body of the victim, Sarah Cherry, and the hairs were visually not identified as belonging to the victim. At Dechaine's 1989 trial, his motion for DNA testing was denied by the trial judge because the period of testing was estimated to delay the trial by several weeks. Only three years later, the State of Maine intentionally destroyed in June 1992 the rape kit, and the referenced hairs and other evidence which may have contained biological traces. At the time there was a pending motion for new trial based on new evidence. The hearing on the motion was heard in July, but the defense did not know about the destruction a month earlier of the critical evidence.

More than twenty years later, the case of Dennis Dechaine continues to be fought in the courts. Fortunately, the material from the victim's fingernails was not destroyed, because through a quirk in the labeling of trial evidence exhibits, it was in the custody of Dechaine's attorney. The DNA in those samples presents the strongest case for Dechaine's innocence.

In the case of Alfred Trenkler, a critical claim by the prosecution's primary witness was that the fatal bomb was previously attached to the underside of that witness's car. However, before the trial, and the opportunity for further examination and testing, that car was returned to the witness – who was also the primary alternate suspect in the case.

In the case of exoneree Joseph Abbitt in North Carolina, the court clerk destroyed the trial exhibits, as preservation was not required by law after Abbitt's 1995 conviction for child abuse. Fortunately, a rape kit was preserved at the Winston-Salem Police Dept and he was exonerated after DNA testing.[23]

In 1982 Walter Swift was convicted of sexual assault in Michigan. In 1997, he contacted the Innocence Project, but the physical evidence, including rape kit, had been destroyed. However, the earlier testing had been done by blood type and that was enough to exclude Swift. His initial attorney had not called the blood test technician to testify, and that technician was later shocked to learn that Swift had initially been convicted because his testing showed innocence.[24] Swift spent 28 years in prison because the state had

23. "Joseph Lamont Abbitt," National Registry of Exonerations, at http://www.law.umich.edu/special/exoneration/Pages/casedetail.aspx?caseid=3807

24. "Walter Swift," National Registry of Exonerations, at http://www.law.umich.edu/special/exoneration/Pages/casedetail.aspx?caseid=3673

destroyed evidence and his own lawyer had provided ineffective assistance of counsel by not pursuing the earlier blood test results.

With the advent of DNA testing, most states now require the retention of evidence for as long as the defendant is in prison. Even if the defendant was not convicted, such evidence should be saved for as long as the unknown perpetrators are likely to be alive.

Proposal 63: That post-trial recantations by witnesses be fairly evaluated for their truthfulness, and that subsequent charges of perjury be initiated only by judges in the interests of promoting truthfulness at all stages of the criminal justice system. And that polygraphs be utilized in that consideration.

With their traditional confidence in verdicts, judges have been too quick to dismiss the credibility of recanting witnesses. In New Hampshire, Gary Howard was convicted in 2000 of sexually assaulting the 12-year old daughter of his former wife and was sentenced to 10-20 years in prison. Three years later, the alleged victim provided the first of several recantations. After a hearing, the judge denied Howard's motion for a new trial, and stated that the recantation was likely not credible and initiated by family pressure. However, there was no evidence at the hearing about such alleged family pressure. There was no consideration given to a polygraph for the recanting accuser/victim and no interviewing of witnesses who might have corroborated part of her recanted story.

In 1985, Cathleen Crowell Webb attempted to recant her claim of rape that led to the 1979 conviction of Gary Dotson in Illinois. The prosecutors refused to believe her, and threatened her with perjury indictments. A Clemency Board refused to grant relief to Dotson on the basis of the recantation, but the recantation was sufficient to enable Dotson to obtain court orders for DNA tests of the evidence. In 1988, those DNA tests proved that Webb had sex with her boyfriend and not with Dotson, but it took another year for prosecutors to agree that they had prosecuted the wrong man. In fact, there was no rape at all. Dotson then became famous as the first DNA exoneree.[25] Nonetheless, it can be said that the wrongful conviction ruined his life and that of his family.

Rob Warden, formerly the Director of the Center on Wrongful Convictions, has written that the hesitation to believe recanting witnesses is not isolated. He researched 26 other cases where initially disbelieved recanting accusers or witnesses were subsequently believed, and justice was improved. In one of those cases, the recantation came 18 years after a wrongful conviction.[26]

In Ohio, a recantation of lies told in trials in 1975 resulted in the release in 2014 of three men: Ricky Jackson, Wiley Bridgeman, and Ronnie Bridgeman (now known as Kwame Ajamu.) Eddie Vernon was 12 years old when he testified against the three men, all of whom were sentenced to death. Somehow, despite exculpatory evidence, the

25. Gary Dotson, National Registry of Exonerations, at http://www.law.umich.edu/special/exoneration/Pages/casedetail.aspx?caseid=3186
26. "Time to Rethink Recantations," by Rob Warden. *Chicago Sun-Times*, November 7, 2013. At http://www.suntimes.com/news/otherviews/23575179-452/time-to-rethink-recantations.html

juries believed him, and beyond a reasonable doubt. In 2014, after several years of agony and prodding, Vernon came forward with his recantation. As is usually the case, no action was reported against the police officers who encouraged his lies. With 39 years, three months and nine days in wrongful imprisonment, Ricky Jackson achieved the new record for exonerees in the National Registry.[27]

When a witness or accuser recants, defense attorneys and prosecutors need to work hard to prove or disprove the recantation. It's an especially difficult credibility test, as it's clear that one of the two statements by the same witness/accuser is false. Corroboration by others of any part of the recantation is helpful. Also, all recanters should be encouraged to take a polygraph exam, and if it is not satisfactory, to take another. With an 80 percent accuracy rate, and 20 percent failure, in exoneration cases, polygraphs are not likely to be wrong twice for the same person.[28] The simple willingness of a recanting accuser or witness is often an indication of truthfulness. In the Gary Dotson case, Cathleen Webb passed a polygraph exam, but the prosecutors still did not believe her, until DNA testing proved her veracity.

In Jason Girts' case in Kentucky, the polygraph worked correctly. He had been convicted in 2006 of sexually abusing his stepson 10 years earlier, almost entirely on the stepson's testimony. Two years after the trial, the stepson recanted, and a

27. "Ricky Jackson," National Registry of Exonerations, at http://www.law.umich.edu/special/exoneration/Pages/casedetail.aspx?caseid=4553. The summaries for Kwame Ajamu and Wiley Bridgeman are nearly identical.
28. See "Polygraphs and 215 Wrongful Conviction Exonerations" by Morrison Bonpasse. *POLYGRAPH*, July 2013. At http://www.bonpasseexonerationservices.com/about.html

polygraph indicated that his recantation was truthful. Girts was released, and the charges were dismissed two years into his seven year sentence.[29]

Proposal 64: That post-trial reviews of cases utilize the maximum use of DNA testing and other up-to-date forensic knowledge where there was insufficient forensic expertise presented at trial.

With the adoption by Massachusetts of a law in 2012, every state now has a statute providing for post-conviction DNA testing, but not all have the provisions[30] below, as recommended by the Innocence Project. These statutes should:

Include a reasonable standard to establish proof of innocence at the stage where an individual is petitioning for post-conviction DNA testing;

Allow access to post-conviction DNA testing wherever it can establish innocence, even if the petitioner is no longer incarcerated, and including cases where the petitioner pled guilty or provided a confession or admission to the crime;

Exclude "sunset provisions," or absolute deadlines, for when access to post-conviction DNA evidence will expire;

29. "Jason Girts," National Registry of Exonerations, at http://www.law.umich.edu/special/exoneration/Pages/casedetail.aspx?caseid=4087
30. Innocence Project, "Access to Post-Conviction DNA Testing" at http://www.innocenceproject.org/Content/Access_To_PostConviction_DNA_Testing.php.

Enable judges to order comparisons of crime scene evidence against national and state-level criminal justice databases, including CODIS [Combined DNA Index System] and IAFIS [Integrated Automated Fingerprint Identification System];

Require state officials to properly preserve and catalogue biological evidence for as long as an individual is incarcerated or otherwise experiences any consequences of a potential wrongful conviction (e.g. probation, parole, civil commitment or mandatory registration as a sex offender), as well as to account for evidence in their custody;

Disallow procedural hurdles that stymie DNA testing petitions and proceedings that govern other forms of post-conviction relief;

Allow convicted persons to appeal from orders denying DNA testing;

Require a full, fair and prompt response to DNA testing petitions, including the avoidance of debate around whether currently available DNA technology was available at the time of the trial;

Avoid unfunded mandates by providing funding to DNA testing statutes; and

Provide flexibility in where, and how, DNA testing is conducted.

In this post-Gary Dotson world, it is sometimes hard to understand why some or most prosecutors resist full DNA testing, besides the issue of cost.

In 2009 Johnnie Lee Savory of Illinois was featured in a *New York Times* article about how prosecutors try to avoid or delay DNA testing. He had been released on parole in 2006 after serving 30 years after a conviction when he was 14 for a double murder. The article reported that prosecutors opposed DNA tests "on the grounds that a jury was convinced of his guilt without DNA and that the 175 convicts already exonerated by DNA were 'statistically insignificant.' "[31] Four years later, it was reported that a county judge finally ordered DNA tests, despite prosecutors' objections.[32] Savory was described as "hitting the roof" when he heard about testing, as he had been trying to get those tests for 15 years. The results are still pending.

Proposal 65: That jurors be encouraged to have a continuing interest in justice in a particular case, and that if they come to believe that the verdict for which they voted is unjust, they be encouraged to step forward individually or as a group with their views.

31. "Prosecutors Block Access to DNA Testing for Inmates," by Shaila Dewan. *New York Times*, May 19, 2009 at http://www.nytimes.com/2009/05/18/us/18dna.html
32. "Judge rules Johnnie Lee Savory can use DNA tests on old evidence," by Andy Kravetz. *Peoria Journal Star*, August 7, 2013. Also, "Johnnie Lee Savory: 30 Seconds To Lose Your Life, 30 Years To Get It Back," by David Smallwood. August 27, 2014, *NDIGO* online, at http://ndigo.com/index.php/30-seconds-lose-life-30-years-get-back/

As noted in the previous chapter, jurors are a collection of nearly randomly selected individuals pulled together to perform an extraordinary task. The nearly universal pattern is for those jurors who actually perform jury duty to leave the courthouse at the end of the proceeding and never see each other again.

The states vary on the amount of secrecy surrounds the identity of jurors, so reporters, defense attorneys and others usually have some difficulty in contacting jurors. In most states, jurors are cautioned to be very careful about talking with the media after a trial. Again, the message to jurors is to do your duty and be gone.

However, some jurors have continued to take an interest in their cases in the interests of justice.

As noted above in Proposals 47 and 56, in other types of decision making, the decision makers usually have the opportunity to change their minds, in light of new information.

In 1928, three North Carolina men were released from prison after receiving a pardon from the Governor. The three were Frank Dove, Fred Dove and George Williams, and they had been sentenced to death in 1922 for murder. Fortunately, the fourth defendant told officials on the day of his execution that the other three had no role in the crime. With that information and other corroboration, the sentences of the three were commuted to life in prison. It took another five years, with support from some of the original jurors and the prosecutor and some arresting officers to convince Governor Angus McLean to completely pardon the men to assure their release.[33]

33. *In Spite of Innocence – The Ordeal of 400 Americans Wrongly Convicted of Crimes Punishable by Death*, by Michael

In 1936 in Arkansas, Ayliff Draper was similarly unlucky to be wrongly convicted, and then lucky that his co-defendant told officers a few hours before his execution that Draper had no part in the murder for which they were both convicted and sentenced to death. Draper's sentence was commuted to life in prison, but for several of the original jurors and local officials, that was not enough for justice. In 1938 Governor Carl Bailey granted Draper a full pardon and he was released.[34]

In 1955, a jury in Texas convicted Gordon Morris of murder and sentenced him to death by electrocution. His brother continued to investigate the case and determined that Gordon Morris was misidentified and that he was physically incapable of the charged murder. Fortunately, the authorities were persuaded of the problem with the conviction and Morris's sentence was commuted to life imprisonment three days before his scheduled death. After learning of the new evidence, the jury foreman conducted his own reinvestigation and then located the other members of the jury. Together, the jurors urged the governor to pardon Morris. Instead, the governor commuted Morris's sentence, three days before his scheduled execution. He was paroled in 1968, but recommitted to prison due to a parole violation in 1973 and re-paroled in 1976.[35]

Radelet, Hugo Bedau and Constance Putnam. Northeastern University Press, 1992. Page 300.
34. Ibid. page 301.
35. *Presumed Guilty*, by Martin Yant. Prometheus Books, 1991. Page 112. See also http://www.victimsofthestate.org/TX/indexHA.html. See also, *The Rope, The Chair, and Needle: Capital Punishment in Texas*, 1923-1990, by James W Marquart, Sheldon Ekland-

In Oregon, a teenaged migrant farm worker, Santiago Morales, was convicted of murder in 1986. One policeman had testified that Morales would not look him in the eye during questioning. Prior to sentencing, three jurors talked about the case and concurred with their doubts about their previous votes for a guilty verdict.

> One juror was so passionate that a friend of the juror, Donna Slepack, visited Morales in prison, befriended him, taught him English and began investigating the case. Ultimately she learned that Mixtec Indians don't speak Spanish, which meant that the translator in the courtroom was largely ineffective not only for Morales, but for the witnesses who testified. Further, the interpretation of Morales' demeanor during his questioning was wrong—Mixtec Indians never look their elders in the eye.[36]

In 1991, a motion for new trial was granted due to the new evidence and the revelation that Morales had told his lawyer that he wanted to testify but the lawyer blocked the request. Oregon Governor Neil Goldschmidt pardoned Morales, and the charges were later dismissed.

In 1997, a Chattanooga, Tennessee, 21-year old Wayne Cservak was tried for sexually molesting the 13-year old son of his girlfriend. He had refused a plea bargain because he said he was innocent. The jury was deadlocked with one juror, Jim Thomas, holding out for not guilty for the last six hours of deliberations. Ultimately, he gave in. When the

Olson and Johnathan R. Sorensen. University of Texas Press, 2010, page 115.

36. "Santiago Ventura Morales," National Registry of Exonerations, at http://www.law.umich.edu/special/exoneration/Pages/casedetail.aspx?caseid=3492.

verdict was announced, an aunt of Cservak yelled to the courtroom, "Thanks for convicting an innocent man."[37]

A few days later, Thomas wrote to the judge to express his doubts about the verdict. He attended Cservak's sentencing, unlike most jurors in general, and he told the judge and court at that time that he believed Cservak to be innocent. Cservak was sentenced to ten years in prison.

Thomas fortunately had the means to then hire an attorney for Cservak who appealed the verdict and a new trial was ordered based on ineffectiveness of trial counsel. Shortly thereafter, the complainant recanted and Cservak was released after serving seven months in prison for something he didn't do.[38] But for the dedication of a juror to justice, he could have remained there nine more years.

In 1999 in Missouri, Theodore White, Jr. was sentenced to 50 years in prison for sexual abuse of his adopted daughter, the daughter of his wife from an earlier marriage. At his retrial, occasioned by an undisclosed romance between his wife and an investigating police officer, the jury was deadlocked 11-1 for acquittal, and a mistrial was declared.

> After the trial four jurors publicly spoke out that there was no credible evidence of White's guilt, but that one juror refused to participate in deliberations or change his guilty vote even though he admitted

37. "Lone Juror's Change of Heart in Child Molestation Case Tips Scales of Justice," by Barry Siegel. *Los Angeles Times*, March 10, 1998. At http://articles.latimes.com/print/1998/mar/10/news/mn-27462

38. For more information about the Czervak case see, "Juror refuses to accept injustice," by Pam Sohn. *The Chattanooga Times*, posted at Justice Denied, www.justicedenied.org/v1issue1.htm on Feb 2, 1999.

> he had 'doubts' about White's guilt. Juror Jill Miller told reporters, 'He is not guilty, for sure. There is not one bit of evidence the state brought us to prove his guilt. When it was over we just cried. It was so outrageous, there are no words to describe it. ... After the [mistrial] verdict, (several jurors) went out together, and said, 'We want to do anything we can to help them out. We just can't let it end like this — we have to do something to help them.' Miller and several jurors began advocating on White's behalf, including writing letters to Missouri's Attorney General Jay Nixon encouraging him to intervene and encourage the Jackson County Prosecuting Attorney's Office to dismiss the charges so White could go free."[39]

Finally, there was a third trial in 2005, and White was acquitted.

In the infamous "Norfolk Four" case, nine of Eric Wilson's jurors (who had previously found him guilty of murder in 1999) joined others who wrote to Virginia Governor Mark Warner to urge him to grant clemency petitions.[40] Wilson was released in 2005, but never formally exonerated, despite the clear evidence of innocence. In any case, for the purposes here, nine of his original twelve jurors sought to revoke their "guilty" votes.

In the Kirstin Lobato manslaughter case in Nevada, two jurors have written to the trial judge to

39. "Theodore White, Jr. Settles Wrongful Conviction Lawsuit For $15.5 Million," by Hans Sherrer at http://justicedenied.org/wordpress/archives/1353

40. "Derek Tice," National Registry of Exonerations, at http://www.law.umich.edu/special/exoneration/Pages/casedetail.aspx?caseid=3820.

modify their views of the case. They both wrote, "I believe that if the jury in 2006 had known Ms. Lobato's new evidence it could have influenced the jury's deliberations, and it could have resulted in either a hung jury or Ms. Lobato's acquittal." And, "I believe it is in the interest of justice that Ms. Lobato be granted a new trial." So far, the judge has found that such an effort is not enough, but it's still important that the public, the media, and the prosecutor know that jurors in a case would have decided otherwise if they had seen the subsequently-developed evidence.[41]

In the Alfred Trenkler case in Massachusetts, four jurors from the 1993 trial wrote separately to the presiding judge in 2008-09 after reading a book which claimed that Trenkler was innocent.[42] They wrote to say that if they had seen the evidence presented to them in a post-trial book, they may have voted otherwise; and they recommended a new trial for Trenkler. A fifth juror also wrote to the judge with concerns about the original verdict, and to also ask for a retrial. He told the author that he didn't read the book because he didn't need to. He said he was the holdout juror who never believed that Trenkler was guilty. Nonetheless, the judge and the U.S. Attorney have not indicated any concern about the substance of the letters.[43]

At least Trenkler's judge thanked the five jurors for their letters. Sometimes, as in the case of David

41. For more information about the Kirstin Lobato case see http://www.justice4kirstin.com and http://www.injustice-anywhere.org/KirstinLobato.html
42. The book was *Perfectly Innocent – The Wrongful Conviction of Alfred Trenkler,* by Morrison Bonpasse. 2006.
43. For the jurors' letters, see the Alfred Trenkler website, at http://www.alfredtrenklerinnocent.org/documents/LetterstoJudgeZobelfromfivejurors.pdf

Flores in Iowa, the interests of jurors in justice is not appreciated.

Flores was convicted in 1997 of killing an innocent bystander during a gang-related gun battle. Samuel McCrorey was the jury foreperson and he told the *Des Moines Register* on the day of Flores's sentencing, "I feel horrible that a young man is going to prison for life for a crime he didn't commit." In part because the jurors had agreed that they would not discuss the verdict with the press, Judge Richard Blane excoriated McCrorey in a letter to the other jurors, saying that he "should be ashamed" and "should live the rest of his life with the knowledge that he has violated your trust and that his word is no good."[44]

That was in 1997. Sixteen years later, David Flores was released from prison after pleading guilty with an Alford plea to something he didn't do. The release came after police misconduct was discovered in the case including the suppression before his trial of an FBI report which stated that another man, now deceased, was the likely killer.[45]

The off-putting legal term for post-conviction letters from jurors is "jurors' remorse," as if to say that it's only their hearts that felt badly for what they decided rather than their doubt-filled minds.

Despite the infrequency of subsequent juror involvement in cases, and despite their uneven record of success in correcting justice, it is still recommended here with this proposal that jurors

44. "Judge Chides Juror for Statements," by Dan Eggen. *The Des Moines Register*, April 25, 1997. At http://truthinjustice.org/flores-juror.htm
45. "David Flores sentenced then released from jail," by Kim St. Onge. *KCCI News*, July 11, 2013, at http://www.kcci.com/news/central-iowa/plea-deal-reached-in-flores-case/20905440

retain a commitment to justice in the cases they judged.

Proposal 66: That victims and their families be encouraged to continue to seek justice in their cases, which will sometimes involve claims of wrongful conviction.

Victims want justice, and sometimes they have assisted the quest for justice for those who were wrongly convicted of crimes against them.

In the not-so-distant past, victims were encouraged to walk away from the criminal justice system after a guilty verdict and forget it. More recently, victims have been more involved and laws have been passed to require notification of victims when their perpetrators are applying for parole or are released from prison.

With the post-1989 advent of the Innocence Movement, researchers have studied the effects of wrongful convictions on victims. In one study, a victim stated,

> For [several] years, I had been quite comfortable with my role as the victim. When the exoneration happens, that exoneree becomes the victim, and I, the rape victim, became the offender. The roles switch, and it's a role you don't know what to do with. And the world is saying 'How could you have made such a terrible mistake?' [46]

46. "Study of Victim Experiences of Wrongful Convictions," by Seri Irazola, Erin Williamson, Julie Stricker and Emily Niedzwiecki for ICF Corporation for a grant from the U.S. Dept of Justice Office of Justice Programs. Page 65. September 2013 at https://www.ncjrs.gov/pdffiles1/nij/grants/244084.pdf

One person who overcame those feelings and became a leading advocate for claimants of wrongful conviction is Jennifer Thompson. She was raped in North Carolina in 1984 and misidentified her assailant as Ronald Cotton, who then spent ten years in prison before his DNA exoneration. She and Cotton later wrote the book, *Picking Cotton*, about their different experiences of the same wrongful conviction and she has publicly spoken many times of her experience.

Thompson became involved in the Innocence Movement after the DNA testing showed that Cotton was not her assailant.[47] Before then, she didn't know that Cotton's claim of wrongful conviction was any more serious than that of other criminals who try to escape responsibility for their actions.

In the case of Ray Krone,[48] the 100th exoneree from death rows since the post-1976 resumption of capital punishment, the mother of the victim became a supporter of his claim of innocence. She was at the prison gate when Krone was released. He said of her, "She was hugging me and apologizing for hating me and asking my forgiveness. I told her that I understood why she hated me and that I never held it against her. She hated the murderer, and that wasn't me."[49]

In Oklahoma, Christy Sheppard grew up with her family's understanding that Ron Williamson and Ron Fritz raped and murdered her cousin. After the 1999 exoneration of both men, Sheppard

47. "Ronald Cotton," National Registry of Exonerations, at http://www.law.umich.edu/special/exoneration/Pages/casedetail.aspx?caseid=3124
48. "Ray Krone," National Registry of Exonerations, at http://www.law.umich.edu/special/exoneration/Pages/casedetail.aspx?caseid=3365
49. *Parade* magazine, February 23, 2003.

became increasingly involved in the Innocence Movement, and has campaigned for an Oklahoma Innocence Commission.[50]

A key aspect of preventing wrongful convictions is the apprehension of the actual perpetrators. As John Pray of the Wisconsin Innocence Project said, "Our reform mission, to get the right person, is something that can be shared by victims. He heads the Victims Committee of the Innocence Network.[51]

In addition to the above-described interest by victims in preventing future wrongful convictions, this proposal urges that defense attorneys, prosecutors and claimants of wrongful conviction reach out sensitively and discreetly to victims to seek their support for the correction of injustice.

The literature on wrongful convictions contains few references to such contacts, but the increasing awareness of the Innocence Movement will make such contacts more acceptable and valuable. In the above mentioned (Fn. 46) study of 11 victims of crimes involving wrongful convictions, one of the 11 "believed in the wrongfully convicted person's innocence from the time of the original trial and was actively involved in the appeal and exoneration process."[52]

Prosecutors often defer to the interests of victims in trial strategy and sentencing, and they should pay more attention to the victims' interest in bringing the right people to justice. Despite their

50. "Common Interests," the Innocence Project at http://www.innocenceproject.org/Content/Common_Interests.php.
51. ibid.
52. "Study of Victim Experiences of Wrongful Convictions," op cit., (Fn 46) SUMMARY at http://nij.gov/journals/274/pages/victim-impact-wrongful-convictions.aspx

anger and grief, victims and their families do not seek the punishment of innocent people.

Such contact by a claimant of wrongful conviction must be done especially carefully, as inmates in most states are forbidden to have direct contact with their victims. Victims' families are often involved in cases, and within those families there are sometimes family members who have doubts about the actual guilt of the person convicted. Finding an appropriate go-between, such as a minister or counselor, is an alternate route to approach victims and such family members.

In the three primary cases with claims of wrongful conviction on which the author has worked, the powerful members of the victims's families have resisted entreaties to explore the truth.

Proposal 67: That defense attorneys, police, prosecutors and judges be encouraged to have a continuing interest in justice in a particular case, and that if they come to believe that the verdict in a case in which they participated is unjust, they be encouraged to proactively seek justice.

This proposal is similar to that for the continuing obligation for jurors, except the professionals in this proposal are employed and paid to provide justice.

By comparison, if an engineer designs a bridge which collapses after that engineer moves to another employer, that engineer must still bear responsibility for his/her design. Of course, a prosecutor has the right to move on in life and not be burdened with a lifelong chain linking him/her back to cases handled when a prosecutor.

On the other hand, when a former prosecutor is presented with evidence of innocence of a person s/he prosecuted to a conviction, it would seem that a former prosecutor should have some ethical obligation to consider the claim and respond in some way supportive of the truth. Such a response could either be directly to the claimant or to his/her successor with support for an inquiry into the truth.

Part of that continuing responsibility should involve acknowledgement of earlier roles in wrongful convictions.

Very few judges who have presided over wrongful convicts have spoken of their concern about what they have done or the overall issue. One exception is former California Superior Court Judge LaDoris Cordell who accepted the guilty plea of Bobby Herrera for a shooting. She sentenced him to five years in prison. By her own later recollection, she heard that Herrera's attorney had been disciplined several times and she had the charges against Herrera dismissed after 11 months in prison. She wrote, "I will always remember Bobby Herrera, the man whom I wrongfully sentenced to prison."[53] The initiative for identifying the injustice to Herrera may have come from his family and his lawyers,[54] but the point remains that former Judge Cordell is one of the very few

53. "LaDoris H. Cordell: I'll always remember the man I wrongfully sentenced to prison." Op-Ed, *Mercury News*, June 13, 2012. At http://www.mercurynews.com/ci_20850837/ladoris-h-cordell-ill-always-remember-man-i
54. "Bobby Paiste Herrera," National Registry of Exonerations, at http://www.law.umich.edu/special/exoneration/Pages/casedetail.aspx?caseid=3293

judges who has publicly regretted his/her own role in a wrongful conviction.

In Australia, retired judge Michael Kirby publicly regretted his role in the wrongful conviction of Andrew Mallard. Said Kirby at a public lecture, "Maybe if I'd paid a little more attention, may be if I'd seen some of these arguments (sooner).... he wouldn't have had to spend a decade in prison; it's something that troubles the mind."[55]

Inside the courtroom, judges express more often their regrets to the exonerees, as with the case of William McCaffrey in New York. He was exonerated after four years in prison for a rape for which the alleged victim later recanted. Judge Richard Carruthers told McCaffrey of his "personal regrets," for having been the judge who sent him to prison.[56]

55. "Wrongful Conviction Reminiscences of an Australian High Court Judge," Wrongful Convictions Blog, May 15, 2012 at http://wrongfulconvictionsblog.org/2012/05/15/wrongful-conviction-reminiscences-of-an-australian-high-court-judge/
56. "Man Wrongfully Convicted of Rape Is Now Free," by Glenn Zimmerman. *New York Channel 4,* December 10, 2009 at http://www.nbcnewyork.com/news/local/Man-Wrongfully-Convicted-of-Rape-Is-Now-Free-78972917.html

Chapter 10: Executive powers for justice: Prisons, Pardons and Clemency

While prosecutors, police and the courts have central roles in creating as well as correcting wrongful convictions, the executive branch of the State and Federal governments can help as well. (In this sense and used here, Departments of Justice or Offices of Attorneys General are considered as "prosecutor" offices.)

Proposal 68: That Governors and the President administer their departments and bureaus of corrections and prisons in order to encourage that all claims of wrongful conviction by inmates, parolees and probationers be presented and fairly considered.

More effectively than individuals and organizations on the outside, Departments of Correction are able to communicate with all the inmates under their control. These departments should facilitate the circulation, understanding and completion of a national "Claim of Innocence Questionnaire" by all inmates and those on probation and parole who claim innocence. (Refer to Proposal 3, Registry of Claims of Innocence.)

Many prisons now offer email services to their inmates, which provide a much faster means of communications with friends and relatives and, most importantly for this book, with legal counsel and advocates for claims of innocence. All U.S. prisons should offer such services by the end of 2015. Incidentally, this service can also be managed by prisons as a reasonable revenue source.

This power of this ability to communicate with inmates was illustrated in the Spring of 2014 when the Federal Bureau of Prisons (BOP) sent emails and hard copy communications to all inmates about the "Clemency Project" initiative of the Department of Justice to reduce the sentences of some inmates convicted of drug offenses. A major part of that communications effort was the use of the BOP's Trulinks/Corrlinks email system. Those communications produced more than 20,000 completed questionnaires from inmates claiming eligibility for the program.

Of course, changing the technology of how to communicate can be much easier than changing the "what to communicate." The scope of this proposal depends upon the degree of implementation of other proposals. For example, the amount of executive branch work for the current proposal might depend upon the extent that the next proposal, regarding the location of Innocence Network offices in prisons, is adopted.

At minimum, prisons, parole and probation offices should have information immediately available for inmates, parolees and probationers who claim innocence. That information would include the addresses of available Innocence Network members and the names and addresses of people at the nearest law schools who have stepped forward to assist claimants of wrongful conviction.

Inmates claiming wrongful conviction should have access to word processors and legal databases on which to do legal research, and printers.

Proposal 69: That Governors and the President invite members of the Innocence Network or related organizations to establish offices within every prison system in the U.S. which can provide inmates with onsite confidential appointments to present and discuss their claims of innocence.

From such offices within the prison system, Innocence Network organizations could schedule office hours in smaller prisons.

With such offices, the Innocence Network would not be some unknown office in a far-away place but represented by a real person who has walked the halls of the prison and met with inmates who are never more than one or two degrees of separation from a claimant.

Proposal 70: That Governors and the President specifically proclaim to their corrections employees and to inmates, parolees and probationers that they will work proactively to ensure that there are no innocent people in their prisons by the end of the 2010s decade.

It is not in the interest of corrections officials to have innocent people under their jurisdictions. It's a waste of corrections resources, and the presence of such people undermines the overall ethos and morale of the organization.

Such an explicit announcement of policy would encourage wardens and corrections employees to make decisions that enhance the abilities of those claiming innocence to present their claims.

In the past, there have been a few dedicated wardens who tried to prevent the execution of wrongly convicted inmates, and assist inmates' claims of innocence.

In West Virginia in 1951, Robert Bailey was days away from his execution for murder, but Warden Orel Skeen believed that Bailey was innocent. Skeen contacted Erle Stanley Garner and his "Court of Last Resort" and Garner and a polygraph examiner arrived quickly. Despite being a "nervous wreck," Bailey passed his polygraph and other evidence of his innocence was gathered. Governor Okey Patterson was persuaded to change his mind about Bailey and commuted his sentence to life. Nine years later, Governor Cecil Underwood granted Bailey a conditional pardon.[1]

In 1916, Thomas Bambrick was executed in Sing Sing Prison for the murder of a policeman, but many people, including reformer Warden Thomas Mott Osborne, believed Bambrick to be innocent. Bambrick knew the identity of the real killer, but he refused to break an honor code or "squeal" on the perpetrator. Said Osborne after the failure of his efforts to save Bambrick, "It is almost as certain that Bambrick is innocent as that the sun will rise tomorrow."[2]

In 1945, Willie Calloway was convicted of murder in Michigan and sentenced to life in prison. In 1953, two prison wardens asked an award-winning *Detroit Free Press* reporter to look into the case after learning that a key witness had admitted his perjury. As the movement for Calloway's innocence proceeded, alibi witnesses were found who said he was working with them at the time of the murder. Calloway was released in late 1953.[3]

Such support for inmates perceived to be innocent by their peers and wardens contrasts with instances in the 21st century where wardens have blocked efforts on behalf of those claiming

1. *In Spite of Innocence – The Ordeal of 400 Americans Wrongly Convicted of Crimes Punishable by Death*, by Michael Radelet, Hugo Bedau and Constance Putnam. Northeastern University Press, 1992. Pages 247-249.
2. Ibid. Page 284.
3. Ibid. Pages 292-293.

innocence. In New Hampshire in 2012, the State Prison warden prohibited Chad Evans[4] from taking a second polygraph after his first exam was determined to be inconclusive. In 2010, Evans passed a voice stress analysis examination when he denied murdering 21-month old Kassidy Bortner. The New Hampshire Commissioner of Corrections and the Governor have declined, so far, to reverse the warden's decision.

There are very few other cases of prisons refusing access to polygraph examinations. One was the case of Alonzo Watts, who was convicted of murder in Pennsylvania. In 2006, a Centurion Ministries volunteer and an investigative reporter were actively working on his case and Watts had agreed to take a polygraph exam, but the prison denied his request. Watts died in prison that year, before he and his supporters had a chance to persuade the prison warden, perhaps via the governor or a court order, to permit the polygraph exam.

Most recently and most dramatically, was the case of Troy Davis of Georgia whose request for a polygraph examination on September 20, 2011 was denied by prison officials. He was executed the next day, on September 21. While Davis's attorneys should have requested the polygraph far earlier in the long struggle, the execution could easily have been delayed to accommodate the late request. It would have been a severe test of the view by polygraph examiners that non-truth-related stress can be filtered out of the bio-feedback monitored during the answering of questions. If Davis failed his polygraph, he could have requested

4. For information about his claim of innocence, see www.chadevanswronglyconvicted.org. He is a client of the author.

a second exam and that request, too, should have been granted. These requests and exams could have taken less than a week to perform. While a polygraph is not perfect, the .04 probability of a double false reading (.2 X .2) surely made the exam worth conducting.

Wardens and other corrections officials should be encouraged to support claims of innocence by inmates and to do what they can to assist the development of such claims. Permitting a privately funded polygraphist to administer a polygraph in the State Prison's own polygraph room would appear to be an extremely minor burden, compared the enormous harm of a continued wrongful conviction and worse, a wrongful execution.

Proposal 71: That Governors and the President direct that the libraries of each of their prisons be connected electronically with the law library of a nearby law school and that inmates receive adequate training and assistance to maximize their utilization of the library's legal resources.

The benefits of such an expansion of the capabilities of prison law library extend beyond the needs of those who claim innocence. There is an enormous amount of legal talent in our prisons. Some inmates are lawyers, but most are self-taught advocates who know the laws relevant to their cases and those of their friends as well as, or better than, their outside-the-walls lawyers. However, legal skills and talent need adequate legal libraries. The connection to the law school law resources could also reinforce the connection to the students and professors at the law school who are working on exonerations of the wrongly convicted.

Proposal 72: That Governors and the President use their powers of pardon and clemency to release inmates or defendants whose claims of innocence have not received a fair decision before the judicial branch. And that the standard of pardon or clemency be the same as for the granting of a new trial, i.e. would it be likely that a contemporary jury, after hearing all the currently available evidence would find "reasonable doubt" or "any doubt" as to the culpability of the defendant.

Governors and the President have played minor roles in the Innocence Movement. Of the 1,520 exonerees in the National Registry of Exonerations since 1989, as of December 31, 2014, approximately 100 were pardoned by their governors and most of those had achieved some judicial relief. None was pardoned by the President.

The powers of pardon and clemency are virtually synonymous and are used to forgive a convicted person for a crime and to cancel the penalty. All rights and privileges of citizenship, including the right to vote are restored upon receipt of a pardon.

Pardons are usually used for reasons other than innocence, such as good conduct in prison combined with excessive sentence, or having a terminal illness. Sometimes a pardon is used as an executive's tool to relieve an innocent person from a wrongful conviction where judicial relief is not available. Often pardons are granted after the judiciary has exonerated a person by vacating a conviction.

The largest batch of pardons on behalf of the wrongly convicted came from Governor George Ryan in Illinois on January 11, 2003, during his last few days of office. He commuted the death sentences of 167 inmates after he had found during his term as governor that he had signed about the same number of death warrants as the number of inmates who had been exonerated from death row. That 50:50 ratio led him to the conclusion that there was too high a risk of executing an innocent person. On that day he also pardoned four inmates on the grounds of innocence.

The pardons contemplated in this proposal are for those cases when the justice system has not worked to the extent of declaring someone exonerated.

In 2011 in Montana, a judge overturned the 1984 murder conviction of Barry Beach and he was released after serving 30 years in prison for a crime he claims he never committed. However, the state appealed and after 17 months of freedom, the Montana Supreme Court reversed the lower court judge with a 4-3 decision. Thus, there were four judges, three at the Supreme Court and one at the lower court who believed that Beach's conviction was unjustified. (By Proposal 61 herein, the four judges' votes of "doubt" would have led to the options for the prosecution of retrial or release.) Nonetheless, Beach was ordered to return to prison in 2013.

Governor Steve Bullock asked the Board of Pardons and Parole in April 2014 to recommend back to him that Beach's 100 year sentence, imposed upon him as a juvenile, be commuted and that he be paroled, without necessarily a concurrence with the views of his innocence. Normally, the Governor in Montana does not make recommendations to the Parole Board. However, in June, the Board rejected the request, in large part because Beach will not show remorse, which he maintains he will never do, as he did not commit the crime.[5]

In Montana, the Governor cannot give a pardon without a positive recommendation by the Parole Board, so one action under consideration, given the wide political support for Beach, is for the legislature to pass a law giving the Governor that additional power.

Restricted to consideration only of those convicted of Federal crimes, the President of the United States currently does not consider innocence as a basis or reason for pardon. From the Department of Justice website comes this statement, "A pardon is not a sign of vindication and does not connote or establish innocence. For that reason, when considering the merits of a pardon petition, pardon officials take into account the petitioner's acceptance of responsibility, remorse, and atonement for the offense."[6]

Currently, the Office of the Pardon Attorney in the Dept. of Justice only accepts petitions from people who have completed their sentences more than five years previous in order to give them time to show their ability to lead productive lives. However, while the power to pardon arises from the U.S. Constitution, that requirement of remorse is not statutory, and presidents may pardon people who do not fit that criterion, such as when President Ford pardoned former President Nixon in 1974 even before he was indicted.

Congress should pass a law which authorizes the President to issue pardons to claimants of innocence, just as do many governors. The

5. "Parole Board Rejects Barry Beach's clemency bid," Associated Press, in the *Billings Gazette*, June 11, 2014.
6. "Pardon Information and Instructions," Dept. of Justice at http://www.justice.gov/pardon/pardon_instructions.htm

standard for such claimants should be whether there is reasonable doubt about their guilt.

Proposal 73: That when governors and the President and their delegates appoint judges and prosecutors, they should consider the proven record of sensitivity to the claims of innocence by defendants and those who have been wrongly convicted.

Lawyers seeking to become prosecutors and judges should be able to show the appointing authority, or the electorate voters, that they are aware of, and concerned about, the problem of wrongful convictions. Such awareness can come as simply as from reading books, or from working on behalf of one or more claimants of wrongful conviction.

On the other hand, appointments to be prosecutors or judges should be denied to those who have demonstrated a bias against claimants of innocence. For example, a prosecutor who is found to have persuaded a jury, with or without misconduct, to convict an innocent person should apologize to that person. A prosecutor who does not apologize or show other signs, ironically, of remorse should not be considered for appointment as a judge. The argument becomes stronger for those prosecutors who have been found to have engaged in some form of prosecutor misconduct during the trials of an exoneree or of any other defendant.

Chapter 11: Post Exoneration

Fair treatment of exonerees after exoneration will assist the country in acknowledging the harm done to them. Often, such exonerees, such as Jeffrey Deskovic, work on behalf of those left behind who claim innocence.

Proposal 74: That fair compensation be paid to all defendants who suffered imprisonment and other deprivations due to wrongful convictions, and that such compensation begin, at some reasonable level, within 30 days after the inmate's release from prison or the vacating of the conviction.

For too many exonerees, there is no compensation for the time they spent in prison or under the reputation-killing weight of a conviction. Only 27 states provide by statute for compensation of exonerees.

The least generous of the 27 is New Hampshire which allows up to $20,000 as a total cap, regardless of the number of months and years of wrongful imprisonment. At the other end of the scale is Texas which, since 2009 with the passage of the Tim Cole Act, has provided lump sum payments of up to $80,000 per year of incarceration and for an equivalent amount set aside for an annuity which would provide payments for the rest of the exonerees' lives.[1]

1. "Exonerated of Crimes, but Compensated Differently," by Brandi Grissom of the Texas Tribune. *New York Times*, September 23, 2011, at http://www.nytimes.com/2011/09/23/us/exonerated-of-crimes-but-compensated-differently.html

Through early 2013, Texas had paid almost $61 million to 89 exonerees since 1992. The annual payouts during recent years have all been over $10 million with 2010's exceeding $20 million.[2]

In addition to the statutory compensation, some exonerees have been able to sue law enforcement wrongdoers and obtain substantial settlements or awards. In 2014, the "Central Park Five" were awarded about $41 million for their convictions in 1990 and subsequent imprisonments in the "Central Park jogger" case.[3] In Putnam County, New York, Jeff Deskovic won a $41 million court judgment against the county and its investigators for their roles in his wrongful conviction in 1990 for raping and murdering a high school classmate.[4]

Even for some of the 27 states that do have a statutory scheme for compensation, there are often exclusions for exonerees who plead guilty or who had prior convictions.[5]

These high-publicity cases mask the harsh reality that approximately 40 percent of exonerees receive no compensation whatsoever for their

2. "Interactive: Payouts to Exonerated Texas Prisoners," by Ryan Murphy and Brandi Grissom. February 19, 2013, *The Texas Tribune*, at http://www.texastribune.org/library/data/texas-exoneree-payouts/
3. "Settlement Is Approved in Central Park Jogger Case, but New York Deflects Blame," by Benjamin Weiser. *New York Times*, Sept. 5, 2014 at http://www.nytimes.com/2014/09/06/nyregion/41-million-settlement-for-5-convicted-in-jogger-case-is-approved.html
4. "Jeff Deskovic, wrongly convicted of rape and murder, awarded $41.6 million in damages," by Radley Balko. *Washington Post*, October 24, 2014 at http://www.washingtonpost.com/news/the-watch/wp/2014/10/24/jeff-deskovic-wrongly-convicted-of-rape-and-murder-awarded-41-6-million-in-damages/
5. "Making Up for Lost Time," by the Innocence Project, at http://www.innocenceproject.org/docs/Innocence_Project_Compensation_Report.pdf

wrongful imprisonments.[6] That means that of the 1,520 exonerees listed on the National Registry of Exonerations on December 31, 2014, approximately 600 will not be compensated in any way.

Aside from the need to meet a moral obligation to compensate the wrongly convicted, such compensation is also necessary in order to force the people and governments who are responsible for these wrongful convictions to pay for them and to incorporate those costs into their plans for future action. Noted above were the compensation costs to Illinois, Texas and a few in New York, where voters are starting to pay attention.

Proposal 75: That all other vestiges of wrongful conviction be remedied for each exoneree, such as criminal records for the vacated wrongful conviction, immediately upon release from prison or the date of vacating of the conviction.

For too many exonerees, the burden of a wrongful conviction continues long after that walk out the prison door. As noted above, about 40 percent of the exonerees are never compensated for their wrongful imprisonment.

For others, the burden of a felony conviction continues to weigh down the prospects for renewed lifes, as exoneration does not mean the same in all contexts. Of the Norfolk Four who were wrongly

6. "Time doesn't pay, wrongfully imprisoned find," by Brian Rokus. *CNN*, March 29, 2012, at http://edition.cnn.com/2012/03/25/justice/wrongful-conviction-payments/index.html. See also "Wrongly Convicted Inmates fight for Compensation," by Molly Hennessy-Fiske. December 20, 2014, *Los Angeles Times*, at http://www.latimes.com/nation/la-na-exoneree-national-20141220-story.htm

convicted of the 1997 rape and murder of 18-year-old Navy wife, Michelle Moore-Bosko, only one, Derek Tice, is listed in the National Registry of Exonerations. Three of them were released from prison, upon the pardon by Governor Tim Kaine. The real perpetrator, Omar Ballard, had confessed to the crimes, and said that no one else was involved with him.

However, Erik Wilson continues to be required to register as a sex offender in Texas where he lives and to report to the local police once a year. Because of that sex offender status, he cannot attend school functions for his daughter, and suffers from numerous other indignities attached to that status.

His exoneration problem was that he had already completed his wrongful sentence for rape and had been released from prison when the Virginia authorities finally conceded the mistakes in the Norfolk Four cases. Because Wilson was no longer in prison, he was not eligible for habeas corpus relief in the Federal Courts, despite a strong dissent from a Fourth Circuit Court judge, James Wynn. He wrote that he was, "deeply troubled that our legal system would be construed to prevent a person with compelling evidence of his actual innocence and wrongful conviction from accessing a forum in which to clear his name."[7] That's the point of this proposal.

Everyone familiar with the stories of the Norfolk Four knows that Erik Wilson had no role in the rape and murder of Michelle Moore-Bosko, but he

7. "Out of Prison? For Some, That Might Mean Out of Luck," by Adam Liptak. *New York Times*, April 1, 2013, at http://www.nytimes.com/2013/04/02/us/eric-wilson-one-of-norfolk-four-challenges-conviction.html

continues to suffer, and not alone. No compensation has been paid to any of the Norfolk Four.

In 2011, the "West Memphis Three" were released from prison, which they had endured since their 1994 convictions for murdering three boys in West Memphis, Arkansas. However, because their release was via a negotiated Alford plea, in which they pled guilty and were released for time-served, they were ineligible for compensation and their criminal records continue to be stained with the wrongful convictions.[8]

John Blume and Rebecca Helm have called such exonerees by Alford pleas "the Unexonerated."[9]

Proposal 76: That the 42 US Code 1983 statute be amended to change the absolute immunity from civil liability for prosecutors in their "advocative" functions to a qualified immunity, as already applies to their "non-advocative" functions.

With rare exceptions, prosecutors whose unethical actions contributed substantially to wrongful convictions have not been held responsible for their actions.

One of the exceptions was the sanction against Judge Kenneth Anderson, who was formerly the prosecutor who obtained the 1987 murder conviction of Michael Morton in Texas. Morton was exonerated in 2011 after 25 years in prison for the

8. "West Memphis Three," *Wikipedia* at http://en.wikipedia.org/wiki/West_Memphis_Three
9. "The Unexonerated: Factually Innocent Defendants Who Plead Guilty," by John H. Blume and Rebecca K. Helm. Cornell Law Faculty Working Papers, January 21, 2014 at http://scholarship.law.cornell.edu/clsops_papers/113/

murder of his wife. For failing to disclose exculpatory evidence to Morton, and other offenses, Anderson was jailed in 2014 for 10 days and forced to resign from his judgeship and abandon his license to practice law.[10]

The current primary source of this immunity for prosecutors is the 1976 U.S. Supreme Court case of Imbler v. Pachtman. Paul Imbler was convicted in 1961 in California state courts of robbery and murder and was sentenced to death. At one point, he was within seven days of execution, but his conviction was vacated in 1971. He then sued the prosecuting district attorney, Richard Pachtman, in Federal Court pursuant to 42 U.S.C. 1983, for his alleged misconduct which included using false testimony and withholding exculpatory evidence favorable to Imbler. Each of the lower courts denied relief on the grounds of "absolute immunity" from civil damages liability for prosecutors. The U.S. Supreme Court affirmed in 1976.[11]

In that decision, the Court opened the door to some liability when it restricted the scope of its ruling to a prosecutor's work as an advocate for the government, rather than in a non-advocate role.

In 1991, the Court ruled in Burns v. Reed[12] that, prosecutors were not immune from Sect. 1983 lawsuits for damages for non-advocacy work, such as providing training to police officers. In such instances, prosecutors were entitled to "qualified

10. For a summary of the Morton case, see the National Registry of Exonerations at http://www.law.umich.edu/special/exoneration/pages/casedetail.aspx?caseid=3834.
11. Imbler v. Pachtman, 424 U.S. 409 (1976), at http://www.law.cornell.edu/supremecourt/text/424/409
12. Burns v. Reed, 500 U.S. 478 (1991) at http://caselaw.lp.findlaw.com/scripts/getcase.pl?court=US&vol=500&invol=478

immunity," subject to the circumstances and the closeness of the work to advocacy.

It is that "qualified immunity" standard which this proposal would extend to advocacy work by prosecutors. The reason for extending such liability is the same as for the use of civil liability for all other professions, which is to deter malpractice and compensate those who are harmed.

The need for such a change in the law became even more apparent in the case of the wrongly convicted John Thompson, whose Louisiana murder case was briefly outlined in Chapter 8. The prosecutor misconduct in that case involved hiding exculpatory evidence from the defense in both the carjacking and murder cases against Thompson. The Louisiana jury was so offended by the prosecutor misconduct and the harm to John Thompson with 14 years of imprisonment, mostly on death row, that it awarded him $14 million. However, in the case of Connick v. Thompson, the U.S. Supreme Court reversed the award, on the grounds of absolute prosecutor immunity and left Thompson with nothing.[13] Later, however, he was awarded $300,000 compensation by the Louisiana statutory compensation system.[14]

For fair compensation to be paid to victims of wrongful conviction due to prosecutorial misconduct, the immunity accorded to prosecutors for their advocacy work should be lowered from "absolute" to "qualified." Under that latter standard, prosecutors would be entitled to some deference for mistakes, but not for egregious misconduct.

13. Connick v. Thompson, Wikipedia at http://en.wikipedia.org/wiki/Connick_v._Thompson
14. "John Thompson," Summary at National Registry of Exonerations at http://www.law.umich.edu/special/exoneration/Pages/casedetail.aspx?caseid=3685

Chapter 12: Substance and Procedure in an Adversarial System.

The Anglo-American justice system is called an "adversarial" system because it is thought to generate truth and justice by two opposing sides presenting their evidence and arguments.

However, it often occurs that the two sides battle each other in order to win, and with a secondary role for the pursuit of the truth.

The motto of the American Polygraph Association is "Dedicated to Truth," and that should be the goal for the legal system.

Proposal 77: That wherever the adversarial system faces a choice between the system, and its procedures, or truth and justice, that truth and justice prevail.

Too often one side of a trial will seek to admit evidence which will seem credible and helpful to establish the truth, but the other side will object due to a superficial violation of an evidentiary rule and the evidence will be excluded.

Similarly, juries will sometimes ask for more information about testimony that was given in the trial, and judges will deny the request because the trial is over. In the 1994 case of exoneree Juan Carlos Pichardo in New York, the jury asked to hear the recording of Pichardo's testimony and the judge denied the request. During that testimony, he denied committing murder. After six years in prison, Pichardo was finally exonerated and later awarded compensation of $200,000 by the City of New York.[1]

When juries ask judges for more information about the cases they have heard, such requests should be honored, or a verdict of not guilty should be entered due to reasonable doubt. That is, if a jury has enough concern about trial testimony or evidence to ask a further question, that questioning should indicate sufficient doubt to require a verdict of Not Guilty if the judge declines to provide an answer or more information.

Proposal 78: That where the enforcement of a procedural rule is likely to deter the presentation of the truth and frustrate justice, a judge would be authorized to waive that enforcement.

In addition to the procedural issue of filing deadlines, as discussed in Chapter 9, there is a general problem in the law of valuing procedure more than justice. This conflict has been called substance vs. procedure or form vs. substance. Actually, there should be no conflict as all procedural issues should be resolved in favor of justice as that is the general purpose of all such rules.

An important case for looking at substance and procedure is Herrera v. Collins as it was called when it reached the United States Supreme Court. In the majority opinion which denied Leonel Herrera the ability get his case back to the district court for a hearing on the merits, Justice

1. "Juan Carlos Pichardo," National Registry of Exonerations, at http://www.law.umich.edu/special/exoneration/Pages/casedetail.aspx?caseid=4122

Rehnquist wrote about deluging the courts with presumably worthless claims of innocence if the case were to be reopened. Herrera's claim included an affidavit from an attorney that the attorney's client, Herrera's brother, had committed the crime, but the Court said the Constitution's Eighth Amendment did not provide a procedural right to a hearing on such new evidence. In other words, if the procedures were followed there was no constitutional protection against executing the innocent.

Sometimes, the procedural problem is what is called "professional ethics." In the two cases below the lawyers' adherence to their ethical standards resulted in injustice for their clients or others.

In 1986 Francis Featherstone was convicted of murder in New York, even though his attorneys knew that another man was the killer. The ethical problem was that Featherstone's attorneys also represented the other man and they felt bound by professional ethics to keep silent while Featherstone was tried and convicted.[2]

Featherstone was not an angel and he went into the Witness Protection program. He never served time in prison for the wrongful conviction because the truth was revealed on the day of his sentencing. Nonetheless, it was legal ethics that valued professional standards over truth and justice that allowed Featherstone to be convicted, and those rules should be changed by raising the priorities of truth and justice and lowering the priorities of procedure and so-called ethics.

2. "Guilty Verdict in Murder Case is Overturned," by Kirk Johnson. *New York Times*, September 6, 1986. At http://www.nytimes.com/1986/09/06/nyregion/guilty-verdict-in-murder-case-is-overturned.htm

Alton Logan's 26 years in prison from a wrongful conviction in Illinois show a far more egregious case where lawyers felt their professional ethics were more important than a man's freedom. Logan was arrested along with Edgar Hope in Chicago for the 1982 murder of a security guard. Hope told his attorney, Marc Miller, that Logan was not his accomplice during the robbery that resulted in the guard's death. Instead, a man named Andrew Wilson was his accomplice. Miller then confirmed with Wilson and Wilson's attorneys, Dale Coventry and Jamie Kunz, that Wilson and Hope were the guilty parties, and not Logan.

Nonetheless, Alton Logan and Edgar Hope were convicted of murder because the three lawyers determined that they would violate their professional ethical obligations to their clients, Wilson and Hope, by telling Logan's attorney what they knew. Instead, Wilson's attorneys Coventry and Kunz wrote an affidavit about their knowledge and sealed it in a container and waited until their client died, which would release them from their obligations of confidentiality to him.

Wilson died in 2007, and the affidavit was unlocked and Logan was released from prison in 2008, after 26 years. The City of Chicago paid him $10.25 million in compensation for his wrongful conviction.[3]

As with so many of the exoneration stories, there was a degree of luck for Logan at the end. In 2007, Harold Winston was a public defender and successor to Coventry and Kunz, now 70 and 64 years old. Winston had heard rumors of the innocence affidavit, without knowing the contents.

3. "Alton Logan" at the National Registry of Exonerations, at http://www.law.umich.edu/special/exoneration/Pages/casedetail.aspx?caseid=3389

Serendipitously, Winston learned of Andrew Wilson's death in prison and he sought out Kunz, and then Coventry, to see if there was truth to the rumor. There was.[4] Without that connected chain of luck, Logan would still be in prison, as are so many other thousands of wrongfully convicted people whose cases do not contain such eventual luck. Logan's luck turned with Wilson's relatively early death at the age of 54.

This case symbolizes the perspective of too many lawyers (prosecutors and defense lawyers) and too many law enforcement officers that sending innocent people to prison for unbelievably long periods of time is a legitimate price to pay for the benefits of our supposedly excellent criminal justice system.

If any of the three lawyers who knew of Logan's innocence had come forward to a judge or to the prosecutors and insisted on justice for Alton Logan, regardless of the possibly absurd consequences for the lawyer breaking a code of conduct rule of confidentiality, Alton would not have gone to prison.

4. "Inmate's freedom may hinge on secret kept for 26 years," by Maurice Possley. *Chicago Tribune*, January 19, 2008, at http://articles.chicagotribune.com/2008-01-19/news/0801180946_1_security-guard-attorney-client-privilege-andrew-wilson

Chapter 13: Conclusion

What is needed to STOP wrongful convictions is a national program on the scale of the Space Program's effort to send an astronaut to the moon by the end of the 1960s.

In 1964, Edward Radin wrote optimistically in *The Innocents* that court reform was necessary. He added, "Beyond court reformation, there still can be no cure unless there is an understanding by both judges and lawyers of the problem and the reasons why it arises. Once they become aware of the patterns that lead to injustice, then many of the primary causes can either be eliminated entirely or reduced sharply to the point where an erroneous conviction becomes a rarity and a justifiable shock to the press and the public."[1]

The elimination of wrongful convictions, or reduction to .1% or less, and a continuous review to detect and resolve those which remain, will take more than some tinkering with police procedures and court rules. Adoption and partial adoption of the proposals in this book will help achieve that goal.

It should be the goal of every level in the criminal justice system to do justice. It is not satisfactory for one level to do its job and let the other levels worry about justice. When responding to overzealous prosecutors, courts have sometimes admonished, "that a prosecutor's 'duty is to seek justice, not merely to convict.' "[2] Similarly, it is not the defense bar's job to find ways for their clients to

1. *The Innocents*, by Edward D. Radin. Tower Publications, 1964. Page.227.
2. State v. Bujnowski, 130 N.H. 1,7 (1987), citing State v. Preston, 121 N.H. 147, 151, 427 A.2d 32, 34 (1981) (quoting ABA Code of Professional Responsibility, EC 7-13).

escape justice, but rather to provide the best justice.

Many groups and individuals have worked thousands of hours to reduce and stop wrongful convictions; and the struggle continues. Both sides of the adversarial system, law enforcement and defense attorneys/defendants have an interest in this goal. Illustrating this mutual effort was the joint report issued in December, 2013 by the International Association of Chiefs of Police, the U.S. Justice Dept's Office of Justice Programs and the Innocence Project. The report has 30 recommendations divided into eight categories for reducing wrongful convictions, which is in everyone's interest except the actual perpetrators of crimes for which others have been held responsible.[3]

Lawyers must play a critical role in correcting the problem of wrongful convictions, just as they have been key to its creation and growth. Lawyers created the laws through their domination of judiciary and criminal justice committees in legislatures. Lawyers are primary players in the criminal justice system as they are the prosecutors, defense attorneys and judges. Only the jurors are not required to be attorneys.

Ironically, it is the legal profession which holds other professions accountable, e.g. doctors, for their negligence, but lawyers are rarely held personally accountable for the horrendous tragedy of wrongful convictions. While most exonerees are not fully compensated for their losses of freedom

3. "National Summit on Wrongful Convictions: Building a Systemic Approach to Prevent Wrongful Convictions," originally to be released in August 2013. At https://www.bja.gov/Publications/IACP-Wrongful_Convictions_Summit_Report.pdf

and income, even fewer receive any compensation from their lawyers' malpractice insurance funds.

If all or most of the foregoing Proposals, and the above-mentioned 30 recommendations of chiefs of police, D.O.J. and the Innocence Project, and the reforms proposed by Daniel Medwed in *Prosecution Complex* had been implemented at the times of the convictions of the currently (as of Dec. 31, 2014) registered 1,520 exonerees at the National Registry of Exonerations, perhaps none of them would have been convicted. At the goaled rate of .1 percent, one or two would have been convicted.

Several of the proposals in this book will cost millions of dollars and a few will cost more than a billion. Many will save money. The savings to the country through the avoidance of prison time, of disruption of work and income, and of legal expenses will be measured in the hundreds of millions of dollars.

The reduction in the use of prisons will bring large savings, to be measured in the billions. In 2010, the country spent $37 billion for operating our prisons, compared to $2.9 billion in 1980[4] ($7.6 billion corrected for inflation). That is a five-fold increase, and crime rates have been declining since 1991.[5]

Several states have implemented "justice reinvestment programs" to improve justice and simultaneously reduce costs. In 2010, North Carolina's prison population rose to 40,000 and the corrections spending had risen 49 percent in ten years and was expected to rise another $500

4. "Direct Expenditures for Correctional Activities, Table 1.9. Sourcebook of Criminal Statistics at http://www.albany.edu/sourcebook/pdf/t192010.pdf.

5. "Crime in the United States," Wikipedia, at http://en.wikipedia.org/wiki/Crime_in_the_United_States

million to accommodate anticipated inmate population growth. The "Justice Reinvestment" reforms were instituted in 2011 and through 2014, the prison population fell to 37,665 and 10 prisons were closed.[6]

Some of the proposals will even generate income for our governments through the taxation of regulated, formerly illegal, activities.

Those savings, plus additional income, may well exceed the costs of most of the proposals. Regardless of the net costs, however, we must embark upon the adoption of these proposals and others in order to achieve a more just society.

Justice is one of the primary obligations of government and is part of the social contract among citizens and the government. For too long our country has deluded itself with the arrogant view that our justice system is the best in the world and by reciting blindly the "Blackstone Ratio" as if its utterance made it true. Reformulating an old idea, Sir William Blackstone wrote in 1765, "It is better that ten guilty persons escape than that one innocent suffer."[7]

Instead, as the large numbers of wrongly convicted show, we have tolerated a system which is far from the best, and for too long we likely have been convicting more innocents than we have allowed guilty persons to go free. We have turned Blackstone's Ratio on its head.

6. "Justice Reinvestment in North Carolina: Three Years Later," November 2014, The Justice Center, Council of State Governments, at http://csgjusticecenter.org/jr/north-carolina/publications/justice-reinvestment-in-north-carolina-three-years-later/

7. *Commentaries on the Laws of England*, by William Blackstone. See Wikipedia at http://en.wikipedia.org/wiki/Commentaries_on_the_Laws_of_England

In his concurring opinion in In Re Winship, Justice John Marshall Harlan put the idea of the Blackstone Ratio into qualitative terms. He wrote that it is "far worse to convict an innocent man than to let a guilty man go free."[8] The connection between the guilty and the innocent is even more direct, as Nancy Petro has noted elegantly and poignantly, "Tragically, this is not an either/or proposition, for when we convict an innocent person, we do both."[9]

By adopting several, many or most of the proposals presented here, we will fulfill a sacred commitment to our citizens to respect their freedom unless they are truly guilty of crimes beyond a reasonable doubt, or any doubt.

Proposal 79: That everyone involved in the criminal justice system, and every citizen, accept a continuing responsibility to ensure that truth and justice prevail.

In previous chapters, the responsibilities of attorneys, prosecutors, judges, jurors, corrections officers and others have been noted. Those duties are often specifically described by statute or ethical codes. Their jobs cover specific sectors of the criminal justice system, but they all are chartered to provide justice. However, this proposal is for a new ethos which goes beyond the job description

8. In Re Winship, 397 U.S. 358 (1970) At http://caselaw.lp.findlaw.com/scripts/getcase.pl?court=US&vol=397&invol=358
9. "Law Schools: Add Wrongful Conviction to Core Curriculum," by Nancy Petro. Wrongful Conviction Blog, April 19, 2012, at http://wrongfulconvictionsblog.org/2012/04/19/law-schools-add-wrongful-conviction-to-core-curriculum/

and asks that everyone work for justice as a continuing responsibility throughout their lives whether on or off the job.

The challenge of this decade is to reduce wrongful convictions to .1 percent of convictions and the number of wrongly convicted in our prisons and parole and probation systems to .1 percent.

If we can place astronauts onto the moon, we can keep innocent people out of prison.

Proposal 80: That enough of the previous 79 proposals be implemented to STOP and CORRECT wrongful convictions before the end of this decade.

Author's Acknowledgments

I thank my wrongly convicted friends, Dennis Dechaine, Chad Evans and Alfred Trenkler for their inspiration and helpful comments on these proposals. Each of them is innocent and must be exonerated before the end of this decade.

Bill Bunting's long term commitment to Dennis Dechaine's struggle is heroic, and his comments on the first draft were helpful.

The writing of this book would have been far more difficult without the information now collected and available from the groundbreaking National Registry of Exonerations (www.exonerationregistry.org). It's a jewel of a resource. A special thank you goes to Samuel Gross and Robert Warden for the creation of the Registry and to Maurice Possley for his ongoing editing, inspiring investigative journalism, and his encouragement for my work.

Also much appreciated is the Wrongful Convictions Blog (www.wrongfulconvictionsblog.org) led by Mark Godsey and its primary contributors Ron Huff, Phil Locke, Nancy Petro and Martin Yant.

I thank my wife, Leah, for her love and patience.

Appendix A

Significant General Books and early articles about Wrongful Convictions, primarily in the U.S., in Chronological Order of Publication.

1913. "European Systems of State Indemnity for Errors of Criminal Justice," by Edwin Borchard. *Journal of Criminal Law and Criminology*, Vol 3, pp. 684-695.

1913. "State Indemnity for Errors of Criminal Justice," Editorial by John H. Wigmore. *Journal of Criminal Law and Criminology*. January, 1913.

1932. *Convicting the Innocent - Sixty-five Actual Errors of Criminal Justice*, by Edwin Borchard. Garden City Publishing. See also, 2013. *Edwin M. Borchard - Convicting The Innocent, and State Indemnity For Errors Of Criminal Justice*, by Edwin Montefiore Borchard, Hans Sherrer (Compiler). The Justice Institute, 2013. (Of the 65 "actual errors," three were in the United Kingdom.)

1952. *The Court of Last Resort*, by Erle Stanley Gardner. William Sloan Associates. AND *The Court of Last Resort*, the 1954 enlarged paperback edition. Cardinal. (Describes eight exonerations, and one of uncertain innocence, who was exonerated in 1960, post-publication.)

1957. *Not Guilty*, by Jerome Frank and Barbara Frank, in association with Harold Hoffman. Doubleday (hardcover), Popular Library (paperback.) *British edition was Not Guilty – 36 comparatively recent cases in which the wrong man was convicted*, by Jerome Frank and Barbara Frank. Victor Gollancz Publisher. See also subsequent edition, _Not Guilty_, by Jerome Frank and Barbara Frank. Panther Books, 1961.

1963. _The Vindicators_, by Eugene B. Block, Doubleday. (12 cases of proven wrongful conviction.)

1964. _The Innocents_, by Edward D Radin. William Morrow and Co. (80 wrongful conviction cases, from 300 the author researched.)

1969. "Convicting the innocent," by D.E.J. MacNamara. *Crime and Delinquency* 15, pp. 57-61.

1973 _Wrongful Imprisonment: Mistaken Convictions and Their Consequences_, by Ruth Brandon and Christie Davies. George Allen and Unwin, Ltd. (London.)

1987. _Miscarriages of justice in potentially capital cases_, by Hugo Adam Bedau and Michael L. Radelet. Stanford University, and the article of the same title in 40 Stanford Law Review 21 (1987)

1988. "Convicted but innocent: Wrongful conviction and the criminal justice system," by Arye Rattner. *Law and Human Behavior*, Vol 12(3), Sept. 1988, pp. 283-293.

1989 -

1991. _Presumed Guilty_, Martin D. Yant. Prometheus Books.

1992. _In Spite of Innocence – Erroneous Convictions in Capital Cases: The Ordeal of 400 Americans Wrongly Convicted of Crimes Punishable by Death_, by Michael L. Radelet, Hugo Adam Bedau and

Constance E. Putnam. Northeastern University Press.

1996. _Convicted But Innocent: Wrongful Conviction and Public Policy_, by C. Ronald Huff, Ayre Rattner, and Edward Sagarin. Sage Publications.

1996. _Convicted by juries, exonerated by science: case studies in the use of DNA evidence to establish innocence after trial_, by Edward Connors, Thomas Lundregan, Neal Miller and Tom McEwan. National Institute of Justice.

1996. _Eyewitness Testimony: With a new preface by the author_, by Elizabeth F. Loftus. Harvard University Press. See also, Witness for the Defense: The Accused, the Eyewitness and the Expert Who Puts Memory on Trial, by Elizabeth Loftus (Author), Katherine Ketcham. St. Martin's Griffin, 1992.

2000. _Actual Innocence – Five Days to Execution, and other Dispatches from the Wrongly Convicted_, by Barry Scheck, Peter Neufeld and Jim Dwyer. Doubleday. See also, the 2003 edition: _Actual Innocence: When Justice Goes Wrong and How to Make it Right_. New American Library.

2001. _Wrongly Convicted: Perspectives on Failed Justice_, by Saundra Westervelt and John Humphrys. Rutgers University Press.

2003. _Errors of Justice: Nature, Sources and Remedies_, by Brian Forst. Cambridge University Press.

2003. _The Wrong Men: America's Epidemic of Wrongful Death Row Convictions_, by Stanley Cohen. Carroll & Graf.

2004. *Innocent: Inside Wrongful Conviction Cases*, by Scott Christianson. New York University Press.

2004. *No Crueler Tyrannies: Accusation, False Witness, and Other Terrors of Our Times*, by Dorothy Rabinowitz. Free Press.

2004. *The Day Care Ritual Abuse Moral Panic*, by Mary De Young. Mcfarland & Co.

2004. *The Death of Innocents: An Eyewitness Account of Wrongful Executions*, by Helen Prejean. Random House.

2004. *True Witness: Cops, Courts, Science, and the Battle against Misidentification*, by James M. Doyle. Palgrave, MacMillan Trade.

2005. *In The Company of Giants: The Ultimate Investigation Guide for Legal Professionals, Activists, Journalists & the Wrongfully Convicted*, by Paul Ciolino. iUniverse.

2005. *Surviving Justice: America's Wrongfully Convicted and Exonerated*, by Dave Eggers, Lola Vollen and Scott Turow. McSweeney's Publishing.

2005. *Wilkie Collins's The Dead Alive: The Novel, the Case, and Wrongful Convictions*, by Rob Warden. Northwestern University Press.

2006. *Achieving Justice: Freeing the Innocent, Convicting the Guilty. Report of the ABA Criminal Justice Section's Ad Hoc Committee to Ensure the Integrity of the Criminal Process*, by Paul Giannelli and Myrna Raeder (editors.) American Bar Association.

2006. *Wrongful Capital Convictions and the Legitimacy of the Death Penalty*, by Karen S. Miller. Lfb Scholarly Publishing.

2007. *Rethinking Miscarriages of Justice: Beyond the Tip of the Iceberg*, by Michael Naughton. Palgrave MacMillan.

2007. *Snitch: Informants, Cooperators, and the Corruption of Justice*, by Ethan Brown. Public Affairs.

2008. *Execution's Doorstep: True Stories of the Innocent and Near Damned*, by Leslie Lytle. Northeastern Univesity Press.

2008. *False Positives Equal False Justice*, by John Kelly and J. Michael Bell. Amazon Digital.

2008. *Criminal Investigative Failures*, by D. Kim Rossmo. CRC Press.

2008. *I Am Innocent!: A Comprehensive Encyclopedic History of the World's Wrongly Convicted Persons*, by Jay Robert Nash. Da Capo Press.

2008. *The Innocence Commission – Preventing Wrongful Convictions and Restoring the Criminal Justice System*, by Jon B. Gould. New York University Press.

2008. *The Innocents*, by Peter Neufeld and Barry Scheck, Althea Wasow (Editor) and Taryn Simon (Photographer). Umbrage Editions, 2008.

2008. *The Decline of the Death Penalty and the Discovery of Innocence*, by Frank R. Baumgartner, Suzanna L. De Boef, and Amber E. Boydstun. Cambridge University Press.

2008. *The Supreme Court on Trial: How the American Justice System Sacrifices Innocent Defendants*, by George C. Thomas III. University of Michigan Press.

2009. *Police Interrogation and American Justice*, by Richard A. Leo. Harvard University Press.

2009. *Snitching: Criminal Informants and the Erosion of American Justice*, by Alexandra Natapoff. NYU Press.

2009. *True Stories of False Confessions*, by Rob Warden and Steven A. Drizin. Northwestern University Press.

2009. *When Law Fails: Making Sense of Miscarriages of Justice*, by Charles J. Ogletree, Jr. (Editor), Austin Sarat (Editor), NYU Press.

2010. *Henry Wade's Tough Justice: How Dallas County Prosecutors Led the Nation in Convicting the Innocent*, by Edward Gray (Author), Dog Ear Publishing, LLC

2010. *Tested: How Twelve Wrongly Imprisoned Men Held Onto Hope*, by Dorothy and Peyton Budd. Brown Books.

2010. *Wrongful Conviction: International Perspectives on Miscarriages of Justice*, by C. Ronald Huff and Martin Killias. Temple University Press.

2011. *American Justice in the Age of Innocence: Understanding the Causes of Wrongful Convictions and How to Prevent Them*, by Sandra Guerra Thompson, Hillary K. Valderrama and Jennifer L. Hopgood. iUniverse Publishing.

2011. *Convicting the Innocent: Where Criminal Prosecutions Go Wrong*, by Brandon L. Garrett. Harvard University Press.

2011, 2014 *False Justice: Eight Myths that Convict the Innocent*, by Jim Petro and Nancy Petro. Simon & Schuster.

2011 *Media depictions of wrongful conviction: Reality or distortion*? by Angela Lynn Overton. ProQuest, UMI Dissertation Publishing.

2011. *The Collapse of American Criminal Justice*, by William J. Stuntz. Belknap Press.

2011. *Three Felonies A Day: How the Feds Target the Innocent*, by Harvey Silverglate. Encounter Books.

2011. *Wrongful Conviction: Law, Science and Policy*, (casebook) by James R. Acker and Allison D. Redlich. Carolina Academic Press.

2011. *Wrongful Convictions: Cases and Materials (textbook, 1st Edition)* AND 2nd Edition, 2014), by Justin Brooks. Vandeplas Publishing.

2012. *Failed Evidence: Why Law Enforcement Resists Science*, by David A. Harris. NYU Press.

2012. *Falsely Accused: After 31 years of law enforcement service, a former Texas police officer explains the shambles of the American criminal justice system-and how to prevent becoming its victim*, by Marian Hoy. Publish Green.

2012. *Life after Death Row: Exonerees' Search for Community and Identity*, by Saundra D. Westervelt, Kimberly J. Cook. Rutgers University Press.

2012. *Not Guilty: Are the Acquitted Innocent*? by Daniel Givelber (Author), Amy Farrell NYU Press.

2012. *Conviction of the Innocent: Lessons From Psychology Research*, by Brian L. Cutler American Psychological Association.

2012. *Failed Evidence: Why Law Enforcement Resists Science*, by David A. Harris. NYU Press.

2012. *In Doubt: The Psychology of the Criminal Justice Process*, by Dan Simon. Harvard University Press.

2012. *International Perspectives on Wrongful Convictions: Workshop Report, September 2010*, by Miranda Jolicoeur. BiblioGov.

2012. *Post-Conviction DNA Testing and Wrongful Conviction*, by John Roman and Kelly Walsh. BiblioGov.

2012. *Prosecution Complex: America's Race to Convict and its Impact on the Innocent*, by Daniel Medwed. New York University Press. [This is an excellent book with a large number of proposals to improve justice and reduce the frequency of wrongful convictions.]

2012. _Race and Justice: Wrongful Convictions of African American Men_, by Marvin D., Jr. Free and Mitch Ruesink. Lynne Rienner Publishers.

2012. _The New Jim Crow: Mass Incarceration in the Age of Colorblindedness_, by Michelle Alexander. The New Press.

2012. _The Psychology of Eyewitness Identification, by James M. Lampinen_, Jeffrey S. Neuschatz and Andrew D. Cling. Psychology Press.

2013. _Grave Injustice: Unearthing Wrongful Executions_, by Richard A. Stack. Potomac Books.

2013. _The Innocent and the Criminal Justice System: A Sociological Analysis of Miscarriages of Justice_, by Michael Naughton. (U.K.) Palgrave MacMillan.

2013. _Unbearable Burden: Wrongful Convictions and the Crisis in American Justice_, by David Patrick Keys. CreateSpace Publishing.

2013. _Understanding Wrongful Convictions_, by John T. Rago. Rowman & Littlefield.
2013. _Working in Innocence Programs: Everything You Always Wanted To Know About Innocence Work But Were Afraid To Ask_, by Sarah A. Mourer. Vandeplas Publishing.

2013. _Wrongful Conviction and Criminal Justice Reform: Making Justice_, by Marvin Zalman and Julia Carrano, Taylor and Francis.

2013. _Wrongful Convictions and Miscarriages of Justice: Causes and Remedies in North American_ *and European Criminal Justice Systems*, by C. Ronald Huff and Martin Killias. Routledge.

2013. *Wrongly Convicted: Miscarriages of Justice*, by Jennifer Davies. RW Press.

2014. *Controversies in Innocence Cases in America*, by Sarah Lucy Cooper. Ashgate Publishing.

2014. *Examining Wrongful Convictions: Stepping Back, Moving Forward*, by Allison D. Redlich, James R. Acker, Robert J. Norris, and Catherine L. Bonventre. Carolina Academic Press.

2014. *Flawed Convictions: "Shaken Baby Syndrome" and the Inertia of Injustice*, by Deborah Tuerkheimer. Oxford University Press.

2014 *Miscarriages of Justice: Actual Innocence, Forensic Evidence, and the Law*, by Brent E. Turvey and Craig M Cooley. Academic Press.

Appendix B

Books about Specific U.S. Exonerations (or close) from Wrongful Convictions in order of State and Chronological Order of Conviction[1]

Alabama, 1931. *Scottsboro: A Tragedy of the American South*, by Dan T. Carter. Louisiana State University Press, 2007. (Olen Montgomery, Clarence Norris, Haywood Patterson, Ozie Powell, Willie Robertson, Charlie Weems, Eugene Williams, Andy Wright, Roy Wright: all posthumously pardoned in 2013.)

Alabama, 1973. *Freeing The Innocent: How We Did It - A Handbook For The Wrongly Convicted*, by Michael Pardue and Becky Pardue. CreateSpace, 2005. (Michael Pardue, 1977.)

Alabama, 1988. *Circumstantial Evidence: Death, Life, and Justice in a Southern Town*, by Pete Earley. Bantam, 1995. *Just Mercy - A Story of Justice and Redemption*, by Bryan Stevenson. Spiegel & Grau, 2014. (Walter "Johnnie D." McMillan, murder, 1993.)

Arizona, 1977. *Manifest Injustice: The True Story of a Convicted Murderer and the Lawyers Who Fought for His Freedom*, by Barry Siegel. Henry Holt & Co., 2013 (Bill Macumber, murder "no contest" 2012)

Arizona, 1992. *Jingle Jangle The Perfect Crime Turned Inside Out*, by Jim Rix. Broken Bench Press, 2007. (Ray Krone, 2002.)

1. Where linked, exonerees are listed in the National Registry of Exonerations at www.exonerationregistry.org. The Registry's list begins in 1989.

Arkansas, 1919. *A Mob Intent on Death: The NAACP and the Arkansas Riot Cases*, by Richard C. Cortner. Wesleyan University Press, 1988.

Arkansas, 1994. *Devils Knot: The True Story Of The West Memphis Three*, by Mara Leveritt. Atria Books, 2003. *Life After Death*, by Damien Echols. Blue Rider Press, 2012. *Dark Spell: Surviving the Sentence* (Justice Knot Trilogy) (Volume 2) by Mara Leveritt and Jason Baldwin. CreateSpace 2014 (Jason Baldwin, Damien Echols, Jessie Miskelley, 2011.)

California, 1916, 1917. *THE MOONEY CASE- The San Francisco Preparedness Day Bombing of 1916 and its aftermath*, by Richard H. Frost. Stanford University Press, 1968. AND *Frame-up; the incredible case of Tom Mooney and Warren Billings*, by Curt Gentry, W.W. Norton & Co, 1967. (Thomas Mooney and Warren Billings, bombing/murder, 1939 pardon.)

California, 1972. *Last Man Standing: The Tragedy and Triumph of Geronimo Pratt*, by Jack Olsen. Anchor, 2001. AND A summary and analysis of the 1972 conviction of Elmer Pratt for the robbery and shooting of Mr. Olsen and the murder of Mrs. Olsen on a Santa Monica tennis court, by Jim McCloskey. Centurion Ministries (Elmer G. Pratt/Geronimo ji-Jaga, 1999, died 2011.)

California, 1986. *Full Circle: A True Story of Murder, Lies, and Vindication*, by Gloria Killian and Sandra Kobrin. New Horizon Press, 2012. (Gloria Killian, 2002.)

California, 2004. _Shattered Justice: A Savage Murder and the Death of Three Families' Innocence_, by John Philpin. HarperCollins eBooks, 2011. (Richard Raymond Tuite, 2013.)

Colorado, 1999. _Drawn to Injustice: The Wrongful Conviction of Timothy Masters_, by Timothy Masters and Steve Lehto. Berkeley, 2012. (Timothy Masters, 2008.)

Connecticut, 1974. _Guilty Until Proven Innocent_, by Donald S. Connery. Putnam Adult, 1977. _A Death in Canaan_, by Joan Barthel. E.P. Dutton, 1978. (Peter Reilly, murder, 1976.)

Delaware, 1947. _The Rape Case: A Young Lawyer's Struggle for Justice in the 1950's_, by Irving Morris. University of Delaware Press, 2011. (Francis J. Curran, Francis J. Maguire and Ira F. Jones, Jr., rape, 1956.)

Florida, 1961. _Gideon's Trumpet_, by Anthony Lewis. Vintage, 1989. (Clarence Earl Gideon, breaking and entering, larceny. Found not guilty at retrial in 1963 after U.S. Supreme Court reversal in Gideon v. Wainwright, 1963.)

Florida, 1963. _Invitation to a Lynching, by Gene Miller_. Doubleday, 1975. (Freddie Lee Pitts and Wilbert Lee, murder. Pardoned, 1975.)

Florida, 1968. _Arcadia_, by Mark Lane. Holt, Rinehart & Winston, 1970. (James J. Richardson, murder, 1989.)

Florida, 1971. _David Charles; the Story of the Quincy Five_, by Jeffrey Lickson. Mockingbird

Press, 1974. (David Keaton, 1973, Johnny Fredrick, 1973.)

Florida, 1976. *The Wrong Man: A True Story of Innocence on Death Row*, by Michael Mello. University of Minnesota Press, 2001. (Joseph Spaziano, murder. 1998, plead "no contest.")

Florida, 1980. *And Justice For All: The Improbable Story of Virginia Snyder, Investigative Reporter and Private Investigator*, by Virginia Snyder. iUniverse, 2008. (Luis Diaz, 2005.)

Florida, 1984. *The Wrong Man*, by Kevin Davis. Avon Books, 1996. (John Gordon Purvis, murder, 1993.)

Georgia, 1913. *The Leo Frank Case*, by Leonard Dinnerstein. University of Georgia Press, 2008. (Leo Frank, murder, lynched in 1915, pardoned in 1986.)

Georgia, 1975. *Sins of Henry County: After Two Wrongful Convictions & the Death of Jerry Banks, a 35-year-old Cold Case is Reinvestigated*, by Charles L. Sargent. CreateSpace, 2012. (Jerry Banks, 1980)

Georgia, 1982. *Midnight in the Garden of Good and Evil*, by John Berendt. Vintage Books, 1999. (James Williams, murder, 1989.)

Georgia, 1983. *Exit to Freedom*, by Calvin C. Johnson Jr. and Greg Hampikian. University of Georgia Press, 2005. (Calvin Johnson, sexual assault, 1999.)

Illinois, 1956. *Scapegoat Justice, Lloyd Miller and the Failure of the American Legal System*, by Willard

J. Lassers. Indiana University Press, 1973. (Lloyd Miller, murder, 1971.)

Illinois, 1978, (1985 for Jimerson). *A Promise of Justice: The Eighteen-Year Fight to Save Four Innocent Men*, by David Protess and Rob Warden. Hyperion, 1998. (Ford Heights Four: Dennis Williams, 1996, Kenny Adams, 1996, Willie Rainge, 1996, and Verneal Jimerson, 1996.)

Illinois, 1979. *Forgive Me*, by Kathleen Crowell Webb. Fleming H Revell Co, 1985. (Gary Dotson, 1989.)

Illinois, 1985. *Mistakes Were Made: Prosecutorial Misjudgment or Misconduct*, by Lettie McSpadden. Booksurge Publishing, 2009. AND *Till Justice is Done*, by Diana Eiranova-Kyle, CreateSpace 2013. AND *Victims of Justice Revisited*, by Thomas Frisbie and Randy Garrett. Northwestern University Press, 2005. (Rolando Cruz, Alejandro Hernandez, murder, 1995)

Illinois, 1989. *Die Free: A True Story of Murder, Betrayal and Miscarried Justice*, by Peter Rooney. Kindle, 2011. (Joe Burrows, murder, 1996.)

Illinois, 1990. Gone in the Night, by David Protess and Rob Warden. Dell, 1994. (David Dowaliby, murder, 1992.)

Illinois, 1993. *In Spite of the System: A Personal Sort of Wrongful Conviction & Exoneration*, by Gary Gauger with Julie von Bergen. Fourcatfarm Press, 2008. (Gary Gauger, murder, 1996.)

Indiana, 2002. *One Deadly Night : A State Trooper, Triple Homicide, and a Search for Justice*, by John Glatt. St. Martin's Press, 2005. (David Camm, murder, 2013.)

Kentucky, 1900. *My Own Story: An Account of the Conditions in Kentucky Leading to the Assassination of William Goebel, who was Declared Governor of the State, and My Indictment and Conviction on the Charge of Complicity in His Murder*, by Caleb Powers. 1905, and Gale, 2010. (Caleb Powers, murder, 1908.)

Louisiana, 1984. *Desire Street: A True Story of Death and Deliverance in New Orleans*, by Jed Horne. Farrar, Straus and Giroux, 2005 (Curtis Kyles, murder,1998.)

Louisiana, 1984. *Killing Time: An 18-Year Odyssey from Death Row to Freedom*, by John Hollway and Ronald M. Gauthier. Skyhorse Publishing, 2010. (John Thompson, robbery, 1999.)

Maryland, 1962. *Where did the justice go? The story of the Giles-Johnson case*, by Frances Strauss. Gambit, 1970. AND An American rape: A true account of the Giles-Johnson case, by A. Robert Smith and James V. Giles. New Republic Book Company, 1975. (John Giles, James Giles, 1967. and Joseph Johnson, pardoned 1968.)

Maryland, 1985. *Bloodsworth: The True Story of One Man's Triumph over Injustice*, by Tim Junkin. Algonquin Books, 2005. (Kirk Bloodsworth, 1993.)

Massachusetts, 1921. *Tragedy in Dedham: The story of the Sacco-Vanzetti case*, by Francis Russell. McGraw Hill, 1971. AND *Sacco & Vanzetti: The*

Case Resolved, by Francis Russell, Harper Collins, 1986. AND *With Malice Aforethought: The Execution of Nicola Sacco and Bartolomeo Vanzetti* by Theodore W. Grippo. iUniverse, 2011. (Nicola Sacco and Bartolomeo Vanzetti, murder, both executed in 1927. Mass. Governor's Proclamation of Injustice, 1977.)

Michigan, 1944. *Sprung: The Release of Willie Calloway*, by Ken McCormick. St. Martin's Press, 1964. (Willie Calloway, murder, 1953.)

Michigan, 1976. *Sweet Freedom: Breaking the Bondage of Maurice Carter*, by Doug Tjapkes. Faithwalk Publishing, 2006. (Maurice Carter, 2004.)

Minnesota, 2008. *A Road to Freedom: Strangers Restore Justice for an Innocent Man*, by Trudy C Baltazar. Trulines Publishing, 2014. (Juoa Fong Lee, vehicular homicide, 2011.)

Mississippi, 2004. *The Skeptical Juror and the Trial of Cory Maye*, by J Bennett Allen. Allen & Allen Semiotics, 2010. (Corey Maye, murder, 2007.)

Missouri, 1979. *St. Joseph's Children: A True Story of Terror and Justice*, by Terry Ganey. Lyle Stewart, 1989. (Melvin Reynolds, murder, 1983.)

Missouri, 2005. *Free Ryan Ferguson: 101 Reasons Why Ryan Should Be Released*, by Brian D'Ambrosio. Smashwords Ebook, 2013. (Ryan Ferguson, murder, 2013.)

Nebraska, 1956. Barbarous Souls, by David L. Strauss and Steven A. Drizin. Northwestern

University Press, 2010. (Darrel Parker, murder, 1991.)

New Jersey, 1948. *Jersey Justice: The Story of the Trenton Six*, by Ms. Cathy D. Knepper. Rivergate, 2011. (Ralph Cooper (plead guilty and released 1954), Collis English (died in prison awaiting new trial 1952). Remaining four: McKinley Forrest, John McKenzie, James Thorpe and Horace Wilson, found not guilty in 1951.)

New Jersey, 1967. *Eye of the Hurricane: My Path from Darkness to Freedom*, by Rubin "Hurricane" Carter and Ken Klonsky. Chicago Review Press, 2011. AND *Rubin "Hurricane" Carter and the American Justice System*, by Paul B. Wice. Rutgers University Press, 2000. AND Hurricane: The Miraculous Journey of Rubin Carter, by James S. Hirsch. Mariner Books, 1999. (Rubin Carter, 1985.)

New Jersey, multi-year. *Innocence Lost in New Jersey*, by Sandra K. Manning and Scott Christianson. (re: 25 wrongly convicted New Jersey citizens)

New York, 1915. *Slaughter on a Snowy Morn: A Tale of Murder, Corruption and the Death Penalty Case That Revolutionised the American Courtroom*, by Colin Evans. Icon Books Ltd 2010. (Charles Frederick Stielow, murder, 1918.)

New York, 1938. *Punishment Without Crime*, by Isidore Zimmerman, and Francis Bond. Manor Books, 1972. (Isidore Zimmerman, murder, 1962.)

New York, 1985. *Giller's Ethics Story: In the Pink Room*, by Stephen Gillers. Foundation Press, 2005. (Alberto Ramos, rape, 1994)

New York, 1989. *Trials of a Forensic Psychologist – A Casebook,* by Charles Patrick Ewing. John Wiley & Sons. (Chapter 8, pp. 177-198, Richard Knupp, child sexual abuse, 1992.)

New York, 1990. *The Central Park Five: The Untold Story Behind One of New York City's Most Infamous Crimes,* by Sarah Burns. Knopf Doubleday Publishing Group, 2012. (Antron McCray, Kevin Richardson, Raymond Santana, Yusef Salaam, Korey Wise, sexual assault, 2002.)

New York, 1990. *A Criminal Injustice: A True Crime, a False Confession, and the Fight to Free Marty Tankleff* , by Richard Firstman and Jay Salpeter. Ballantine Books, 2008. (Martin Tankleff, murder, 2007.)

North Carolina, 1985. *Picking Cotton: Our Memoir of Justice and Redemption,* by Ron Cotton and Jennifer Thompson-Cannino. St. Martin's Press, 2009. (Ronald Cotton, rape, 1995.)

North Carolina, 1985. *Making Justice Our Business: The Wrongful Conviction of Darryl Hunt and the Work of Faith*, by Stephen B. Boyd. Wipf & Stock, 2011. and *From Freedom to Victory: The Story of Regina Lane, the Integon Victim of Winston-Salem*, by Linda Felker and Regina Lane. Smashwords Ebook, 2012. (Darryl Hunt, murder, 2004.)

North Carolina, 1994. *Life After Death Row: The true story of Glen Edward Chapman*, by Edward

Chapman and Alex Cury. CreateSpace, 2010. (Glen Edward Chapman, murder, 2008.)

Ohio, 1984. *Guilty by Popular Demand: A True Story of Small Town Injustice*, by Bill Osinki. Kent State University Press, 2012. (Dale Johnston, murder, 1990.)

Oklahoma, 1988. *The Innocent Man: Murder and Injustice in a Small Town*, by John Grisham. Doubleday, 2006. (Ronald Williamson, murder, 1999.)

Oklahoma, 1988. *Journey Toward Justice*, by Dennis Fritz. Seven Locks Press, 2006. (Dennis Fritz, murder, 1999.)

Pennsylvania, 1982. *7 Days to Live*, by Nick Yarris. Severn House, 2011. (Nicholas Yarris, murder, 2003.)

South Carolina, 1982. *Anatomy of Injustice: A Murder Case Gone Wrong*, by Raymond Bonner, 2012. (Edward Lee Elmore, murder, 2012.)

Texas, 1974, *Insufficient Funds*, by Robert McCandless. Smashwords Ebook, 2011. (Robert McCandless, robbery, 1980.)

Texas, 1977. *Adams v. Texas*, by Randall Adams and William Hoffer. St. Martin's Press, 1991. (Randall Adams, murder, 1989.)

Texas, 1977. *Chasing Justice: My Story of Freeing Myself After Two Decades on Death Row for a Crime I Didn't Commit*, by Kerry Max Cook. Harper Collins, 2007. (Kerry Max Cook, 1997.)

Texas, 1981. *Exonerated: A Brief and Dangerous Freedom*, by Joyce King. River Grove Books, 2014. (James Woodard, murder, 2008.)

Texas, 1981. *White Lies: Rape, Murder, and Justice Texas Style*, by Nick Davies. Pantheon, 1991. (Clarence Brandley, murder, 1991)

Texas, 1982. *Overcome, Succeed and Prosper*, by Lenell Geter. Marzinza Publishing Group, 2001. (Lenell Geter, robbery, 1984.)

Texas, 1986. *A Plea For Justice: The Timothy Cole Story*, by Fred B. McKinley Eakin Press, 2010. (Timothy Cole, sexual assault, 2009)

Texas, 1987. *Getting Life: An Innocent Man's 25-Year Journey from Prison to Peace*, by Michael Morton. Simon and Schuster, 2014. (Michael Morton, murder, 2011.)

Texas, 1989, 1990. *Mortal Justice: A True Story of Murder and Vindication*, by Jeanette Popp. New Horizon Press. (Christopher Ochoa, murder, 2002. Richard Danzinger, sexual assault, 2002.)

Texas, 1999. *Tulia: Race, Cocaine, and Corruption in a Small Texas Town*, by Nate Blakeslee. Public Affairs, 2006. (Many defendants convicted and exonerated.)

Texas, 1999. *The Cowboy Chronicles*, by Bill Davis. Smashwords Ebook, 2009. (Michael Toney, murder. 2009.)

Vermont, 1819. *The Counterfeit Man*, by Gerald McFarland. Pantheon. 1990. (Jesse and Stephen Boorn, murder, 1819.)

Virginia, 1982. *Why Me? When It Could've Been You!: The Life of Julius Earl Ruffin*, by Magnolia Holiday. Magnolia Productions, 2007. (Julius Earl Ruffin, rape, 2003.)

Virginia, 1984. *An Expendable Man: The Near-Execution of Earl Washington, Jr.*, by Margaret Edds. NYU Press, 2003 (Earl Washington, Jr., murder, 2000.)

Virginia, 2000. *The Wrong Guys: Murder, False Confessions, and the Norfolk Four*, by Tom Wells and Richard A. Leo. New Press, 2008. (Derek Tice, 2011. Joseph J. Dick Jr., Danial Williams and Eric Wilson.)

Washington, 1981. *Predator: Rape, Madness, And Injustice In Seattle*, by Jack Olsen. Delacorte Press, 1991. (Steve Titus, 1981.)

Wisconsin, 1996. *It happened to Audrey: A Terrifying Journey from Loving Mom to Accused Baby Killer* , by Jill Wellington and Audrey Edmunds. Titletown Publishing, 2012. (Audrey Edmunds, murder, 2008.)

Wisconsin, 2014. *The Innocent Killer: A True Story of a Wrongful Conviction and its Astonishing Aftermath*, by Michael Griesbach. American Bar Association. AND 2010 *Unreasonable Inferences: The True Story of a Wrongful Conviction and Its Astonishing Aftermath*, by Michael Griesbach. Point Beach Publishing. (Steven Avery, sexual assault, 2003.)

Multi-state, 1976-1993. *The Exonerated: A Play*, by Jessica Blank and Erik Jensen. Faber and Faber,

2003. AND *Living Justice: Love, Freedom, and the Making of The Exonerated*, by Jessica Blank and Erik Jensen. Atria Books, 2006. (Kerry Max Cook, TX, 1977, 1997; Gary Gauger, IL, 1993, 1996; Robert Earl Hayes, FL, 1991, 1997; Sonia "Sunny" Jacobs, FL, 1976, 1992; David Keaton, FL, 1971, 1973; Delbert Tibbs, FL, 1974, 1977.

Appendix C

Books about Specific U.S. Wrongful Conviction Cases - Not Yet Exonerated (in chronological order by state and date of conviction)

California, 1937. *Colder Case: How California Executed the Wrong Man and Left a Serial Killer Free to Stalk Children*, by George Sherwood. Amazon Digital Services, 2014. (Albert Dyer, murder, executed 1938).

California, 1948. *Cell 2455: Death Row: A Condemned Man's Own Story*, by Caryl Chessman. Da Capo Press (reprint) 2006. (Caryl Chessman, rape, executed 1960.)

California, 1982. *Mean Justice*, by Edward Humes. Pocket, 2003. (over 100 cases of claimed innocence, including Patrick Dunn, in Bakersfield, California area.)

California, 2002. *Rush to Judgement: a critical examination of the David Westerfield, Danielle van Dam child kidnapping and murder case*, by C. Stevenson. CreateSpace, 2011. (David Westerfield, kidnapping and murder)

Connecticut, 1989. *Justice Denied - The Trial of Erik Rasmussen*, by Eric Rasmussen. iUniverse, 2004. (Erik Rasmussen, murder.)

Connecticut, 1989. *Convicting the Innocent: The Story of a Murder, a False Confession and the Struggle to Free a "wrong man."* by Donald Connery, 1996 (Richard LaPointe, murder.)

Connecticut 2005. *No Evidence, No Jury, No Justice: The True Story of Jeremy Barney, Prisoner #318764*, by Christian Peet. GenPop books, 2014. (Jeremy Barney, sexual assault.)

Federal, Alaska, 2006. *KU KLUX KOURTS--America's Hidden Injustice*, by Roderick Williams. self-published. 2013. (Roderick O. Williams, drug distribution.)

Federal, Illinois, 2007. *Tilted: The Trials of Conrad Black*, Second Edition, by Steven Skurka. Dundurn, 2011. (Conrad Black, embezzlement, fraud.)

Federal, Massachusetts, 1993. *Perfectly Innocent – The Wrongful Conviction of Alfred Trenkler*, by Morrison Bonpasse. CreateSpace, 2007. (Alfred Trenkler, Attempted Malicious Destruction by Explosives, Aiding and Abetting.)

Federal, North Carolina, 1979. *A Wilderness of Error: The Trials of Jeffrey MacDonald*, by Errol Morris. Penguin Press HC, 2012. AND *Fatal Vision*, by Joe McGinniss. Signet, 1983. (Jeffrey MacDonald, murder.)

Federal, South Dakota, 1977. *The Trial of Leonard Peltier*, by Jim Messerschmidt. South End Press, 1999. AND In the Spirit of Crazy Horse, by Peter Matthiessen. Penquin Books, 1992. (Leonard Peltier, murder.)

Federal, U.S. Air Force, 2012. *The Whole Truth: The Tainted Prosecution of an American Fighter Pilot*, by Bob Harvey. Viper Pilot Press, 2013. (Lt. Col. James Wilkerson, sexual assault.)

Florida, 1987. *Injustice System: A Murder in Miami and a Trial Gone Wrong*, by Clive Stafford Smith, (Krishna Maharaj, murder)

Florida, 1976. *Fatal Flaw: A True Story of Malice and Murder in a Small Southern Town*, by Phillip Finch, Villard Books, New York, 1992. Zeigler, Through Vidster's Eyes; A Wrongful Conviction In A 1975 Quadruple Capital Murder, by Nic H. Vicocq. Smashwords, 2012. (William Zeigler, murder)

Florida, 1985. *Unanswered Cries: A True Story of Friends, Neighbors, and Murder in a Small Town*, by Thomas French, St. Martins Press, 1992. (George Lewis, murder)

Florida, 1988. *The Truth Shall Set Him Free: A True Story of Murder, Lies and a Police Officer's Conviction of Convenience*, by Jeanne Bragg. Morris Publishing, 2001. (James Duckett, murder.)

Georgia, 1991. *I am Troy Davis*, by Jen Marlowe, Martina Davis-Correia and Troy Anthony Davis. Haymarket Books, 2013. (Troy Davis, murder.)

Illinois, 1946. *William Heirens: His Day in Court/Did an Innocent Man Confess to Three Grisly Murders?* by Dolores Kennedy. Bonus Books, 1991. (William Heirens, murder, died in prison 2012.) AND Before I Kill More, by Lucy Freeman. Pocket, 1977. (with contrary view, that Heirens was guilty.)

Illinois, 1997. *Shadow in the Rain*, by Harriett Ford. Helm Publishing, 2007. (fictionalized story of Ted Kuhl, murder.)

Louisiana, 1977. _Louisiana v. Vincent Simmons: Frame-up in Avoyelles Parish_, by Katja Pumm. CreateSpace, 2011. (Vincent Simmons, rape.)

Maine, 1989. _Human Sacrifice_, by James Moore. Blackberry Press, 2002. (Dennis Dechaine, murder)

Massachusetts, 1963. _A Death in Belmont (P.S.)_, by Sebastian Junger. Harper Perennial, 2007. (Roy Smith, murder.)

Massachusetts, 2006. _Reasonable Doubt: The Fashion Writer, Cape Cod, and the Trial of Chris McCowen_, by Peter Manso. Atria Books, 2011. AND _Invisible Eden: A Story of Love and Murder on Cape Cod_, by Maria Flook. Broadway Books, 2004. (Christopher McCowen, murder.)

Michigan, 2012. _A Mother's Plea and Journey to Forgiveness_, by Laura Schupbach Ouellette. Xulon Press, 2013. (Corrine Baker, murder.)

Minnesota, 2008. _Conversations With Crystal - The Woman Who Fell Off the Bridge_, by Crystal Manning and B. P. Storm. CreateSpace, 2012. (Michael Stoner, Jr., child abuse.)

Missouri, 1994. _Damned to Eternity: The Story of the Man Who They Said Caused the Flood_, by Adam Pitluk. Da Capo Press, 2007. (James Scott, causing a flood.)

Missouri, 2002. _The Skeptical Juror and the Trial of Byron Case_, by J Bennett Allen. Allen & Allen Semiotics, 2010. (Byron Case, murder.)

Nevada, 2002. _Kirstin Blaise Lobato's Unreasonable Conviction: Possibility of Guilt Replaces Proof_

Beyond A Reasonable Doubt, by Hans Sherrer. CreateSpace, 2006, 2008, 2010. AND *Kirstin Blaise Lobato vs State of Nevada: Habeas Corpus Petition with Grounds and Exhibits*, by Hans Sherrer and Michelle Ravell. CreateSpace, 2010. (Kirstin Lobato, murder)

New Hampshire, 2001. *EYE CONTACT – The Mysterious Death in 2000 of Kassidy Bortner, and the Wrongful Convictions of Chad Evans and Amanda Bortner*, by Morrison Bonpasse, CreateSpace, 2011. (Chad Evans, murder)

New Jersey, 1935. *The Airman and the Carpenter: the Lindbergh Kidnapping and the Framing of Richard Hauptmann*, by Ludovic Kennedy. Viking Press, 1985. (Richard Hauptmann, murder, executed 1936.) (one of many books about this case.)

New Mexico, 1931. *Justice Betrayed: A Double Killing in Old Santa Fe*, by Ralph Melnick. University of New Mexico Press, 2002. (Thomas Johnson, murder, executed 1933.)

New York, 1912. *Against the evidence;: The Becker-Rosenthal affair*, by Andy Logan. McCall Publishing Company, 1971. (Charles Becker, murder. Executed 1915.)

New York, 1988. *Destruction of Innocence: The Friedman Case & How Coerced Testimony and Confessions Harm Children, Families and Communities for Decades After the Wrongful Convictions Occur*, by Gavin de Becker and Emily Horowitz. Amazon Digital Services, 2013. (Kindle Edition) (Arnold and Jesse Friedman, abuse of children.)

Ohio, 1909. *Who Killed Ora Lee?: The Trial of Daniel Guy Rasor*, by Linda Thomson Buesch Booksurge, 2007. AND *Reasonable Minds: A Conclusion (Who Killed Ora Lee?)*, by Linda Thompson Buesch. CreateSpace, 2013. (Daniel Guy Rasor, murder.)

Ohio, 1954. *The Wrong Man: The Final Verdict on the Dr. Sam Sheppard Murder Case*, by James Neff. Random House, 2001. *From "The Fugitive" to Freedom - The Real Sam Sheppard Story*, by David Pietras. CreateSpace, 2014. (Sam Sheppard, murder.)

Ohio, 1996. *System Failure: A Critique of the Judicial System of the United States*, by James F. Love IV and Hans Sherrer (Editor). CreateSpace 2009. (James F. Love, rape.)

Oklahoma, 1985. *The Dreams of Ada*, by Robert Mayer. Broadway Books, 2006. (Tommy Ward and Karl Fontenot, murder.)

Oregon, 1995. *Improper Submission: Records of a Wrongful Conviction*, by Erma Armstrong. Tanglewood Hill Press, 2005. (Karlyn Eklof, murder.)

Pennsylvania, 1960. *Murdered Innocence: The Maryann Mitchell Murder Revisited*, by Donna Persico. Lulu.com, 2013. (Elmo Smith, murder, executed 1962.)

Pennsylvania, 1982. *The Case of Mumia Abu-Jamal: A Life in the Balance*, by Amnesty International. Seven Stories Press, 2001. (Mumia Abu-Jamal, murder.)

Texas, 1982. *LAST WORDS FROM DEATH ROW --- The Wall Unit, by Norma Herrera*, Nightengale Press, 2007. (Leonel Herrera, plaintiff in U.S. Supreme Court case, Herrera v. Collins (1993), executed 1993.)

Texas, 1983. *The Wrong Carlos: Anatomy of a Wrongful Execution*, by James S. Liebman, Shawn Crowley, Andrew Markquart, Lauren Rosenberg, Lauren White and Daniel Zharkovsky. Columbia University Press, 2014. (Carlos DeLuna, murder, executed 1989.)

Texas, 1987. *Twisted Truth*, by Wendy Schmid-Eastwood. Athena Press, 2004. (Richard Wayne Jones, murder, executed in 2000.)

Texas, 1992. *The Skeptical Juror and the Trial of Cameron Todd Willingham* by J Bennett Allen. Allen & Allen Semiotics, 2010. AND *Inferno: An Inquiry Into the Willingham Fire*, by J. Bennett Allen. Allen & Allen Semiotics, Inc, 2011. (Cameron Todd Willingham, arson/murder, executed 2004.)

Texas, 1993. *A Saint on Death Row: How a Forgotten Child Became a Man and Changed a World*, by Thomas Cahill Anchor, 2010. (Dominique Jerome Green, murder, executed 2004.)

Texas, 1996. *Just Point At Him*, by Snjezana Marinkovic and Gregory L Torti (Contributor). CreateSpace, 2013. (Gregory Lee Torti, sexual assault.)

Texas, 1997. *A Texas Style Witch Hunt "Justice Denied" The Darlie Lynn Routier Story*, by David Pietras. CreateSpace Publishing, 2013. AND *Innocent on Death Row*, by David Pietras. CreateSpace Publishing, 2014. (Darlie Routier, murder.)

Texas, 1998. *Texas, He Was Innocent*, by Bente Hjortshoej and Connie Wright. Lulu. 2011. AND *Texas, I Was Innocent*, by Tony Wright and Peter Bellamy. Lulu, 2011. (Gregory Edward "Tony" Wright, murder, executed 2008)

Texas, 2004. *999489: From Foster Care To Texas Death Row*, by Gerald E. Marshall and the European Association for Human Rights (Editor). CreateSpace, 2013. (Gerald Marshall, murder.)

Virginia, 1977. *Case of a Lifetime: A Criminal Defense Lawyer's Story*, by Abbe Smith. Palgrave MacMillan Trade, 2008. (Patsy Kelly Jarrett, murder, paroled in 2005.)

Virginia, 1982. *May God Have Mercy: A True Story of Crime and Punishment*, by John C. Tucker. Delta, 1998. (Roger Keith Coleman, murder, executed 1991. DNA tests in 2006 showed guilt.)

Virginia, 1983. *Dead Run: The Shocking Story of Dennis Stockton and Life on Death Row in America*, by Joe Jackson and William F. Burke, Jr. Walker & Co., 2000. (Dennis Stockton, murder. Executed 1995.)

Virginia, 1985. *The Corruption of Innocence: A Journey for Justice*, by Lori St John. Creative

Production Services, 2013. (Joseph O'Dell, murder, executed 1997)

Washington, 1994. *STATE RAISED: A Deep Look into the World of Prison*, by Matthew Wright. iUniverse, 2008. (Matthew Wright, murder.)

West Virginia, 1983. *The Chaparral Murders: Dollar Store Justice*, by Margaret Stoddart. iUniverse, 2007. (Russell Clark Phillips, murder.)

West Virginia, 2006. *My Journey to Hell and Back*, by Jason Lively. Kindle, 2014. AND *Reflections by Jason Lively: My Journey to Hell and Back*. BMF Publishing, 2014. (Jason Lively, murder.)

Wisconsin, 1995. *The Monfils Conspiracy: The Conviction of Six Innocent Men*, by Denis Gullickson, John Gaie. iUniverse, 2009. (Dale Basten, Michael Hirn, Michael Johnson, Keith Kutska, Rey Moore, and Michael Piaskowski, only one of the six to be exonerated, in 2001.)

Wisconsin, 1995. *Who Killed Sarah? Shedding new light on a questionable conviction*, by Doug and Sheila Berry, 2005. (Penny Brummer, murder.)

Wisconsin, 1999. *Full Circle: How a Veteran Cop was Sentenced to Life in Prison for Crimes That Never Happened*, by Sheila Berry and Doug Berry, 2011. (John Maloney, murder)

Multi-state, 1692. *Law & Disorder:: Inside the Dark Heart of Murder*, by John Douglas and Mark Olshaker. Pinnacle, Reissue Edition, 2014. (reviewing sympathetically the claims of many wrongly convicted people since the Salem witch trials.)

Multi-state. *Catholic Priests Falsely Accused: The Facts, The Fraud, The Stories*, by David F. Pierre Jr. CreateSpace, 2011.

Multi-state. *Wrongfully Accused: 15 People Sentenced to Prison for a Crime They Didn't Commit*, by William Webb. CreateSpace 2013.

Multi-state. *Wrongfully Accused #2: 15 More People Sentenced to Prison for a Crime They Didn't Commit*, by William Webb. CreateSpace, 2013.

Appendix D

Books about U.S. Wrongful Conviction Cases – fiction (in alphabetical order by author)

Baldwin, Timothy, C. *Justice Delayed*. CreateSpace, 2013.

Bonpasse, Morrison. *2121*. CreateSpace, 2014.

Bonpasse, Morrison. *Jesus and Jesusa*. Two combined into one volume: *2121* and *Jesus and Jesusa*, CreateSpace, 2014.

Burcell, Robin. *Face of a Killer*. Harper, 2008.

Burke, Alafair. *All Day and a Night: A Novel of Suspense (Ellie Hatcher)*. Harper, 2014

Clark, Jack. *Dancing on Graves*. CreateSpace, 2012.

Dale, Lisa. *A Promise of Safekeeping*. Berkley, 20121.

Fister, Barbara. *Through the Cracks*. Minotaur Books, 2010.

Fleming, David Alex. *Dying Innocence*. Riverside Publishing Group, 2011.

Fowler, Dane. *The Sex Offender: Falsley Accused, Wrongly Convicted, Labeled for Life*. RocksWorld, 2013.

Grisham, John. *The Confession*. Dell, 2011.

Harvey, Michael. *The Innocence Game*. Knopf Publishing Group, 2013.

Hylton, Bill. *The Vindication Obsession*. CreateSpace, 2013.

Long, Al. *The Tamperers*. iUniverse, 2001.

Patterson, Richard North. *Conviction, A Novel*. Ballantine Books, 2005.

Picoult, Jodi. *Salem Falls*. Washington Square Press, 2002.

Sanchez, Dennis. The Big Exoneration. CreateSpace, 2013.

Stevens, Chevy. *That Night*. St. Martin's Press, 2014.

Watts, Larry, and Wright, Cyndi and Bingham, Linda. *Cheating Justice*. Larry Watts Publisher, 2013.

West, Mary Ann. *And Justice For None - The Life and Death of an Innocent Man*. Lulu, 2010.

Printed in Dunstable, United Kingdom

91218257R00167